UNITY IN THE FAITH

PUBLISHED IN HONOR OF

THE CENTENNIAL CELEBRATION

OF

THE UNIVERSITY OF THE SOUTH

1857-1957

UNITY IN
THE FAITH

BY

WILLIAM PORCHER DUBOSE

EDITED BY

W. NORMAN PITTENGER

GREENWICH, CONNECTICUT
1957

© 1957 by The Seabury Press, Incorporated

Library of Congress Catalog Card Number: 57-9536

Design by P. Atkinson Dymock

Printed in the United States of America

FOREWORD

THE honor of writing an introduction to any work which concerns William Porcher DuBose is one of which I am deeply sensible. Dr. DuBose was unmistakably one of the most scholarly, one of the most original, one of the most saintly, and one of the most influential of those personalities whose lives and labors have molded the character and established the reputation of The University of the South.

His education, to begin with, was a purely military one which would not ordinarily be expected to lead to the career he actually followed. The change in his life's course came abruptly in his eighteenth year in the form of a mystical experience as clear and unmistakable as that of Saul of Tarsus. Such clear vocations are the privilege of very few persons, and they sanctify the lives they touch as perhaps nothing else can. Thereafter nothing could divert him—not even the frightful digression of a long war which interrupted and delayed his theological education almost as soon

v

as it had begun. He found himself most fully at Sewanee where he lived the major portion of his life.

For the first twenty years of his academic career he published nothing. It is said that he did not even save his lecture notes from one year to the next, but prepared for every class as if it were his first. He gave himself wholly to his students, and to the University and community of Sewanee, upon which he left an indelible impression. He was the real founder of the School of Theology and he gave the Order of Gownsmen essentially its present form.

During those twenty years his principal intellectual food was the Greek New Testament and Aristotle's *Nichomachean Ethics,* both of which he digested with a thoroughness which could hardly be surpassed. When he was finally ready to write, he published an astonishing series of books all of which were so mature as to require no subsequent revisions.

Between 1892 and his retirement in 1908 he produced five major works which immediately gave him an international reputation. During his remaining ten years he wrote three more books and the series of articles in the *Constructive Quarterly* which are here being republished for, we hope, a wider audience. When death ended his labors, he was rounding out his life's work by integrating his whole system of theology with the source from which it sprang. The book was to have been called *From Aristotle to Christ.*

But Dr. DuBose is with us yet. His works have never ceased to be studied in foreign universities, and now his native land is awakening to do him homage. It is a remarkable thing that a man who spent most of his life in a small university in a forest on an isolated mountain top in Tennessee, and who steeped himself so deeply in so few and such ancient sources, should have produced a system of thought which looks so new, so fresh, so contemporary a half century after much of it was written, and some twoscore years after his death. Who could be more modern than an author who translates "a theology that was cast in a Scholastic mould into a theology based on psychology," and who expresses the truth of the Creed in language "which can appeal to those who are accustomed to think in the terms not of metaphysics but of personality"?

But none would have been quicker than he to disclaim any break with the past. The textbooks to which he gave almost all of his attention were written two thousand years ago. He would have considered naive the proposal of some of our present sociologists to discard all old moralities, and make for ourselves a new one. He once remarked in such a connection, "The individual is as incapable of making morality as he is of making language or civilization. We can never be emancipated from the authority of a slowly developing experience." He believed that no one man and no one group at any time in history ever had more than a partial apprehension of the truth about any important question.

"Truth is not an individual thing; no one of us has all of it—even all of it that is known. Truth is a corporate possession, and the knowledge of it is a corporate process. It enters slowly and painfully into the common sense, the common experience, the common use and life of man. There is a corporate, Catholic Christianity, actually extant on the earth, which no one or no set of us holds all of, or perfectly even what we do hold. Christianity, even so far as actualized in the world, is more and greater than any one or any body of us, and the full actualization of Christianity will come only with the fruition of the world's destiny, in the end of the ages."

DuBose believed in complete freedom of enquiry. He believed that the truths of religion like the truths of natural science progressively extend their command of common consent and have nothing to fear from unrestrained criticism. For him those who would try to prohibit freedom of enquiry (like so many authoritarians of our time) are those who have no deep assurance of the truth of what they profess to

believe. He thus embraced that combination of conserva-
tism, courage, and imagination which characterizes wisdom
in any age; and The University of the South rejoices that
the celebration of her Centennial can be graced by the further extension of the influence of this man of God who did
so much to guide and strengthen and beautify her youth.

Edward McCrady,
VICE-CHANCELLOR OF THE UNIVERSITY
OF THE SOUTH

SEWANEE, 1957

W E HAVE good dominical authority that a prophet is often without honor in his own country. And American Episcopalians should take the saying to heart when they come to see that William Porcher DuBose, who is the only important original theologian in our tradition on this side of the water, has been very nearly forgotten in his own communion as well as in the American religious world generally—an honourable exception being Professor John S. Marshall, author of *The Word Was Made Flesh*—while in Britain and even in France his significance has been recognized and emphasized.

DuBose's name is inextricably associated with the University of the South, of which he was for many years the distinguished ornament. He was instrumental in the founding of St. Luke's, its theological department; he taught both there and in the university itself for many years; his heart and soul belonged to "the mountain."

It is highly appropriate, therefore, that in conjunction

with the one hundredth anniversary of the founding of The
University of the South, this volume of essays from DuBose
should make its appearance. The essays were originally
published in *The Constructive Quarterly*, from 1913 to
1920; this quarterly was edited by Dr. Silas McBee,
DuBose's close friend, and for a decade it drew contributions from both sides of the Atlantic as it sought to promote
ecumenical understanding among Christians of all traditions.
Dr. DuBose died before the journal ceased to appear; evidently it occurred to no one to gather together his dozen
essays and publish them in book-form. So the fact, strange
as it may seem, is that this present book is the first actual
appearance, in permanent form, of DuBose's last—and in
many ways his greatest—work.

I say his greatest work because in these essays, written
in a style much more easily readable than some of his longer
books, Dr. DuBose summarized his whole way of understanding and living the Christian faith as the Anglican Communion holds that faith. The book is not only his "last will
and testament," although it is that; it is the final flowering
of the thought of this great Christian thinker, touching on
practically every important theme in Christian theology but
touching on each of them from a highly *vital* point of view:
here is *Christian theology for living*.

I have been highly honored by being given the opportunity
to arrange and edit for publication this series of essays. I
am not a "Sewanee man," but like all Episcopalians I hold
in great esteem that noble institution and its work for
Church and nation. The only reason that I have under-
taken this task is that my Sewanee friends, and notably the
present dean of its theological faculty, the Reverend George
M. Alexander, have felt that my long interest in and, if I
may so phrase it, concern to proselytize for, Dr. DuBose's
theological point of view, gave me a certain capacity for
the work. The others who have written introductory material are much more competent in this matter than I; yet I

am most happy to have had a small part in the preparation
of this book.

Someone once remarked in my hearing that Dr. DuBose
is "a dead duck." I think that whoever reads this collection
of essays, with care and attention, will see that no judgment
could be more mistaken. Here is a living thinker, much more
living than many who happen to be physically alive at the
present day. His thought is as vital, as relevant, and as
theologically impressive now as it was thirty and forty years
ago. And it is my own opinion that when the "neo-ortho-
doxy" which is now having its day comes to an end, and men
and women are looking once more for some intelligible
and believable theological orientation, Dr. DuBose's work
will be there for them to study—and, especially as summed
up in this book, will be as useful and helpful to them as it
was to the thousands who studied under, and with all their
hearts loved and revered "the Doctor."

W. NORMAN PITTENGER

General Theological Seminary,
New York City

CONTENTS

THE SAGE AND SEER OF SEWANEE

BY GEORGE BOGGAN MYERS

WILLIAM PORCHER DuBOSE came from South Carolina originally, from the Military College of Charleston known as the Citadel, from the University of Virginia, from the Confederate Army, and last, but not least as he himself would agree, from Sewanee, The University of the South, where he did his teaching and writing and where he lies buried,—soldier, philosopher, theologian, as his epitaph fittingly describes him.

The privilege has been given me of writing about Dr. DuBose from my personal experience, both as student and as teacher of his philosophy of Christianity. As one of his students, I sat under him five days in the week for three years and heard his lectures in New Testament Exegesis in the Theological Department of the University, and on Ethics, "From Aristotle to Christ," which both theological and college students were required to take.[1] For the past thirty-two years I have given lectures, both required and elective, in Dr. DuBose's teaching. When I came to Sewanee as a theological student in 1904, St. Luke's Hall, as the building housing the Theological Department was called, was full and no room was available for me. St. Luke's Hall had been built in four sections or "entries," each shut off from the others, while the first floor was occupied by chapel and classrooms. The Doctor had his private suite, with a capacious study in which he could work uninterruptedly, but enjoyed common fellowship with his students in dining-hall and classrooms and in the open house to students which Mrs. DuBose had maintained during her lifetime. Mrs. DuBose died in 1887 and the Doctor was now living alone. At once he took me in, and for several months, until I could move into one of the student suites, I shared his apartment. I well remember how at night, slipping into my own bedroom very quietly so as not to disturb him, I would find him at his desk or walking up and down his study, preparing the next day's lecture, for he prepared each lecture anew and never taught from old lecture notes. So absorbed would I find him, that he rarely noticed my presence.

BEFORE SEWANEE (1836-1873)

William Porcher DuBose was born on April 11, 1836, in Winnsboro, South Carolina, near his father's plantation. As his name indicates, he was of Huguenot descent on both sides. His own was the sixth generation in this country. His grandfather was Samuel DuBose, adjutant in the Revolutionary War, on the staff of Francis Marion, whose niece

[1] The original manuscript of his Ethics in the Doctor's handwriting (with the exception of two or three chapters which have been lost), was given to me by his son, the late Dr. William Haskell DuBose, professor of Old Testament at Sewanee, and has never been published.

he married. He was the son of Theodore Marion and Jane Porcher DuBose whose home had been in the South Carolina Low-Country where they had inherited extensive estates, but who had moved to Winnsboro, about thirty miles from Columbia, shortly before their son William was born. At about the time of his birth, his father bought a permanent home in the Up-Country, Farmington in Fairfield County, a beautiful plantation of 2500 acres, which with its rolling lime prairie and sand-clay hills was perfectly adapted to the diversified farming to which the Huguenot families were accustomed. The plantation was a self-sustaining community. Theodore DuBose, his father, was a scientific farmer and an administrator of ability. A graduate of Yale, he was also a man of wide culture, as was his wife. The classics and the Bible were read aloud in the family circle; their home was its own cultural centre. "The home was both school and church," writes the late Bishop Bratton, "and the children grew into its dual character and were cultured by it without thought that the spirit of home could be otherwise." [2]

When William was eight years old, his father bought another plantation, Roseland, three miles from Winnsboro, so that his sons could attend their first school, although teachers had already been provided at Farmington for their early training. With the move to Roseland their school days began, first in a woman's school where we read William took a prize in scholarship and, in fact, led the whole school.

Then came his entrance into Mt. Zion College, Winnsboro. In preparation his parents presented him with a beautiful mare, Bagatelle, on which he rode into school, and during the holidays enjoyed that boy-horse comradeship which Bishop Bratton calls boy-heaven. At Mt. Zion was laid the foundation of his complete at-homeness with Greek. "His

[2] For a fuller account of the early life of DuBose, see *An Apostle of Reality* —a series of lectures on the DuBose Foundation, delivered at the University of the South by his nephew, the Rt. Rev. Theodore DuBose Bratton, late Bishop of Mississippi and Chancellor of the University of the South.

aptitude for the classical tongues was a talent from God, but his love of them was inspired, and the foundation of accurate familiarity with every mood and tense and delicate tint of Greek, particularly, was permanently laid by Mr. Hudson and his capable masters." In everything except mathematics he was the leading pupil. His father, who was an excellent mathematician, determined to overcome this deficiency, and so after delaying his entrance into college for a full year that he might receive special tutoring in algebra, sent him to a military college, the Citadel in Charleston, for which he himself says he was "physically unprepared, and mentally, also, owing to his trouble with mathematics." This difficulty he overcame, and except for a short period in his junior year, he led the student body at the Citadel and during his senior year, was the ranking officer, which entailed a great deal of responsibility, and was likewise appointed assistant professor in the Department of English. In December 1855 he graduated with first honors.

The following October he was ready to enter the University of Virginia. Visits of some length to the plantations of his numerous kinsfolk in the Low-Country and participation in the charming social life of these gracious homes marked the interim period, along with hard study in preparation for the University. This was necessitated by the fact that his curriculum at the Citadel had been dominated by mathematics with consequent neglect of the classics. Now he had to regain this loss and make considerable advance before he was ready for the University of Virginia. His preparation was further complicated by serious trouble with his eyes which yielded only to the most careful treatment and which still persisted throughout his life.

It was during his student days at the Citadel that he experienced a great religious awakening. The Huguenots who immigrated to South Carolina for the most part affiliated with the Church of England, although for several generations the men resisted confirmation and only the women became communicants. A change in attitude is attributed largely to the remarkable career of "Aunt Betsy Porcher." Later Aunt Betsy taught Sunday school in Winnsboro, and it was from her that the DuBose children learned to love her attractive instruction and her bright and cheerful religion. However it was not until his junior year at the Citadel that William Porcher DuBose experienced a deepening and vivifying of his religious life as the result of a genuine mystical experience—the direct, unmediated apprehension and experience of Ultimate Reality which religion calls God. His confirmation at St. Michael's Church in Charleston followed, and in due time a definite call to the ministry, "although he kept this sacred in his inner temple for several years." In his own description of his experience written more than fifty years later, Dr. DuBose sums up this great turning point as follows: "My verification of the fact of God's coming to me, apart from all the mystery of the way, may be expressed in this simple truth of experience that in finding Him, I found myself: a man's own self, when he has once truly come to himself, is his best and only experimental proof of God." [3]

There followed three years at the University of Virginia. At the University at this time each school was separate; the degree was awarded upon graduation in the required number of schools, as was the case in Sewanee in the earlier years. DuBose matriculated in four schools, those of Latin, Greek, French and "Moral Science." In spite of his heavy course and of continued trouble with his eyes, he graduated in three years with the degree of Master of Arts, having given especial attention to the Greek of which he was to make use throughout his life. After his graduation from the University, he entered the diocesan seminary at Camden, South Carolina, to begin his preparation for Holy Orders.

[3] For a full and vivid account of this very real conversion, see *Turning Points*, pp. 17 ff.

The happy climax of a holiday in the summer of 1860 was his meeting with Miss Nannie Peronneau of Charleston. "At first sight of her," he later wrote, "my fate seemed determined." It was not long before they became engaged, but it was not until April 1863, when on furlough after his recovery from wounds received in battle, that he and Miss Peronneau were married in Anderson, S.C. To them were born two daughters and two sons, the last little son soon after the DuBoses moved to Sewanee in 1872. The following April Mrs. DuBose, whose health had been gradually failing, died, and within a year her baby followed her. Five years later Dr. DuBose married Maria Louisa Yerger of Mississippi. The second Mrs. DuBose died in 1887. During the later years of his life, his daughters, Miss Susie and Miss May, cared for their father with great tenderness and devotion.

To return to DuBose's seminary career. By the April of 1861 the War between the States was a tragic fact. The commandant of the Citadel, at the command of the governor of South Carolina, organized the Holcombe Legion for state defense. William DuBose was appointed Adjutant of the Legion. DuBose waited only long enough to consult his bishop and his father; he then left Camden for his new post. The story of his war experiences is graphically told in *Turning Points*. After months of hard drill, the legion was mustered out of State into Confederate service. DuBose was in the midst of the fighting around Richmond and in the advance on Washington. In one of these engagements he was painfully hurt, but not disabled. In the terrible battles of Second Manasses and Second Bull Run he was twice wounded, and was the only field officer of the Legion who was left able to fight through the battle. It devolved upon him to reorganize the shattered regiment and command it in the first Maryland invasion which immediately followed.

Two weeks later, after a forced march to Boonesboro

Gap, he was taken prisoner on a scouting expedition and was for several months a prisoner at Fort Delaware. He was allowed to rejoin his command just in time to be dangerously wounded in an engagement near Kinston. "Within four months," writes Dr. DuBose, "death had three times touched me as closely as was consistent with escape . . . On my return to Richmond from prison I was personally informed that I was dead . . . In 1863 my service was along the coasts from Virginia as far as Vicksburg. During that year influential friends in Church and State, probably to preserve what remained of me for service of another kind, entirely without my knowledge or consent, procured for me a commission as chaplain . . . with Kershaw's Brigade . . . In 1864 in Greeneville, Tennessee, as a newly ordained deacon, I began my ministry with the most brilliant congregation of major-generals down to privates that I have ever had to address . . . In April 1865 the final surrender took place, and I returned home to find it a picture of the most utter desolation, having lain in the centre of Sherman's famous march."

The War had not, however, put a complete stop to DuBose's preparation for the real work of his life. An airtight ammunition box, which soon became well known and was always tossed into the headquarters wagon, contained his library—the Greek Testament, Pascal's *Thoughts*, Xenophon's *Memorabilia*, and a little blue and gold copy of Tennyson's poems which had been given to him by Nannie Peronneau. St. Paul's was his only theology. "I can distinctly remember lying on my back while my men were constructing earthworks, and with closed eyes constructing for myself the vital spiritual sequence, unity and completeness of the first eight chapters of the *Epistle to the Romans*," he says. This book was really his *pièce de résistance*. Tennyson was his constant companion. Leg over saddle, on the march through the mountains of Virginia, he drank in the music of his songs and the mysteries of *In Memoriam*.

"Some of the students at Sewanee will remember that I knew in those early days, how to enter into the romance as well as into the severer, if not more serious, business of their lives." DuBose was repeatedly cited by the commanding general and recommended for promotion. General Capers, later Bishop of South Carolina and Chancellor of the University of the South, tells how he read these citations many years after, and was much impressed since they related to one who had become known to him as a distinguished theologian.

At last the War was over, and DuBose was able to return to his little family at Winnsboro. Soon after, he was called to the rectorship of St. John's Church, Fairfield. At the first visit of the Bishop, almost a year after he had taken charge of the parish, he was ordained priest, on September 9, 1866. To supplement the almost non-existent salary he taught Greek at Mt. Zion College. In January 1868 he moved to Abbeville to become the rector of Trinity Church. Three years later, he was very nearly elected bishop to assist the then aging and blind Bishop Davis. "One of the most fortunate escapes of my life," he later wrote. "His pupils and disciples share the great Doctor's feelings," says Bishop Bratton, "not that he would have been any less the Bishop, but that he was so much more the Doctor, the Teacher, the Interpreter."

After a year and a half of happy pastoral life at Abbeville, "suddenly there came to me a communication which was to determine the course of my whole life. It was a telegram informing me that I had been elected chaplain of The University of the South and Professor of Moral Science."

Until the "Rectory" could be built in the Chapel Yard, and his family moved from Abbeville, the new chaplain lived with the Vice-Chancellor, General Gorgas. At once the chaplain became the adviser and counselor of both faculty and students, and during those years in which the old "Grammar School" evolved into the University, and indeed throughout his forty years as chaplain, professor and Dean of the Theological Department, Dr. DuBose, as Bishop Bratton says, "represented the Spirit of Sewanee. To the students, he became the Sage of Sewanee, revered by every generation that came under his influence." It was the chaplain who organized the Order of Gownsmen, an Honor Order, "to stand among the students for excellence in scholarship, deportment, and culture." In 1873 it fell to him to establish classes for the candidates for Holy Orders, the beginning of the School of Theology, the creation of which had always been in the mind of the founders of the University. In 1878 St. Luke's Hall was opened and the Theological Department of the University permanently established. The Rev. Telfair Hodgson, Vice-Chancellor, became its first Dean, and on his death in 1893 Dr. DuBose succeeded to the deanship which he held until his retirement in 1908.

SEWANEE (1873-1918)

Until recently America has produced few philosophical theologians of the first rank, but in Dr. W. P. DuBose America has produced an original thinker of the very highest order. In *The Life of Christ in Recent Research* the late Dr. William Sanday of Oxford University says: "America should make much of Dr. DuBose. I strongly suspect that in his own proper field—which I might perhaps describe as the Philosophy of the Christian Religion—he is the wisest writer on the other side of the Atlantic; indeed it may not be too much to say, the wisest Anglican writer (with so French-looking a name it seems wrong to speak of Anglo-Saxon, and it narrows the ground a little to confine it to a single communion) on both sides of the Atlantic." [4] However, in conversation with Dr. Sanday later, Dr. Du-Bose said, "I am Anglican through and through." The

---

[4] Quoted by the Rev. W. H. Ralston, Jr., in his Master's thesis, *Theology of DuBose*, deposited in the General Theological Seminary Library.

French scholar, the Abbé Brémond, speaks of him as a "great light."[5] An Anglican bishop, in a letter to a fellow bishop, speaks of him as "a perfect sunburst from the West." These estimates by British and European scholars found an echo in his own countrymen. Speaking of the importance of the psychological method in contemporary theology, Dr. Frederick Grant of the Union Seminary in New York assigned among its exponents in America the chief place to Dr. DuBose—"in America, above all, the late Dr. W. P. DuBose and those whom he influenced, including more than one outstanding theologian of the present day."[6] The late Dr. J. O. F. Murray, Master of Selwyn College and Canon of Ely, also interpreted his method as that of spiritual psychology.[7] His method, he says, was essentially psychological, in close touch with modern demands. "His study of the Religious Consciousness is distinguished from that of other psychologists (a) by his use of the Bible as his textbook, and (b) by his analysis of the Religious Consciousness first of St. Paul and of the other writers of the New Testament, and then of Jesus Himself."

His philosophy and theology is Christology. The Incarnation in its completeness and finality as the accomplished fact of the oneness, or at-one-ment, as he terms it, in the Person of Jesus Christ, is the heart and mind of his message and teaching—of Deity and our humanity in the Person of Jesus Christ as two sides of the same Reality, if distinct, in the Deity and the humanly accomplished divinity of our humanity as he calls it.[8] Thus it is that Dr. DuBose accomplished in his thought with a striking originality of style and treatment the most difficult task that has con-

[5] Quoted by Silas McBee in the *Constructive Quarterly*, September 1920.
[6] *Anglican Theological Review*, July 1927.
[7] *DuBose, Prophet of Unity*, DuBose Foundation lectures delivered by the Rev. J. O. F. Murry at The University of the South.
[8] *The Reason of Life:* The Divinity and Deity of Jesus Christ, Chapter XIX.

fronted Christian philosophy, the mutual inclusiveness and dependence of Deity and humanity in the person of Jesus as the two sides of the same Reality, although distinct. It is in his method of treatment, that of spiritual psychology, that he is most original and contemporary. He insists upon Christ's complete humanity as not different from ours in kind. "It was not sinful in Him, because He was sinless in it." "Nature" is ethically neutral; it is personality that is righteous or sinful. Thus he breaks with the conventional doctrine of original sin. "Christ took all of original sin except the sin." [9] To which I might add, by way of interpretation, God did not create an evil world, including human nature as such. As Genesis has it, "God saw everything that He had made, and behold, it was very good." Evil is not the exclusive opposite of good, it is the perversion of good—good gone wrong and that is why it is so infernally evil. It exists only by "permission" of good. Evil (and sin) is possible because of freedom of choice. Evil does not exist in its own right; it has no right to exist. "Deep, deeper than we believe, lie the roots of sin; it is in the good that they exist; it is in the good that they thrive and send up sap and produce the black fruit of hell." [10] Herein lies the real terror and pity of tragedy. Dr. DuBose did not underrate the tragedy of sin, but he did not take the tragic view of human nature. Our Lord took our nature upon Him, and "it was not sinful in Him because He was sinless in it." The end and meaning of human life is union with God in Christ by the power of the Holy Spirit. The Incarnation would have happened had man never sinned. The immediate purpose of the Incarnation is to redeem us from sin; the ultimate purpose is union with God in Christ, our sonship in and with and through Him. "Incarnation was no after-thought of God, no after-need of man." [11]

[9] *Soteriology,* p. 272.
[10] Charles Williams, *Descent of the Dove,* p. 108.
[11] *Reason of Life,* p. 68.

Dr. DuBose's mind was so profound and original and bold that many of his statements seem startling, if not shocking, even to trained theologians. "Without any fireworks he can take the reader's breath away," says the late Canon J. K. Mozley of St. Paul's, London, in his work on the Atonement. "God is the infinite of what we are, and we are the finite of what God is." "It is not true because the Church or the Bible says so; the Church and the Bible say so because it is true." "We do not believe because we argue; we argue because we believe." "God is not in the world to find Himself, but to find Himself in the world." "Contraries do not necessarily contradict nor need opposites oppose." "Controversy is of the devil." Are we seeking truth, or to drive our opponent to the wall? There is a truth on both sides. *Audire alteram partem.*" He said to us in class one day, "If you can lose your faith, God will take care of His truth." [12]

Dr. Mozley assigns Dr. DuBose a chief place in one of the three schools of interpretation of the Atonement. For him Christ, he notes, is not our substitute, nor our example. He is our representative. [13]

Dr. DuBose says that the *Logos* was in Nature, not substantially but rationally. He avoided the pitfalls of deism on the one hand and pantheism on the other. The *Logos* was *in* Nature, not *qua.* Nature, but as the mind and reason and will of Nature, so that he could boldly say, is not God Nature, and is not Nature God? [14] "Is it not true that God is the Infinite of what we are, and that we are the finite of what God is? The first word of religion is the recognition of the fact that we are in the image of God. To know God at all we have to know ourselves; to know ourselves unto perfection, we have to know God. To be

[12] *Christian Defense,* an essay by DuBose in the *Sunday School Teacher's Manual,* the Rev. William M. Groton, ed.

[13] J. K. Mozley, *The Doctrine of the Atonement,* p. 173 and particularly p. 196.

[14] *Turning Points in My Life,* p. 88.

ourselves unto perfection, we have to be what God is. It is a natural and metaphysical fact that we 'do not the truth,' that we are not the truth of ourselves, are not our real selves, until we walk in the light, and are what God is. There is no other end or limit or goal for man than God. What we want from Him is nothing less than Himself, seeing that He is our own and only perfect Self." [15]

In the chapter on "Catholic Principles" in *Turning Points,* Dr. DuBose says, "I am a thorough-going Trinitarian in prayer: I find God personally only in the person of Jesus Christ, and Christ only by His presence to me and with me and in me by the Holy Ghost." [16]

The conventional-minded became alarmed, and more than once he was charged with heresy. On the occasion of a hostile review of one of his books, I said to him, "Doctor, they call you a heretic." He was shining his shoes at the time, and raising his brush and shaking it he said, "Yes, they call me a heretic, but they'll see; they'll see." One of his close friends, Bishop Gregg of Texas, became alarmed until a patient explanation set his fears at rest. After one of his books was published, another bishop attacked him in the Board of Trustees as heretical. It must have been the *Soteriology,* hard sledding even for trained minds. Bishop Gailor, who had been chaplain of the University and devoted to Dr. DuBose, and who had written the Introduction to the *Ecumenical Councils,* said he had read the book, but it was too profound for him to say whether it was heretical or not. It developed that the other bishop had not read the book, and that was that.

Dr. DuBose had been teaching for twenty years before his first book was published in 1892 when he was fifty-six years old. As a result he never found it necessary to revise an edition; his positions had been thought through.

Dr. DuBose was small in stature, but this was the only

[15] *The Reason of Life,* pp. 142-143.
[16] *Turning Points,* p. 90.

way in which he could be called small. His appearance and personality were so striking that even the undiscerning were impressed. His massive forehead and deep-set eyes betokened the thinker. He was gentle but with the strength of gentleness, and although his students knew that they were in the presence of a great and good man, they did not stand in awe of him. "A tiny silver saint," Will Percy calls him in the chapter on Sewanee in *Lanterns on the Levee*. He was as approachable as a friendly child, and he had a keen sense of humor. His lectures were often enlivened with good stories. In his lectures on Ethics he would come down from the platform and imitate Aristotle's *Megalopsucos* with his deep voice and dignified gait. His students were at ease in his presence. On one occasion he was hurrying to eight o'clock chapel with his gown ballooning in the wind. I said to him, "Doctor, I thought you told us that *Megalopsucos* was not in a hurry." His reply was to the effect that "A Christian can do as he pleases"—reminiscent of St. Augustine's, "Love and do as you please."

His personality was impressive but never overpowering, and he encouraged his students to think for themselves. His lectures were difficult for those who were not philosophically minded, but even these never went empty away; they "got the man" when they did not get his subtleties of thought. He lectured without notes to the whole student body, with only his Greek New Testament before him. His lecture hour was eleven o'clock and at the stroke of noon, he led the student body in noon-day prayers for missions. At times he would get lost in the Lord's Prayer and had to be prompted by his son, Professor Haskell DuBose.

Throughout his active association with the University the Doctor entered with enthusiasm into the life of the students. His enthusiasm for athletics was well known. To quote Bishop Bratton again, "The traditional spectacle will live . . . of the Doctor on the side lines of Hardee Field, bare headed and with face aflame, jostling and being jostled by equally excited students contending for a clear view of the field and of every movement of the players. No one knew better than he what the 'Sewanee spirit' meant, nor what was its power to overcome odds,—for no one had contributed more to its making and persistence"—and no one has understood the meaning and mission of Sewanee better than Dr. DuBose and few as thoroughly and as well. Bishop Bratton also brings out Dr. DuBose's love of music and poetry. He enjoyed the Negro melodies our quartet used to sing after supper under his study windows.

With the opening of the Theological Department the southern dioceses assumed the salaries of the theological professors. Sewanee was living in poverty; as Dr. Shoup, professor of metaphysics, expressed it in a toast, Sewanee is a "place where people of eminent respectability live together in cheerful poverty." At this time the DuBose family income ranged from $500 in a lean year to $1000 in a fat one.

In 1873 there had been opened at Monteagle, seven miles from Sewanee, the celebrated Fairmount School for Young Ladies, and Dr. DuBose became its chaplain and later, as we have said, married its founder, Mrs. Maria Louisa Yerger. In those days Dr. DuBose kept a horse and often spent Sunday afternoons riding back into the mountains or down into the valleys and coves to conduct services; and so on horseback he often visited Fairmount and frequently celebrated the Holy Communion for the school girls. It was at Fairmount that he lived after his retirement, with his daughters who had succeeded to the headship of the school. It was here that most of his great books were written, his daughter Susie acting as his secretary. For many years before his retirement he had been accustomed to spend the weekends at Fairmount where he preached to the girls and in the evenings read and talked with them. As part of their training the students briefed his sermons, and in the evening the girls gathered around him and he would read to them such stories as *Uncle Remus* and *The Brushwood Boy,* or delight them with his own. When the school was finally closed, he and his daughters moved back to the old Rectory at Sewanee. There he spent his closing years, near old friends and the family of his son Haskell. And it was here in the summer of 1918 that he died.

HIS CHURCHMANSHIP

Dr. DuBose might be called a high churchman, but not in any party or partisan sense. He was a high churchman because he took a high view of the Church, a high view of the Scriptures, a high view of the Sacraments. He had, as he tells us in *Turning Points in My Life*, his Evangelical phase, his Broad Church phase, his High Church phase, but they were phases, not stages, in his life. "If the extreme danger of churchliness is one-sided objectivism, that of evangelicism is one-sided subjectivism. What I have wished, and wish, to see at Sewanee, as a religious and educational centre is a high, dignified, and truly typical worship, fully expressive of the reality with which we are dealing and of what we are doing; neither manifesting by our careless-ness and indifference our contempt of, or superiority to, forms, nor, on the other hand, supposing that we have to be oriental or Latin in our exhibitions of reverence. If there were a ritual exactly and distinctively expressive of the truest and the most real reverence of our race, it would be a simple and severe one. We are least demonstrative when we think the most seriously and feel the most deeply, and least of all in matters the most sacred. At the same time, the highest good manners in the world are those that show them-selves in the presence of divine realities." [17]

He was a high churchman in no partisan sense—"tremen-dously so," to use one of his expressions, and set the tone

[17] *Turning Points*, pp. 66-67.

of the Seminary which he founded. It has kept the peace, for the most part, and caused the few fanatics, whether high, low or broad, to travel a lonely road. *Esto perpetua*. In the teaching and the spirit of Dr. DuBose, the distinctiveness and exclusiveness of Christianity were combined. In this sense, he was "broad" and "catholic." "This accounts," he writes in regard to the gathering of his former students in August 1911, "for the fact that the gathering is made up, not of those of one way, but of those of all the ways of thinking and believing in the Church. No one thinks of asking which way is most or least in evidence among us, because with whatever differences, we have learned here to think and live together without sense or recognition of parties and partisanship. All honest and reasonable differences or con- victions have been met and treated with equal interest, sympathy, and mutual respect and understanding. There are men now at home and happy in the Church who could not have entered or remained in it outside of such a wel- coming atmosphere of large-mindedness and large-hearted- ness." [18]

At the reunion of his old students, he insisted that we must be not the mere objects of God's love, but the subjects. "It is not *mere* giving, of course, that is the true expression of Christ, but giving life, soul, self. And there is no either true giving of self, or true self or life to give, that is not Love."

Commenting on this thought of Dr. DuBose, I have often added in teaching and preaching that the greatest gift of God to us is Himself as Love,—save one, and that is to love Him back with the same love wherewith He loves us.

Dr. DuBose insists that we must be not the mere objects of God's love, but the subjects as well. He requires as He gives. It is better to give than to receive even the love of God. But this, too, is a matter of grace. "We love because

[18] *Turning Points*, pp. 8-9.

He loved us first." Not truth or righteousness are adequate fully to describe the nature and character of God. Only Love can do that—"those four little letters."

In class on one occasion he told us that someone asked him if he believed in the "real presence." His answer was, "I believe in anything real."

In his celebration of the Holy Communion in the Theological Chapel, he wore white eucharistic vestments. With his snow-white hair and beard, in the candle-light of the early morning, he was completely absorbed in worship. It was a combination of meditation and contemplation in worship. Worship was a reality to him and impressed his students so.

The founders of Sewanee were mainly old-fashioned high churchmen, in the tradition of Bishop Hobart whom Bishop Gailor considered the greatest bishop of the American Church—such men as Elliott, Otey, Green, Quintard, Gailor and Guerry. They were not interested particularly in ceremonial. The liturgical revival came later, in our own day. We have always had good, if not extreme, services at Sewanee. In my student days, as now, eucharistic vestments were worn both at the University and the Theological Chapel and we have always had sung Evensong at the University Chapel. When I was a student, the late Bishop Guerry was chaplain of the University and professor of homiletics in the seminary. He had been one of Dr. DuBose's students and was thoroughly versed in his teaching. When Dr. Murray, Warden of Selwyn College, Cambridge, gave the DuBose Lectures at Sewanee in 1922, Bishop Guerry, then Bishop of South Carolina, said that some day South Carolina would recognize Dr. DuBose as its greatest citizen. That he was South Carolina's greatest citizen I think is undoubtedly true, but I fear it would be going a long way for any state to recognize a theologian as its greatest citizen.

THE END AND THE NEW BEGINNING (1918)

In the fall of 1917 on a visit to Sewanee just nine months before he died Dr. DuBose and I had a long walk together, and he was as alert and active as ever. "His mind was keenly alive and active, and clear almost to the last moment," writes his son, the late Dr. Haskell DuBose. "We could not but stand by in awe at this miracle of holy living and holy dying, vaguely aware that behind and within the veil, there was being enacted a mystical experience of which we could not be but partly conscious."[19] "Shortly before the end as his children were gathered about his bedside, he said: '. . . I am prepared and ready to go to my real home. If God should take me tonight, I would be glad. The Eternal Father, the risen Christ, the Blessed Holy Ghost have been my companions . . .' He fell asleep on August 18th, 1918. . . . 'The new life was at hand before the old ended.' The two were ever blending and perfecting him as he walked with God."[20]

His family was impoverished after the War between the States and Sherman's invasion which swept across Winnsboro, his home. In class one day he told us that after the War, he had lost his fortune and his civilization. The Church was all that he had left. To the Church he gave himself, and in it he lived and moved and had his being at Sewanee. The Church and Christianity and Sewanee became his life. "He is one of the few 'Voices' in the world; not one of the many echoes."[21]

He was a grammarian, but how much more! Nevertheless the last stanza of Browning's *A Grammarian's Funeral* applies peculiarly to him, and to his last earthly resting place on Sewanee's Mountain top.

[19] *An Apostle of Reality,* p. 213.
[20] *Ibid.,* p. 214.
[21] *DuBose as a Prophet of Unity,* p. 7.

Here's the top-peak; the multitudes below
    Live, for they can, there:
This man decided not to Live, but to Know—
    Bury this man here?
Here—here's the place, where meteors shoot, clouds form,
    Lightenings are loosened,
Stars come and go! Let joy break with the storm,
    Peace let the dew send!
Lofty designs must close in like effects:
    Loftily lying,
Leave him—still loftier than the world suspects,
    Living and dying.

THE SIGNIFICANCE OF
DuBOSE'S THEOLOGY

BY W. NORMAN PITTENGER

WILLIAM PORCHER DuBOSE was the only important creative theologian that the Episcopal Church in the United States has produced.

To put it as bluntly as this may seem extreme; but I am convinced that the statement is true and that it is highly important for Episcopalians to recognize its truth, to study his work, and to give him the place in their thinking that he so richly deserves. And this is especially necessary at this time, since DuBose not only has value in and for himself and for his theology in the abstract; he also is a corrective to tendencies in our contemporary religious thought which his constructive approach is peculiarly able to meet.

Dr. Myers, in his charming essay in this volume, has given us a biographical account and an appreciation of "the

Doctor" which will provide the reader with the information about, and with the understanding of, the man himself, particularly in his long relationship to the University of the South. Such information and such an understanding is essential, since with DuBose it is true that the man and his theology were so at one that neither can be apprehended properly without the other. Furthermore, the "style" of his writing, with its play upon words, its inversion of phrasing, its commingling of the vernacular with the technical and theological, is part of his contribution to thought. He *forced* the English language to serve his purposes. In the essays here collected and published in book-form for the first time, the literary style is much simpler and more direct than in most of his hitherto published work. Yet there is still that demand for attention, that requirement that we note with care the way he uses words and the use that he makes of them, which in a real sense is part of his contribution: we have to master, and make our own, the ideas that he is stating; we become, in a deep sense, sharers in thought with him as we read and ponder what he has to say.

MAJOR THEMES OF DuBOSE

The fact is that in these essays we have a kind of summation, and summary, of DuBose's thought about the meaning of the Christian religion, both theologically and practically. We have his loyalty to the great historical tradition of Christian faith, as the Anglican Communion has received and taught it; we have his daring use of ideas which to many at his time, and to many today, seem hardly compatible with such loyalty; we have his bold assertion of the interpenetration of God and man, his insistence on God's immanence in and work through his creation—and this in an age when Christian teachers like Barth, Brunner, Reinhold Niebuhr and many others, have emphasized almost exclusively the transcendence of God and the sinfulness and alienation of man. And we have so much more. We have his strong church-loyalty, his high valuation of the sacramental life of the Church, his deep personal piety, his courageous insistence that in Christian faith, and there supremely, the truth about man as well as the truth about God is spoken to us for our salvation.

In pointing out DuBose's theological significance, therefore, I can do no better than by listing *seriatim,* and then commenting upon, what seem to me the half-dozen major themes which run through his writings and which are expressed clearly in the essays from *The Constructive Quarterly* here printed.

CHRISTIANITY AS LIFE

Christianity, for DuBose, is primarily a *life.* That is to say, the major importance of the Christian religion is that it offers to men a participation in the life of faith, hope, charity, obedience, which is our response to the grace, love, possibility of fellowship made available in Jesus Christ. "For me to live *is* Christ," said St. Paul; and DuBose took this saying very seriously. We are to *become* Christ; his life of free obedience to the Father, his participation in the divine love, his bestowal of grace becoming the inner secret of our own lives and leading to a life in the world in which Christ is placarded before men as the truth about themselves.

This does not mean that DuBose minimized the theological structure of the Christian religion. On the contrary he insisted upon it; but he insisted upon it as derivative from the life which men live in relationship with God in Christ, and as the expression of the truth about themselves which they know and experience in their acceptance of and assimilation to the Christ who is in them. Theology as an arid, intellectual discipline did not interest DuBose; his concern for it was, in our modern idiom, entirely existential.

It is because it *concerns* us, because it speaks out of and speaks to the depths of our life, that we must attend to it.

THE IMMANENCE OF GOD

DuBose sees that man, made for this life in Christ, in the Image of God, and indwelt by the personal Word of God, is in actual fact a sinner. But he does not exaggerate this sinfulness of man in the style of many of our contemporaries. He recognizes man's deviation from the divine purpose, his estrangement from the divine love, his willful choice of ends which are not in accord with his true (i.e., God-intended) nature. But his teaching does not concentrate on sin; it concentrates on the redemption wrought in Christ and the universal scope of that already-accomplished fact. In the life, teaching, death, and resurrection of our Lord, all has been done that need ever be done to establish the conditions necessary for our restoration. Our task is now given us: it is to accept that which has been done, to live ourselves into it and make it our own, "to become Christ" (as I phrased it above).

Hence DuBose, while agreeing with the Augustinian analysis of man's situation, is unwilling to accept the corollary which post-Augustinianism often made. He cannot say that man is utterly helpless and hopeless, because for him man is *never*, even in his sin, without the presence and the power, the grace and help, which God grants to all his children. He takes very seriously the truth of our participation—by virtue of our personal humanity—in the Word of God, the Word who was incarnate in Christ. And he refuses to separate our feeble, stumbling human efforts from the always present, ever operative, grace of God in the Word. We must work. We must in fact "work out our own salvation in fear and trembling," precisely because in that very work, done by us in all freedom, *God* works in us, "both to will and to do of his good pleasure." It is when we are doing *our* best, humanly speaking (and thus with complete safeguarding of our human responsibility and freedom), that God is doing *his* best (thus safeguarding the divine action); and it is in our doing that God's doing is effectively manifest, for God comes first with his prevenient grace, his initiating love, his determining action.

Our awareness of sinfulness is not therefore a token of our hopeless state, so much as it is the recognition of a fact which God overcomes in us; which he *has* overcome and which he wills that we overcome through him and in his power.

CHRIST THE WORD

This leads us to a consideration of DuBose's view of Christ our Lord. Here "the Doctor" was at one with the early Church in his insistence on the truth in the doctrine of the *Logos* or Word. In the whole creation the Word is at work, indwelling it and operative through it. There is a general immanence of God in that sense, although I fancy that DuBose preferred to think of "immanence" as properly attributed to the Holy Spirit, and would have preferred some such phrasing as "the general concomitance of God the Word in and through the creation." It is this Word—God in that mode of his being which "proceeds forth" in creation and revelation—who is known in human history and in human experience in a personal manner. Because men are persons, the Word works in, speaks to, and expresses himself through them, *personally*. Thus, "in the fullness of the times," when all was seen by God as "ready," Jesus was born. In him the Word of God dwelt and through him the Word of God acted, with such fullness and intensity that it was appropriate for the Johannine writer to say of him that "the Word was made flesh and dwelt among us, full of grace and truth."

DuBose was very emphatic about the full reality of the humanity of Jesus; he had no patience with a docetic Christology, in which the Word simply masqueraded "in flesh," nor had he any patience with Apollinarian and similar points of view, in which our Lord's mind, or some other aspect of his human nature, is supplanted by the Word. In the *fullest* sense, Jesus is human, our Brother; and it is exactly because he is man in this complete sense —and that means man in free, responsible, obedient, loving relationship with God—that he is also divine in a genuine sense, too.

God and man, therefore, are not seen by DuBose as separated by a chasm so utter and so deep that only by a catastrophic intrusion from outside can they be brought together. They are *for* each other; God originatively as creator and source, man derivatively as dependent upon and needing God for his fulfillment as man. Furthermore, DuBose is prepared to go even further and to say, in daring phrase, that God "needs" man—not for his being, not lest God fail, but simply and solely because in the divine love God "made man for himself" and his heart of love is not satisfied until that great intention is realized and accomplished. In Christ it *was* accomplished; in him, the Image of God is fully imaged; in him, the Truth about man is spoken and enacted and realized. *Now* the process of God's operation is the taking of men, through their free response in obedient love, into that relationship, so that they become in him that which in the divine intention they already are.

THE UNITY OF GOD AND MEN IN CHRIST

    This is the context in which DuBose sees the Church. The Church is no mechanical affair, no simply human organization; it is a living, dynamic fellowship in which the life of God in Christ is shared with men, incorporating them into that which was achieved by God, through and in man, in Christ.

As the essays in this volume show, "unity" was for DuBose the great goal and purpose of the Church. Unity between God and man in Christ; unity between man and

man in Christ; unity of all Christians in the Body of Christ
—here are recurrent themes which we need to emphasize
over again in our own time. This unity is to be expressed
outwardly as the Christian communions, now divided, find
their common centre in Christ and the life in him. Problems
of ministry, and the like, are to be viewed in this light; and
there will be, for DuBose, no solution of them unless they
are thus viewed. The episcopate, for example, is not so
much a bone of contention between divided Christians as it
is a symbol and expression of the unity which can be theirs.
To commend the episcopate, therefore, is not to fight for
it; it is to show, in concrete fact, that it does symbolize and
express the unity of Christians in their Lord in his Body,
where he is at work to bring them into a one-ness with God
and their fellows through common unity in him.

The sacraments are also understood in this way. DuBose
liked to quote Luther's dictum that the Christian life was a
realizing of the fact of our baptism. That meant for him
that the baptized person is one who has now been united
with God, and his fellows, in Christ; his whole Christian
life is an explication and amplification of that unity once
given—it is a taking for ourselves and on ourselves of all
that baptism gives. Similarly, the Holy Communion (upon
which DuBose wrote with an eloquence and passion which
must move us deeply) is a continuing action in which the
life of unity is nourished, strengthened, renewed, given again
and again for our acceptance and assimilation.

GOD'S CONTINUING REVELATION

DuBose believed that the world-view as-
sociated with the evolutionary description of nature, especially biological nature, fitted well the Christian faith.
Indeed one might say that he regarded it as a kind of "new
revelation" to our own day. Some will think that he over-
emphasized both its significance and its Christian relevance.
I for one do not believe that he did so. It seems to me that

here is one of his themes which, with whatever modifications may be required in detail, gives him a particular importance. For him, evolution did not mean the simple unpacking of what was already there; it meant the ever-fresh appearing of life and the dynamic, vital, process of change and development—in a phrase of my own which, I think, expresses DuBose's view of this, "continuity of process with emergence of genuine novelty." I am convinced that the turning of our theologians, during the years since DuBose's death, from this deep appreciation of the scientific contribution to our knowledge, and their interesting themselves in a kind of "domestic housekeeping," in which they talk to themselves about their theologies, has contributed very largely to that alienation of religion from life, that apparent irrelevance of Christianity to the common affairs and the common knowledge of ordinary men and women, which is so much a phenomenon of the quarter-century now past.

In any event, DuBose both welcomed and used the general evolutionary picture. A world in which God is ceaselessly at work, bringing his purposes to pass in most varied ways; a world in which there is life, movement, change, growth; a world which is, so to say, the material out of which God brings the new life—here is his theme. And he will not permit pre-scientific notions of irruption into the world, or un-natural ideas of the crudely miraculous to be central to the basic Christian affirmation, although he has a real place for what miracle *means* in his insistence that God works ever in the world to bring to pass fresh and novel emergences, juxtapositions and coincidences.

He emphasized strongly God's providential care of his creation. In fact one might say that God's "providence" was for him only another way of saying that God is ceaselessly at work in his world, ever moving through it and in it to accomplish his designs. Providence meant the *personal* action of the *personal* God. It was a general providence, in that God is in all that happens, whether for good or for ill

—he is in it when it is for good because it is then the direct expression of himself; he is in it when ill is found, because then he works to make the very evil a means to a good, or better, end. Providence was also special, in that a man who commits himself to God finds that God "works all things together for good," not by removing obstacles nor by easing life but by giving himself in and through the hardships, accidents, evils as they occur.

In his autobiographical addresses published under the title *Turning Points of My Life,* DuBose beautifully relates prayer to this conception. He remarks that there is indeed no limit to what God will do for us in answer to our prayer; but he goes on to insist that this is never in complete opposition to us, but it is in us and through us that God answers. He says that God will not make us holy, in spite of ourselves; he will make us holy through and in and by our own seeking of holiness. Even in petitionary prayer for "things," DuBose says, God does not *change for us* the order which he has established, but in that order he adapts both it and us to the end that we may become his better children, more dependent upon him, more loving towards him, more expressive of the Christ who is in us. Prayer, then, is not a magical coercion; it is a religious devotion.

THE BIBLE

There is one other point upon which I must dwell. This is the biblical note which is found throughout DuBose's writing—notably found in these essays. He began his theologizing with, and from, the Bible. He did this, not without full attention to the results of biblical research (and little incidental remarks in his writing show that he had taken full account of all this), but with great regard for the predominantly *religious* nature of the Scriptures. One might say that he used the Bible as the record of man's continuing *experience* of the fact of God's continuing *self-revelation;* or one might say that he took the Bible as the supreme and normative account of the fact of God and of God's ways with his children. But he never used the Scriptures woodenly or unimaginatively. He did not try to force St. Paul's varied and changing religious insight into a "system"; he saw his epistles as the reflection of a vivid experience which impelled him to "be all things to all men," if he could by any means bring them to share his discovery by Christ and his acceptance of the new life in him. In my judgment, DuBose used the Bible in the right way; he did not treat it after the fashion of those biblical theologians who are enamoured of the letter of Scripture, but he read it and used it spiritually. His was what some contemporary German scholars would call a "spiritual exegesis." Thus he was able to see the Bible in closest relationship with, rather than as the eternal enemy of, the rest of man's life and the rich multiplicity of his experience.

THE RICHNESS OF DuBOSE'S THOUGHT

I am quite aware of the unhappy fact that I have not been able to do justice to William Porcher DuBose. Not only have I failed to give as fully as I ought, and as I should have liked, the analysis of the themes that I have chosen; I have also failed to include half a dozen other themes which are almost equally important. But perhaps it is just as well that I have failed. For this will send the reader to DuBose's own writings; and there he will find, in all its richness, a Christian theology which is thoroughly alive, thoroughly alert, appealing not in spite of, but because of, the style and manner of its presentation.

He will also find that DuBose makes him *think*. The "Doctor" told his hearers, at the anniversary celebration whose report is found in the volume to which I have already referred, *Turning Points,* that he did not aim, that he never had aimed, at making disciples who would simply accept what he said as he said it. What he had sought to do was to inculcate an attitude, a way of looking at our faith, which they could then use for themselves. It would be contrary to his strongest desires if we were to become "apers," so to say, of his thought. But in the themes which I have discussed and in the others which the reader will discover for himself as he reads these essays and then (as we may hope) goes on to the big books and the two or three little books which appeared in DuBose's lifetime, he will be stimulated and inspired to do some hard thinking. And it is my judgment that he will find that in the emphases which I have noted, and in others too, there will be given him new and deeper insight into the Christian faith. Above all, there will be new and deeper impulsion towards Christian life— towards the conscientious yet joyful appropriation for himself of the grace, the love, the fellowship, with God, in the loyal, obedient, faithful life which is proper to the sons of men.

UNITY IN THE FAITH

A CONSTRUCTIVE TREATMENT
OF CHRISTIANITY

It is absurd to say that there can be a religion of
God without a theology, or a life of Christ without
a Christology . . . faith without creed . . . sacra-
ments or worship without forms. We do not know
anything without body . . .

Before venturing upon a construction, or even a constructive
treatment, of Christianity, let me first carefully limit and
define the term, as I purpose to use it. "Constructive" and
"construction" may attach either to the verb to construct or
to the verb to construe, and these two, though the same in
origin, have a very different force in use. I do not undertake
to construct but only to *construe* Christianity.

Christianity *is*, and is what it is: I cannot conceive it as at
this late day either needing to be or capable of being "made"
or "made over." Jesus Christ is Christianity, and He is The
Same, yesterday, today, and forever. Nor can I see that
He is not as nearly The Same to us all as any Reality can be
which is subject to the deficiencies and varieties of our
human construing, the imperfections of our understanding

and the inadequacy of our spiritual appropriation and experience. There is nothing in the world, or out of it, that is the same to every man, or even to any two men,— not even God, or God perhaps least of all. However He is The Same in Himself, He is to us only that which, and so much as, each of us construes Him.

This therefore is only my own construction, or construing, of Christianity: probably no single reader will accept it as his own. And yet I believe that among us all, or all who will call themselves Christians, there will be a consensus or agreement, a unity, of faith and experience, so far as I shall express these, in comparison with which our differences ought to count as nothing. Our agreement will be as to the real end, matter, and fact of the Life in Christ. Our disagreements will begin and end with our theories, explanations, philosophies and doctrines, all which are in the sphere of our human construing, and outside that of the divine facts. Nevertheless, not only are all these too, all this human handling of the truth, inevitable and necessary, but the differences they engender are equally necessary to the completeness and totality of the truth. No man can see all the truth, or the truth on all its sides, and the more living and in earnest he is the more will he magnify the part he sees out of proportion with, and even to the exclusion of, what he does not see. There is a divine wisdom in the promise of truth not to the individual but to the Church. No genius or honesty or spirituality has ever exempted any individual from the possibility and danger of error. Our Lord has placed the security and conservation of His truth where it naturally and rationally belongs, in the reconciliation of differences, the inner and higher unity of outer and partial diversities, in the essential and ultimate oneness of the many and not in the excellence or superiority of the one or the few. The Church is divinely organized and constituted Unity,—a unity within which by free interrelation and interaction different points of view, impressions, emphases, perspectives, and so theories, doctrines, systems, etc., may correct, supplement, and complete one another and bring all to the essential and sufficient unity that not only belongs to them but can come only through their all-sided contributions. Incidentally we may say of Sects in Christianity that their evil is expressed in the word itself: they are organized and isolated differences and diversities. Their partial and emphasized good is withdrawn from communication to and influence upon others; their deficiencies, ignorances or errors are removed from supplementing or correction by others. They are destructive of that Oneness in Christ which is the essence and definition of Christianity, which is ours in spite of our differences, and within which our differences would quickly melt down into not merely pardonable or permissible but even contributory and completive diversities.

It seems to be the general experience and conclusion of missionaries that in such other civilizations as the Chinese, Japanese, or East Indian, our Western differences and divisions are incomprehensible and a serious hindrance to the reception of Christianity. While, on the other hand, these civilizations are as open and susceptible to Christian truth and life as our own is. There is as little doubt that at home, thinking, living and active Christians are growing more and more restive and dissatisfied under what they are coming to look upon as senseless internecine strifes and are demanding substitution of unity and co-operation for division and competition. And outside of organized and visible Christianity, there is a growing multitude of those who say that they have no use for the churches as they are, but nevertheless not only disclaim irreligion, but profess faith in God and in Christ.

Now the matters of our human disagreements, while outside the objective, divine and unchangeable fact of Christianity itself, cannot therefore be all swept away and done without. It is absurd to say that there can be a religion of

God without a theology, or a life of Christ without a
Christology, truth without doctrine, faith without creed,
Church without order or orders, sacraments or worship without forms. We do not know anything without body, or until
we have embodied it: the most spiritual or the most abstract
truth or idea must be in some way expressed, uttered or
"outered," before it can be ours. We can know nothing
of God Himself except through His Word,—that which in
some way expresses Him, or that which eternally and
universally expresses Him. There is no question that there
is an objectively and transcendently true Theology and
Christology, a true divine intention and meaning of Church
and Sacraments; and that all these are to be more and more
known by us,—and known in the sense and by the means
of being expressed, embodied, realized. Spiritual or intellectual, immaterial and invisible forms of conception are
just as much forms as material and visible ones, and we
cannot know or do without them.

Our differences, therefore, and the matter and forms of
our differences, have to be reckoned with, and the propriety
and necessity of their being either composed and done away
or else reconciled and harmonized is not to be surrendered
to the difficulty or seeming impossibility of the task. The
time seems to be ripe in Christendom for the assuming
and entering upon that task, and I have no further suggestion to make upon the conduct of it. But preliminary to
it,—admitting as we must the impossibility of simply wiping
out our differences and divisions, and the necessity of in
some way that is God's way settling them—our present day
construing of Christianity must meet the needs and demands
of the time with that in Christianity which is before and
above and without our controversies, which is outside the
field of our human versions and perversions of it. May we
not interpret and accept the "Back to Christ"—with all its
vagueness, diversity, and conflict of meanings, within and
without the Churches—as not merely a desire of escape

from the confusions of current Christianity, but something deeper and more positive, a feeling of the drawing of the Christ?

Our Lord says, "I, if I be lifted up, will draw all men unto Me." He also says, "No man can come unto Me except the Father draw him." Not on these words alone do we base the assertion that there is a universal drawing of humanity to Christ—a drawing both from within and from without, both natural and supernatural, not only from the Divine without us to the divine within us, but also from the divine within us to the Divine without us. That is, religion has a double origin: it comes alike from God to us and from us to God. Therefore it can be treated equally as a human production and as a divine communication, as the act of God in man, and as the act of man in God. All attraction is on both sides, whether between matter and matter, between man and woman, or between the soul and God. The assertion that there is a universal drawing of humanity to Christ is based upon the fact of the natural drawing of all life, of every form of life, to its proper end and destiny, to its predestined complement and completion. All acorns do not become oaks, because there lie many conditions and many hindrances between; but every acorn has an inherent impulse and disposition to be an oak.

I believe that the times are full of this natural and universal drawing to Christ. I believe that there is a great deal of Christianity in men outside of the Churches, to whom the Churches are a hindrance and an obstacle to their coming to Christ. It is because Christ is the reason and the meaning and the end of every man that all men are drawn to Him, unless hindered by conditions or by sin. It is a fearful thing if in any way the Churches are standing between men and Christ, if in any sense or with any truth it can be said, as was once said of the Church of God, "The name of God [that should be glorified] is blasphemed among men because of you."

It is this too general condition that we have to meet and deal with: we have to confess that at this late date of the Christian Era men are still asking, Who is Christ, and What is Christianity? We have more need than ever to get behind our logomachies, and be making straighter approaches and simpler answers to these questions. The way must be open to all true comers, no matter what or how, or how indirect, the drawing: Christ would have all men come unto Him. There must be made "straight paths for the feet, that that which is lame be not turned out of the way, but rather be healed."

There are three directions or points of view from which, prior to all differences among Christians, I should approach the matter of our common Christianity. The first I will call the Conceptual or Intuitional,—by which I mean Christianity viewed and considered from the standpoint of ourselves. Religion is primarily a matter of human conception—as well as of divine generation. There must be the womb or the soil as well as the seed, mother as well as father,—and the offspring is of the one as well as the other, or rather of the union of the two. Considering the former of the two sources, it is a truth, though only a half truth, to treat religion as a product or function of humanity itself, as having a human cause and origin. It is the highest instance of the natural impulse and effort of a finite being to find itself, to compass its end, to realize its nature and accomplish its destiny. The end of man is as far above and beyond that of any other being within our knowledge as his reason, his freedom, his personality is superior to anything else in nature, of which he is the head and crown. That God is the true and supreme end of man we know by the simple fact that the end of man can lie only on true lines of himself, and all these lines lead directly and only to God. The end of his mind is Truth, the end of his feelings or affections is Love, the end of his will and activities is Goodness and Good: and the completeness and perfection of all these is God. No finite spirit, seeking and striving to be all itself, can will or conceive for itself anything short of the infinitely True, Beautiful, and Good—infinite Wisdom, Virtue, Happiness—infinite Holiness, Righteousness, Life. God, so far as we can know Him, is the Infinite, Eternal, Perfect of ourselves, as we are the finite, incomplete, and imperfect of Him. If this is a conceiving or creating God in our own image, I admit it and justify it. It is the only way and form in which we can know God at all. When God would fully reveal or manifest Himself to us, it was necessarily on this same line—in a Human Son, One who was fully He and fully We. It is impossible to think of God except as the infinite and perfect of ourselves. If it was a human conception, then it was a true human conception or intuition, of God, of ourselves, and of our relation to God, that in the beginning laid the foundation of religion in the fact that we are created or constituted in the image of God; and that the beginning and principle of all spiritual instinct and impulse is the natural movement and effort of the spirit in us to fulfil itself in that image, to realize itself as Son of God, to become perfect as our Father in Heaven is perfect.

The spiritual nature and life of man has had its aeons, and may yet have to pass through aeons, of evolution, but we can take its bearings and read its direction. It is moving on to God, and even when it is not, or we cannot see that it is, we know that it ought to be doing so, that that Good is its goal. I have so far treated all this as pure human conception or intuition, but it may be this without being only this. It may be ourselves and yet God in us, or God in us and still completely and perfectly ourselves—as we see manifested in the divine-human person of our Lord. Whatever of higher or divine there is in all our truly spiritual selves and acts, the truth remains that the divine in this world works only in, with, and through the natural, and above all the human. All creation, natural and spiritual, is through evolution: everything that is made also makes itself, —is made to make itself through a process immanent and operative in itself. There is nothing natural or human in which or of which science, carried far enough, might not discover natural or human causes or conditions,—unless we distinguish between these, and recognize that conditions are never causes—that there is but one Cause. As nothing ever comes of God in things except through things, so nothing ever comes from God to man except through man, and except through the organs or faculties and laws of human transmission. If God has spoken to the prophet and through the prophet, how has He done so? It was the prophet's own consciousness and conscience of God that spoke in him in the name and with the authority of God. God was indeed in him and with him, but in his own consciousness and as his own conscience. The spirit of man, as any other part of him, is fallible, and there are false prophets; we must try the spirits whether they be of God. But that no more proves that the spirit of man is not a medium of actual relation with God and of true communication from God, than false impressions or conclusions prove that our senses or our reason are not proper instruments of natural fact and truth. Let any man's consciousness and conscience be that of God in a matter, and he will speak, and have a right to speak, in the name and with the authority of God. It will be no blasphemy in him to say, Thus saith the Lord.

Our Lord Himself had a human spiritual as well as natural genealogy. The human faith and character in Him that conquered the world and brings it into oneness with God, the human love that in Him was stronger than death and brought life and immortality to light, were older than His own supreme manifestation of them, and only culminated in Himself in the fulness of a time of age-long growth and preparation. He humanly inherited the faith, the hope, the love that so supremely characterized Himself. If in all these human endowments He also transcended their human origin and degree, so as in His sole person to manifest and to render possible and assured their ultimate triumph in our common humanity, if Christianity now claims as distinctly and immediately a divine as a human origin and operation, yet the divine in it is absolutely and perfectly along the lines of the human, is simply redemptive and completive of the human. Whatever our Lord humanly was, suffered, or accomplished in the matter of our salvation, was precisely what our nature demanded, what ourselves need, as constituting our salvation. He was all that we are, in order that we might through Him become all that He is, that we might become all ourselves in and with Him. All that was supernatural in Jesus Christ, His birth from above, His human life, sufferings, death, resurrection and ascension, was but the process of our own further and higher nature and destination.

If it is necessary to construe Christianity thus to ourselves as a genuinely human conception, as an instinct and intuition of ourselves, born of the divine within us and looking for completion through union with the Divine without us, as the outcome of our own "feeling after" that we may "find" God—all this, however essential a part it may be of the religion of Christ, is but the ante-chamber, the precondition, of His Gospel. The Gospel, as such, comes wholly after any and all immanent or prevenient or merely natural and human want or search or anticipation of it. However much of religion may have come *of* us, as the groping and search of the divine in ourselves, the Gospel comes only and wholly as the response of the Divine from *without* us. Eliminate from Jesus Christ the truths and facts expressed in the distinctively and specifically Christian terms Incarnation and Resurrection, and you drop Him out of the category of Realizer, Revealer, and Giver, into that of, still, Seeker. He is not even, in any real sense, Seer; for it is manifestly true in itself, quite apart from our Lord's having said so, that "No man hath seen God at any time," or is able to know or empowered to communicate "the things freely given us of God" which constitute The Gospel.

It is not enough to say that, however truly human our Lord was, the very completeness and perfection of His humanity, the fact of His having humanly conquered sin and transcended death, proves a something more than human with Him and in Him. Not only in Christ but in Christianity every single term or element of properly called Gospel means, and necessarily means, something more than human with us and in us through Christ. What then is it in Christianity that makes it distinctively and specifically a gospel, and The Gospel? It is not that it is the truest human guess at truth or intuition of truth. It is not that it is the rightest human rule or law of righteousness. It is not that it is the purest human spirit of love and goodness. It is neither the highest human example nor the most consummate exposition of all these that makes Christianity The Gospel. Of course if we carry them to the limit of the perfection which we claim for Christ, then at once all this truth and righteousness and holiness is lifted out of the merely human —even with all its natural divinity. We must say with Nicodemus, "Thou art a teacher come from God." But then such a divine teaching and example would not itself be a Gospel. Christ is more than a Teacher, and Christianity is more than a teaching.

The essence of Christianity is expressed in the word Incarnation, and its function in the fact of Resurrection and Eternal Life. We need of course to be told and shown, and to know, what truth and holiness and righteousness and life are; but that, however both humanly and divinely it were accomplished for us and by us, would not meet and satisfy our real need. What we want is not to know Truth, Beauty, and Goodness—though that is necessary by the way; it is to be true, beautiful, and good. We want God in us and with us,—not immanently and naturally as He is in everything, but personally and transcendently as He is only in those who are themselves in Him, whose faith and hope and love are in Him, and whose holiness, righteousness, and life are His in them. The beginning of the Gospel is God in Christ, the end of it is that God in Christ not only means, but is, God in Humanity, God in Us. By Us I mean not our mere being or nature, but our conscious, free, personal, and living Selves.

The Gospel not only makes God one with us in Christ, but makes all the human life of Christ ours. The essence of that life was, not merely its attitude, but the completeness and finality of its attitude, toward Sin on the one hand, and Holiness or God on the other. No spiritual intuition or conception of the end or destiny of man can picture it otherwise than as the final extinction in him of all that we call sin, and the fulfilling in him of all we call holiness: sin meaning all transgression or contradiction of nature, Self, or God, and holiness all fulfilling of nature and Self in God. The finality of Christ's attitude and act in us is that, as toward sin it was "unto death," that is, unto the human extinction of sin; and as toward holiness it was "unto eternal life," that is, unto the completion and perfection of nature and self, the fulness of life, in God.

The Gospel, finally, provides for such a relation of ourselves to all that Christ did, and was, and is in our humanity, such a relation to it and to Him of faith and hope and love on our part, and of love, grace, and fellowship or oneness with us on His part, as constitutes the most perfect assurance and guarantee, both human and divine, of its being made actually and entirely our own. So God becomes through Christ our Holiness, our Righteousness, and our Life,—and that so completely through ourselves, through the free action and co-operation of our own minds and hearts, our own wills and activities, that His righteousness or life in us is equally ours in Him.

Our task, then, in the second place, is to construe Christ as completely on the divine side as on the human, to see in

Him as truly a Divine Act, an act of God's Love and Grace and Fellowship enacted in, with, and through human faith, hope, and love,—as on the other hand we see in Him a true human act, an act of human faith, hope and love, realizing itself or attaining its end of eternal life, through the love, grace, and fellowship of God working with and in it. The question is how best to emphasize anew, to bring afresh to human need and vision, this divine aspect of the person and work of Christ. I know no other way than the perpetual task of ever renewing and revitalizing the old way—the way of the Historic Christ, the Scriptures, and the Catholic Faith and Life of the Church. The truer our human powers of spiritual intuition and conception, the better will we see the divine and eternal truth and necessity expressed in the terms Incarnation and Resurrection, the human and superhuman meaning of the Birth, Life, Death, and Life Again of Jesus Christ. The difficulties in the letter of all these facts will never, in a true and complete human experience, prevail against the spiritual necessity and inevitableness of their truth.

But we have yet, in the third place, to meet our sorest and most immediate need in the construction, or construing, of our Christianity. It is not enough that Christianity should be, in itself, true to, the very truth of, human nature, human aspiration, and human destination. It is not enough that it should have been historically true in Christ, in the actual fact of an Incarnation of God and a resurrection of humanity in His person. The greatest need remains,—namely, that Christianity shall be a living Fact today, co-ordinate and co-equal in us with what it was in Christ, and what it means and is for us. How shall we go about, not merely conceptually or historically, but actually and practically and presently, construing it for ourselves? I can only suggest some considerations that are as old as Christianity itself,—with the reminder that, as far back as St. John, the task of the individual, the task of each age and time, the task of conscious, intelligent, free, and responsible life forever, is to keep "That which was from the beginning" true and new and alive to the end. It is our business ever to make and keep Christianity as actual and active and living a thing as it was in Christ Himself. The weakness and unreality of so much of our present day Christianity is not so much the consequence as the cause of the doubt and scepticism and criticism to which it has been not unjustly subjected.

Christianity came once, but it did not come for once only: it came once for all, and for all time. It came to be as much in the world today as on the day of our Lord's nativity or of His resurrection. We want the full sense and meaning, if we would realize the full actuality of that truth. We say that Christianity is the Incarnation of God. So far from true is it that the Incarnation ended, even on earth, with the human life and ascension of Christ, that neither did it begin with His birth. The Incarnation is the whole matter of the eternal spiritual—as distinguished from natural or immanent or encosmic—relation, and ultimate unity, of God and man. That process began on earth so soon as the very first inchoate spiritual interrelation and communion were possible and actual between God and man; it will end when humanity, so far as may or shall be, shall be of one spirit, one divine law, one eternal life with God. The expression is, We shall be "One Man" in Christ Jesus, One Humanity in the One Perfected Manhood. The distinctively Christian work of Christ on earth began properly and historically on the Day of Pentecost,—that is, with His session at the right hand of God and His return in the Spirit. All that went before, even the Death and the Resurrection, were only preparing the conditions and laying the foundation. The Life was being lived and made perfect for us, which was to be re-lived and perfected in us and with us and by us. If Christ in us now, in the Mystical Body of which He is Head and we are members, is not as living, and the same Christ, as He was on earth in His natural body,—then most assuredly has there been with us a solution, or dissolution, of the continuity of the Incarnation.

The actual and active presence and operation of Christ as human or universal salvation began properly on the Day of Pentecost. When Christ was glorified the Holy Ghost came, not to supply the place of His absence but to effect His truer, universal and permanent, presence. The supposition that underlay that inception of Christianity as the World Religion may be gathered from the New Testament at almost any point. Let us consider, for example, the tacit assumption of certain questions addressed by St. Paul to the Corinthians: "Is Christ divided?" "Was Paul crucified for you?" "Were ye baptized into Paul?" These questions assume the inclusiveness and universality of Christ. A new humanity, or stage of humanity, a new birth and a new life of humanity, has come into actuality in Him. He is no longer a divine Person only, but divine Humanity. Whatever of incarnation of God, whatever of regeneration and resurrection of humanity, was in Him and was His, was for us and to be ours.

How was this to come about? As a matter of fact it did come about immediately; He was the Head in heaven, and the Church through His spiritual presence in it was His Body upon earth. All that He had Himself accomplished and attained and become in the matter of human salvation, to the limit of the human death to sin and resurrection to eternal life, was now to be appropriated by, reproduced in and re-enacted by those in whom He returns to live on earth. In the fulness of faith it is assumed that all this is actually the case: so true and assured is all this to faith, that to faith it is already true in fact. And just that quality and character of faith is the sole condition and means of its becoming true in fact. "We are dead, We are risen, We have overcome, and are more than conquerors through Him that loved us." "In that He died, He died unto sin; in that He liveth, He liveth unto God: likewise we account ourselves to be dead unto sin and alive unto God through Jesus Christ our Lord." "As many of us as were baptized into Christ were baptized into His death. We were buried with Him by baptism into death, that as He rose from the dead by the glory of the Father, even so should we walk in newness of life." Now all this language—and it is the assumption and foundation of the whole New Testament—is either the most hyperbolic and extravagant of figures, or else it is that transcendent divine truth and reality which we best justify in our Lord's historical appearance upon earth by recognizing and manifesting it in ourselves as His permanent presence still.

Christianity has been sometimes represented as "Salvation by Sample or Example." We do see and know our own salvation perfectly enacted and represented in the life and death—or rather, in the death and life—of our human Lord. And since God draws us to Himself "with cords of a man," we may say that we are saved after the manner of Christ, by walking in His steps, by taking up His cross and following Him, by reflecting His likeness, and so being conformed to or transformed into His image. But faith makes Jesus Christ very much more than a mere example to us: it makes Him not only sample but cause and substance of our salvation. "Because I live, ye shall live also." "I am the Way, the Truth, and the Life." So that we may say, "I live no longer, Christ lives in me." And yet only then do we truly live, because Christ is the only true life and Self of every man.

My word and my spirit may go a little way in influencing and changing others; they may go beyond myself, for I cannot accompany them. God's Word and Spirit cannot go beyond Him: where they are He is, for they are always and livingly Himself. If we are in right relation (of faith, hope, and love) with Christ and His salvation, in the fellowship of His death and the participation of His resurrection, then God's presence and power in us will manifest themselves much more potently than after the manner of mere human influence and example. His Word and Spirit will new-create us into the substance and likeness of what we would be.

If to our newer or truer constructions both of the Human and of the Divine Christ, the Christ of our Intuition and the Christ of History, we are to add a newer and truer construction of Christianity Today,—we are to remember that the New of God is always the Old: the newness is in us, not in Him or in It. What we shall accomplish will not be wholly on newly invented or modern lines,—as though nothing of what we seek has existed before or from the very beginning: "Let that which was from the beginning abide with you and in you," says St. John. If Christianity since Christ has been a continuous fact and factor in the world, if in any sense (actually or ideally) it has been and remains One,—it has done so and been so under the form and entity of the Christian Church and Sacraments. Whatever differences of interpretation or of appreciation of these may exist among us, we will agree that, at the very least, they are intended to signify and symbolize, to express and emphasize, what is essential and vital in Christianity as an integral and permanent factor in the world. And the Church and the Sacraments have no other significance than the continued presence of Jesus Christ Himself upon earth, and our human part and participation in Him—that is to say, in the Incarnate Life of God in humanity which He is. What else can the Church mean and be, than the Body of our Lord's presence and operation upon earth? What is Baptism but our incorporation into that Body, being made participants in that Life? What is the Lord's Supper but our actual, personal, continuous participation in that Life of God in Christ?

There is a line of cleavage in Christian thought upon the question, How far, on the one hand, the Church and the Sacraments only humanly *mean* what they mean,—and, on the other hand, how far they divinely *are* what they mean; and so ought to *be* to us all that they mean. All signs, symbols, types, or figures are only words, spoken to the eye rather than to the ear: different modes of expressing *things*. Ought we not to make a difference between God's words (if we believe them to be such) and men's words? Our words may only mean, but God's words *are*. What we need in our Christianity is, To Take God at His Word, to believe that What He Says to us in Christ Is. It is as much a part of Christianity to know that Christ is in His Church, as it is to know that God is in Christ. If we truly believed that the Church is Christ's Body, the actual and sole organ and instrument of His life and work upon earth; if we truly knew that we are members of His body, partakers of His life, and doers of all that He is in the world to do; if Baptism were to our faith the death and life of Christ, and the Bread and Wine were His Body and Blood, instead of only signs of something not there,—how would the Gospel begin to manifest itself as that which in itself it is—as that which but for us it would be—the Power of God unto salvation, because a Righteousness of God in us through Faith!

With all our mutual understandings and agreements, there will always be certain differences among us, because of certain inevitable liabilities and dangers equally to be found on opposite sides of the above truth of the Church. Some will always be thinking that others are making too much of the outward and visible for the proper emphasis and operation of the inward and spiritual. The others will be equally sure that these are making too much of their own subjective states and selves, and denying or ignoring the objective divine presence and grace upon which the internal state is and ought to be directly conditioned. Are not these two opposite attitudes both necessary and wholesome offsets, and does not the truth and life of Christianity depend upon its ability to meet and compose such differences?

WHY THE CHURCH—IN CHRISTIANITY

In a word, Christianity is:—to realize or to make real (not in themselves but only in ourselves) the truths and facts of God in Christ, of Christ in His Church or Body, of the Church, in all its fulness of the life of Christ and of God, in humanity and in us. Faith is the doing this; and where Faith is, and in proportion as it is real, will ensue Holiness, Righteousness, and Eternal Life, which are the elements and process of our conversion into the Life and Likeness of God.

A very popular evangelist was recently asked, "Are the churches, or the Church, essential to Christianity?" He is reported to have answered, indirectly and practically as follows: "If you want to get to Europe—there are the ships. If you object to the ships and think they are in the way—of course, there is swimming." I wish, in the first place, to point in the simplest way to the notorious fact that there is in our time a wide-spread disposition to dispense with the Church, or the Churches, in Christianity. None of us, I think, wish to deny that there is a great deal of Christianity outside of the Churches: Why does it so much, and apparently increasingly, prefer to remain outside? But again—within the Churches, is there not an equal disposition to make as little of the Church, and as little use of the Church, as such, as possible? Of course I know that this is true only of one of the great sections of Christianity, and that there are other sections which to this one seem to make far too much of the Church and to depend disproportionately upon its "mere" acts and offices. To those who make however much of the Church and its office, I hope that what I shall say will commend itself as true so far as it goes. To those who, even I think, make much too little, I hope it will approve itself as having in it much more of truth than most of us are in the habit of seeing or remembering. At any rate, I am going to try in this paper to mean by the Church what none of us will disclaim as being the truth and essence of it, —though some may not have consciously realized its full reality, and others may feel that fulness of it is still lacking.

The "Why" of the Church depends of course upon its "What." To know precisely What the Church is would answer completely and satisfactorily all questions of Why it is,—that is, Why it is *de jure* and why it ought to be *de facto*. The statement I shall make of it is consistently that of the New Testament taken as a whole. Already we find there all of Christianity that we know, and increasingly more of it that we know not yet and are more and more coming to know. For the fulness of knowledge depends less upon the completeness of the thing to be known than upon the growth and progress of our power to know it.

What the Church is depends immediately and wholly upon what Christ is,—for the Church is the "Body" and the "Fulness" of Christ; and the body and fulness of One are inseparable from Oneself. In the Gospel from the very beginning Christ transcends any human individuality. If He is a man, He is also Man—in a universal and inclusive sense whose beginning and end of truth and meaning we shall be forever engaged in fathoming and understanding. But He is Man because He is not only Man, but God in Man— which is the whole and only truth and meaning of Man. Christ is Man from three points of view: He is Man in divine Conception, in divine process or operation, and in divine consummation and fulfilment. He is thus the Past, Present, and Future of humanity. Before Abraham, or even Adam, was—He is. Because He is the divine Mind or Thought of Man above all time. Christ as Logos, or eternal reason, meaning, and end of Man, is never for one moment severed from the universal *logos,* the reason and meaning of all creation as One Whole;—but it is in that immediate and special function, of humanity as the end at least of terrestrial evolutional existence, that He is "manifested" to us in our own Gospel history.

Christ is Man, not only thus eternally in divine thought or meaning, but also temporally in humanity's own actual process of being and becoming. As Adam stands to us for humanity within the scope and activity of all that we call Nature, so Christ stands to us for that same humanity in all its predestined, accomplishing, and accomplished personal oneness with God. He is the Way; the Truth, Fact or Act; and the Fruit in Eternal Life, of Man's Atone-ment with God: that is to say, of his own conscious, free, and personally accomplished Oneness with God. He is the Oneness, potential by nature, made and become actual by the necessary reciprocal action of Grace and Faith. In the One person of Jesus Christ Humanity has actually passed, undergone transformation, regeneration, or new creation, from its own inchoate and incomplete life in ourselves into life in God, the Eternal, the Infinite, and the Perfect. The process of that transition is given us in the life, death, and resurrection of Jesus Christ. In one sense, which we call "in faith," we have accomplished that transition in Christ. In another sense, which we may call "in fact," the task for us in time, and, for aught we know in eternity, is to accomplish that transition in ourselves in Christ. It is God only Who can work it in us to will and to do; but God can work it in us only in our willing and doing. Christ is God's Will and Word to work it in us; so far as He is concerned, it is done.

He tells us in His Gospel how on our part, in faith, hope, and love, it shall be done just so fast as we are able to receive, appropriate and assimilate to ourselves the Word of Life which alone is able to save our souls.

Now Christ without the Church, or short of the Church, was and is an individual man. He may have been never so divine a man—never so much God in the flesh, his individual flesh; but He was not God in Man but only God in a man. He was not, and is not, *God in us*. His individual flesh was only His one natural body; the Flesh of His true and complete Incarnation was the Whole Body of our humanity. It is the Church only that is His true and abiding Body, the real Incarnation—"the Fulness of Him that filleth all in all," that which He fills with Himself as the soul or spirits fills the body and makes it all Itself. So true is it that the Church is Christ's body and self, and that we are in Him only as we are in it, that we need not hesitate at the *extra ecclesiam nulla salus*,—if we mean Christian salvation: "Christ is the Head of the Church, Himself the Saviour of the Body." As only the soul can save the body, only the spirit can sanctify and save the flesh, so only Christ as the Head and Heart, the Soul and Body, of our humanity is Christian salvation. We are fallen away from the meaning and actuality of the Church, if not of the fact of Christ Himself in the world, and of ourselves in Him, when we allow ourselves to come down to and acquiesce in the conception and use of it as a creation and matter of mere human expediency or utility. The easy and endless existence and multiplication of Churches, as against The Church, has been the natural result as well as the clear evidence of a growing loss of any real sense of the divine and necessary fact of the latter; and this, I hope, we are all more and more coming to realize and feel. I can best indicate, perhaps, what I hope and believe to be the growing attitude of many by trying to express my own. I am commonly and popularly called an Episcopalian. I have always been much more inclined to call myself a Churchman,—and this, more and more, distinctly in the broadest instead of in (what it might easily be, and often is) the narrowest of senses. The narrow sense is, that *my* Church is The Church, which is only less far from the truth than that there is *no* "The Church,"—that a Church or any Church, is only the way or form in which any body or kind of Christian embodies Christianity for itself.

The broad view is that The Church is essentially and necessarily One: that Unity is, implicitly if not explicitly, its sole and whole being and definition. The Church is Oneness with God, and oneness with all else in God. There may be, and are, churches, but only in some sectional (not sectarian) sense—in the sense of being a part of (not cut off from) the whole. There was a church in Corinth, but only as being part of The Church which is Christ. Anything more raised the question of a divided Christ. My being a Churchman therefore does not mean "Only *my* Church," in the restricted or sectional sense; it means distinctively *"not* only my Church" in that sense. I am anythingsoever else only that I may thereby be best and most a member of The Body and a partaker of the Fulness of Christ Himself. A man in order to be an American has to be something else of a narrower or more sectional designation—a New Yorker or a Tennesseean; but there is a great distinction between a Section and a Sect. And there may be sections, and yet not sects, other and otherwise than merely local or geographical. Whatever I may be as part, and in whatever distinction from other parts of the Church, the vital and essential point is that I must be in The Church, and in the most living relation to it possible for me.

The most needed new, and ever to be renewed, beginning of Christianity—certainly for that section of Christianity of which I am, and for which I am now speaking—is an ever fresh realization and valuation of Christ, not for what He merely means but for what He actually is. The only available and real knowledge of Christ is to know Him in what

He always and everywhere is, and not only for what He ever in any time or place was or did. We must know Christ as an Eternal relation, attitude, and disposition to us of God; as an actual, constant operation, process and order of life in us of God; as God's not only expressive but creative and completive Word to us of all that we essentially are and all that we ought to be.

What human word best expresses our own proper and possible relation, our available attitude and status toward that Word of God that Christ is—that at once declaration, commandment, promise and gift of all of Himself in us that we can contain? Is our response to it expressed adequately or possibly in the word "Obedience"? I mean in any sense or fact of present or terrestrial obedience to which we give the name of "Righteousness." Is not true Christianity a perpetual and ever-deepening sense and consciousness of unrighteousness? It does indeed express and demand obedience, righteousness; but if that were all, it would only demand an eternal and infinite impossibility. It would bring to us only condemnation and death, never justification and life. But no,—Christianity is not the demand upon us for righteousness; it is infinitely and eternally more than that. It is the demand upon us—because it is also the promise and gift to us—of God our Righteousness. God-in-us is no mere act of obedience on our part; righteousness is no natural or moral or human endowment. It is the fruit of a personal and spiritual union with God; it is an incarnation of God and a regeneration and resurrection of man. Consequently our proper and possible status and relation to Christ is not obedience, but the infinitely more potent and available one of Faith. Obedience is limited to what we are or can be, faith unites and allies us with the omnipotence of God. A true obedience or will to obey only more and more discovers its impotence as it the more realizes the endless and limitless demand upon it. A true faith can say and will say, "I can bear all things, do all things, be all things, through Him that helpeth me."—But it has to be a very true faith: a faith that at-one-s itself in truth with God in Christ.

There is every reason in the world why the righteousness of faith—both in *esse* and in *posse*—is immeasurably superior to that of obedience,—besides the quite sufficient one that only in faith alone, and in hope and love which are the substance and form of faith, is obedience even thinkably possible. But I will give just one additional reason. The end of Christ as God-in-Man is human perfection and blessedness,—it is *our* perfection and blessedness, *i.e.* our holiness, righteousness, and eternal life. But while all these are ours, and are nothing to us except as actually also ours, they are given to us, they are made the supreme object of our faith, hope, and love, of our deathless desire, pursuit, and progressive attainment—not *as* ours, but as always without, beyond, and above us. Instead of centring us in ourselves, in *us* and *ours*, they are for ever leading us out of ourselves to seek and find ourselves in Other and others. The selfhood we want, the personal perfection and blessedness we love and seek we know in ourselves only in the want of them; we have them only in Christ in whom God has given them to us—not as possible objects of *our* attainment, but as certain results of Christ in us through the one effective means and method of our faith, and hope, and love in and of Him. What one knows, loves, desires and wills—that one most certainly and effectually does and is. That perfect faith in Christ, which includes all these, will not only now make us Christ's, but will in the end make us Christ, in all that fulness of Christ which is His Body and Himself, which is His Church and includes us.

I will not now undertake to define The Church further than as our Lord Himself defines it, or as Christianity from the beginning has received and taken it—as the Body and Fulness of Himself. Our relation, both as to its what and its how, its matter and its means, to the living and life-giving Body of Christ, He Himself has expressed and appointed in the two sacraments of His Life,—the sacrament of birth into Him, and the sacrament of continuous life in and through Him; Baptism and the Lord's Supper. It seems to me that, for not merely the meaning but for the reality and the actuality of our Christianity, everything both rests upon and turns upon our understanding and our practical use of these two sacraments. Some will say, "Yes, so far as they go." Others, and very many of us, need to go much further than we do in our understanding and living up to them. One side thinks that the other makes excessive and superstitious use of them; the other thinks that the one has lost all virtue and reality out of them. The point upon which all may stand together as a mean between all possible excess or defect I shall endeavour to determine as follows:

Christianity does not only humanly mean something,—it divinely is something. It is in itself infinitely and eternally more than at present it can mean for us. Whatever of true it may mean to us, it *is* all that, and as much more as it will take an eternity fully to realize. Christ is indeed an Ideal, but the whole value and religion of Him as such is that He is All the Actual of that Ideal. A word of God not only means, but Is. What is needed to make Christ to us Everything of God and ourselves, is faith enough to know Him as such. He can be to us only so much as we can know Him. The function of faith is to see God in all that He is, and to hear Him in all that He says. If Christ is the Word of God to us, then is He God of God, Light of Light, Very God of very God to us. So again, if true sacraments are words of Christ, words of God, to us—then *are* they what they say to us. They only *are not* so to so many, or to any at all, because *we* do not see them, or hear them, or take them so. The sacrament actually *is* to every one all it means—not merely what *he* means by it but what God means by it— Who takes it so. It is not that our faith puts all its reality into the sacrament *in itself,* but only that our lack of faith takes all realization or actualization of the sacrament *out of us.* We either receive God in Christ or else reject and deny Him in every sacramental act. He is always there in all the significance of the act to be either taken or refused.

I can easily sympathize with the Quaker who prefers to take his religion in inward experiences rather than in external acts which, while such awful realities with God, are so often such lifeless forms with us. But soon the Quaker in his silent and invisible acts of religion must think and feel in terms of the Sacraments of Life. He must realize, or make real to and in himself, the gracious Act of God in both bringing and receiving him into Christ; and no less the continuous grace which through that union, sustained and fed by Communion, imparts to him as his daily bread the eternal life of Christ. The question for the Quaker (apart from the fact that Christ Himself instituted and ordained relation with Himself in and through sacraments) is whether independence of outward expression or form ensures, or is the true and best way to, inward spirituality. In fact there is for us no such thing as independence of form; there are mental and even spiritual, as well as material, forms; which are quite as liable to lapse into formality. The very silence and invisibility of the Quaker's spiritual acts are themselves only other forms which mean and express the same thing. All human life consists in putting into the manifold necessary forms of our existence the substance or reality which they mean, and so often are not. The whole business and difficulty of life is to realize the things that make life, to enter into the reason, meaning, end and purpose of ourselves and all else, to actualize existence. We will not do this by merely changing one form into another, but only by going through the form or expression given us into the reality or substance of which it is the vehicle and which can be conveyed to us only through *some* form.

So I say with Luther that the beginning and end of our Christianity is to realize or make real our baptism—to *be* what God (not only by His Word which is Christ, but by

His individual word to each of us in our baptism) has not only pronounced us but made us—parts and members of Christ. I know too well what it means to say that baptism *only* makes us members of the Church (and with many of us not even that)—by no means always, perhaps never, *really* members of Christ. That comes from dividing the whole truth of baptism into two parts, God's part and our part—God's part of grace or making us, and our part of becoming or being made. Now which of these two parts is the *res* or *thing* in baptism; for both are probably never simultaneously together in the act. What I mean is, that of course God's part is always in the act; but man's part (if that means his subjective or personal appropriation and consciousness of membership in Christ and sonship of God) hardly ever originates in the moment and act of baptism: that takes place either before or after. Upon that point let us pause a moment. To concentrate onesidedly upon man's part in baptism will necessitate the insistence upon only what is called "believer's baptism"; one must bring faith and obedience as the precondition of the reception of whatever of distinctive divine gift is conveyed in the instrument of baptism. The other side takes the position that God's whole part is prior to and unconditioned by man's part in baptism. God gives the whole Christ unconditionally to every human being: the command to us is to go forth and include all nations, all men, in Christ. There is absolutely no limit or condition to the gift; faith and obedience are the conditions only of our reception of the gift and any consequent profit by it. "God gives us life, and this life is in His Son. He that hath the Son hath the life, and he that hath not the Son hath not the life." Now this, "having," not God's giving, is an act of faith and obedience, and so it is conditional upon these. Whether this faith comes before or in or after baptism, it makes good *in us* and *for us* the absolutely unconditional gift to every human being of the life of God in Christ—which baptism in itself *is*, but which it is *in us* only through faith and obedience. And so I repeat that to make good, to realize or make real and actual, our baptism, is the sum and substance of our Christianity.

Now to make good the act and fact of our birth in Christ, we need equally to make good the perpetual fact and continuous act of our life in Him. For life in Christ is never only a fact, it is ever the most strenuous of human acts. To live God in this world is nothing else or less than the life of Christ even as He lived it: "I have overcome the world" is the only full and free and final expression of it. It cannot be anything less than all that baptism says it is, a death to sin and a new and risen life in God. And life cannot be intermitted; it must be lived every day and all the time. Man lives not only by the bread of the body: he needs to labour for that which perishes not, which nourishes unto life eternal. Union is maintained only through communion.

Christianity is expressed in terms which are preserved largely only through inherited reverence and habit. The Cross is still with many both weakness and foolishness; daily dying and living is an absurd extravagance of speech. When Christianity is emptied of its eternal and infinite reality it naturally relapses into what it seemed to Jew and Greek in the beginning. As a requirement and obligation upon ourselves for today and tomorrow it is not only an impossibility but an absurdity. It is an actual and a possible truth and reality to us only in faith, hope, and love—only as God's Word says it, promises it, gives it to us in Christ. In no other sense or way could it all become and be ours, as it is, now and here. But it must be ours here and now: only faith in it here can ever make it fact in us hereafter.

Bishop Butler somewhere (not now at hand) shows the analogy between the Christian conception of humanity as One Man under the headship of Christ, and the natural fact of the solidarity of Mankind, of all men as members one of another under the highest ideal unity—which (and not their actual diversity) is the eternally *real*. He proves that the social or other-regarding instincts, impulses, and affections of men are as much a primitive and integral part of their natures as the individual or self-regarding. Christianity in its Love-oneness in Christ (not only all men but all things One in Him) is not the alteration of nature or humanity, but their fulfilment and completion. It is true as far as it goes, that revealed religion is a republication of natural religion; that baptism is a declaration of what we already are,—that is, children of God and members one of another in the Family of God. Only, this great truth of the oneness of Nature and Christ—or of nature and religion—does not and must not deny the necessity and the fact of a new birth or creation, a regeneration and resurrection, from one to the other. Creation is not so much an act as a process: we become more and more not only by the natural growth or our own increase of what we are already, but by the constant addition to us, from without and above, of what we were not in ourselves, of what God Himself is becoming in us and so we in Him. The new-born or twice-born man, the spiritual man, is indeed still his old or natural self, but he is that self *plus* that which he was not before, *plus* what God, through His Word and by His Spirit (i.e. through Christ by the Holy Ghost) is now in him as He never was before. To put on Christ is not a fact of, nor a process of, nature or ourselves; it is a continuous act or process of God in us, which we make our own only through faith. The new birth or the new life is indeed ours too, our own act and our own work,—but it is ours only as it is not *only* ours, but God's in us. It is only the faith that takes life as God's work in us—that can convert it into, and enable, the obedience or righteousness which makes it our work in God. Jesus Christ is God "to usward"—in all the fulness of that relation—as Purpose, Promise and Fulfilment, as Alpha and Omega of ourselves. Faith, Hope, and Love in Christ as "God to us," if given free scope as the divine and only Way, will work out in response all the fulness of "Us to God." God's holiness, righteousness, life—made thus ours in faith, will (thus too) best and most surely make themselves ours in fact.

Thus the spiritual, the Christ, in us is all the natural,—just as the man of maturest reason is all that the unconscious and insensible foetus was in the womb: he is its reason, meaning, end and purpose. But the spiritual or Christ in us, while in a sense in us from the beginning—that is to say while potential even in our natural selves or our nature —is far more in its actuality than our natural selves or our nature: as much more as Christ Himself, while all of man, was also more than man, was God-Man. This truth to be seen in its Wholeness (and its truth is only in its Wholeness) must be looked at completely on both sides. Christ is as truly God as man, and as truly man as God: just as man is as truly son of God as he is product of Nature, and as truly product of Nature as he is son of God. He has to realize Himself (whether we mean Christ or Man) in both sides or stages of His (or his) being: to do either is to do, or is only through doing, the other. God-Manhood is already a reality in Christ, and has got to be an actuality in us and in the world—if it takes eternity and all of God to make it. But in the meantime, whether possible or not (or *when* only possible), for the individual man or for humanity there is none other goal, there is no other end either natural or spiritual, than God-Manhood. It must be a Faith, a Hope, a Love to us, and no *mere* ideal but an Actual, though it be as high as God and as distant as Eternity. There is no limit to Truth, Beauty, or Goodness and Good, to Holiness, Righteousness, or Life; and since these are our nature, as well as our Super-nature or destinature—there can and must be no limit to Faith, Hope, and Love. I have implied that Christ is the end or goal not only of the individual soul, in whatever Heaven is (in fact heaven needs no other definition than simply "To be where and what Christ is"),—but also of Humanity where it is, here on earth. Our Lord Himself teaches us to pray not that we may be in heaven, but that heaven may come and be on earth: the Kingdom of Heaven is within us. That we shall make a heaven of earth is a vastly other and harder task than that we shall be taken out of this world of pain and impossibilities into a heaven of pure and endless ease. Our Lord at the threshold of His ministry—that ministry which was primarily the solving for us in His own Person the problem and process of eternal life (or of God-Manhood)—was met by the doubt (because the human impossibility) expressed in the words: "If thou be the son of God, command these stones that they be made bread." He knew that He was undertaking the impossible; and His victory over the natural fear or doubt found one expression out of many in the utterance several years after, "God is able out of these stones to raise up children unto Abraham." Abraham is the great exemplar of that human faith which at-ones itself with God who "quickens the dead and calls things that are not as though they were." Such a faith will not stagger at the Word that even "the kingdom of this world shall become the kingdom of our Lord." I who can see God in me, who can foresee all myself in God—why shall I hesitate to look further and farther, and see not only God in the world but all the world in God? Is God farther relatively from being in humanity, in society, in business, in politics, in war, in not only the Church but the State, and in even international relations,—than in us who yet can believe that He *is* in us and can hope that we shall be as wholly in Him? And are not that faith and hope, however far off, ground enough and cause enough to justify all possible love, service, and sacrifice that we can expend upon it? Especially when we know that, whether or no justified by infinite and eternal fact and reality, just that love, service, and sacrifice thus expended, and in proportion to the expenditure, as a matter of fact constitutes all the greatness, glory, and blessedness of even our present and temporal being.

I can see the whole field of compromises that might be necessary, and even right for the time, in the endless process of the transition of the natural into the spiritual, from the human into the divine, from the creature to God. For example I can conceive how despotism, how slavery, how a thousand violences, such as not only wars but massacres and exterminations, persecutions, etc., can have seemed to have been more than merely permitted by God and so to have had the positive sanction and even command of religion. I can myself recall a time and conditions under which duelling, lynch-law, and similar practices, could naturally seem more than necessities, even reasonable and right, in the face and in lieu of worse and greater and no otherwise to be dealt with evils. There might be some things, purely natural and even anti-spiritual, which can be displaced and replaced only by purely spiritual substitutes,—and therefore can be abolished only when adequate spiritual principles and motives exist and proper spiritual conditions permit. I might recount an instance, in the (forever) past, where nothing could— there *was* nothing that could—absolve or excuse a man from fighting a duel, but the actually higher reason and motive of a genuinely Christian courage and manhood. When this arrives, despotism, slavery, violences, irrationalities, and inequities of all sorts, that were inevitable until there were higher reasons, and motives, and forces to replace and abolish them, become, or at least can be seen, felt, known, acknowledged and abandoned as sins. So, in Christianity we have to be redeemed not merely from evils, but from the *mere* nature and natural, and from the mere human selfhood, in which such evils are both inevitable and incurable.

To come back to the very superficial question and answer with which this paper began,—Nothing less than all the truth and reality of What the Church is will answer all the question of Why it is necessary in Christianity. Even treating the Church, as is done in that purely popular form, as only a way or means of "getting there,"—as the ships are certainly only a conveyance to the other and complete end and fact of Europe itself,—in us and in our world the mat-

ter of means is not a negligible one: we do not attain ends
without the use of means. And the Church as the Sacrament
of Christ stands in the Origins of Christianity very much on
the same level as Christ Himself as the Sacrament of God.
But the sacrament is not a sacrament indeed—is not a truly
divine sign, a word, or The Word, of God,—unless it is
more than a sign; unless it is The Thing signified. Christ
is not an outward and visible sign—*minus* the inward and
spiritual grace (the gift and fact and reality) of God Himself with us and in us. And as God is in Christ as the Sacrament of Himself and His Life,—just so is Christ in His
Church which is His Body, and the Fulness of Himself in
our humanity and in ourselves.

Christ, the Church, the Sacraments,—all represent (and
are) what Baron von Hügel so aptly calls the *Givenness* in
Christianity: that is, not what we must be in ourselves in
order to have, but what we must have in and of God in order
to be. One is not in any sense, either of birth or adoption,
the son of another by first himself being it and then being
received and treated as such. On the contrary, only by having become sons or been made sons by The Other, prior to
ourselves and from without ourselves, by nature or by grace
or by both,—can we either know or call ourselves sons, or
begin to realize in ourselves the meaning and reality of sonship. Because we are sons of God—by creation and by incarnation, by nature and by grace, by double birth of Him,
in Adam and in Christ,—God sends forth into our hearts the
Spirit of His Son, or of sonship indeed, whereby we cry
"Abba, Father." We do not become, or are not made, sons
through having the spirit, we have the spirit through having
been made, and (by act of God) *being*, sons. Our part is not
to become, but to realize that we, through grace and act of
God in Christ, *are* sons of God. In a word, Christianity is:
—to realize or to make real (not in themselves but only in
ourselves) the truths and facts of God in Christ, of Christ
in His Church or Body, of the Church, in all its fulness of

the life of Christ and of God, in humanity and in us. Faith is the doing this; and where Faith is, and in proportion as it is real, will ensue Holiness, Righteousness, and Eternal Life, which are the elements and process of our conversion into the Life and Likeness of God.

I have described only what the Church is, so far as it is embodied in the two universally accepted sacraments of Spiritual Birth and Life in Christ. This is not to exclude or ignore whatever more, of organization, of order, of practice, or of worship or devotion, may be necessary to secure and preserve the primal and vital essentials—of Unity, Holiness, Universality, and Continuity. These latter are the Church, are Christ and Christianity. All else are only means or modes or conditions of these. About those means or modes or manners are practically all our difficulties and differences within what we are not hopelessly disagreed in our willingness to call The Church. Unless our variant principles and conscientious insistences are, in the sight of God, honestly and sincerely subordinated to the Things that we agree in knowing are Christianity—namely, Oneness with God in Christ, and Oneness with Humanity in Christ—they are Sin.

INCARNATION

———

The Incarnation was not the mere fact of Christ, it was the entire act of Christ in our flesh or our nature. It was not only that God was in our nature in Him—but what God was in our nature in Him, and what our nature (in its redemption and completion) became in Him.

The question well up before us for our consent and agreement, and so as the basis of our Christian unity, is primarily that of our Christian Faith. So far as that faith is immediately connected with and rooted in the facts and acts of our Lord's human life, they are expressed for some of us in a brief series of "Proper Prefaces" in the services for Christmas Day, Easter Day, Ascension Day, Whitsunday, and Trinity Sunday. Those prefaces are all expressed in terms of the physical facts and acts of our Lord's life, birth, death and resurrection, etc. Anything that one may have to say upon any essential point of our common faith can be no more than a single aspect of a many-sided fact or truth, one's own point of view at the moment: and that is all I claim for what I have to say upon one most vital point. I will put it in the form of a discussion of the Proper Preface for Christmas Day or Season: "Because Thou didst give Jesus Christ, Thine only Son, to be born as at this time for us; Who, by the operation of the Holy Ghost, was made very man, of the substance of the Virgin Mary His Mother: and that without spot of sin, to make us clean from all sin. Therefore, etc."

The particular, and very partial, treatment of those words which I have in view will appear to many in the light of an evasion of their literal and manifest meaning. It may just as well appear to others a far-fetched attempt, by bringing in other matter, to justify the language, and so to make possible and probable the fact or truth of the Preface. My motive is neither of these but simply the following: The doubts and difficulties of Christianity today are mainly in the natural or physical and not in the spiritual sphere whether of thought or of reality. Yet Christianity as an incarnation must needs include and cover both of those spheres. The trouble as found, for example, in the preface before us is: that, coming to us wholly in the language of the physical (which is practically our only language, even for purely spiritual things) the subject-matter, the fact or truth sought to be conveyed, is met by us on the material side and discussed and questioned by us only in the material plane. The real and whole question is not—Can a man be born of a virgin? but—Can God be born "in the flesh"? The latter is what we are called to believe and meant to believe; and if we do believe and know that God was born in the flesh and that incarnation necessitates virgin birth, then we believe the Virgin Birth. What I mean to say now is simply this: To be Christian we must believe the Incarnation: If we do believe that, in reality, we *may* (I need go no farther just here) believe the Virgin Birth. If we do not really believe that, then we *cannot* believe the Virgin Birth. Therefore to stop and attempt to settle the matter of the Virgin Birth *before* we will accept the Incarnation is an absurdity, because it attempts an impossibility.

If therefore I were coming to Christianity for the first time, and were confronted at the door with the dogma of the Virgin Birth, I should ask, "Why do you ask me to believe that?"—and if the answer was, "As part of the Incarnation"—then I should say: Let me see it in and with and as part of the Incarnation that I may believe it. What the result of such a position would be, we can only see in due course.

The accounts in Sts. Matthew and Luke of the "genesis" or human origin of Jesus are written in full consciousness of the spiritual truth and meaning of their Subject. St. Matthew has to account for the thoroughly supernatural fact of "God with us" (Immanuel) in the person of Jesus; and he sees expressed already in that human and historical name the specific and distinctive function of the Incarnation: "He it is that shall save His people from their sins." St. Luke sees in Him who is to be born the long-promised Messiah, the true David, Founder and Maker of the Kingdom of God upon earth. Both recognize in the event of Christmas Day the positive and emphatic fact of a supernatural birth—a birth that is not wholly or only "of blood, or of the will of the flesh, or of the will of man, but of God." That which was born was indeed in the highest sense to be "Son of Man"—"Man from heaven"—but so only because in a yet higher and highest sense He was antecedently "Son of God."

Both evangelists, as the accounts stand, ascribe the divine element in the birth to the operation of the Holy Ghost. It is questionable whether the name (here without the article) is limited to the Third Person of the Trinity. If we presume to distribute the divine operation in the matter, the Father is the Begetter, the Son or Word is the Seed, and the Holy Spirit is the Preparer of the soil or the womb—the principle immanent in and productive of the human conception, as of all human susceptibility and receptivity of the divine. The accounts make Faith the medium of reception and conception of the heavenly Word: "Blessed is she that believed"! For to such "No word from God shall be void of power."

Thus all the spiritual elements and understanding of our Lord's human "becoming" are present in the accounts of the unquestionably supernatural birth. Now here, and here only in the New Testament, these are connected and bound up with certain physical or material postulates, or facts in the flesh, expressed in the terms "Virgin Birth" and deemed necessary to and inseparable from either their actuality or their comprehensibility. But, however neces- sitated this fact, or unanswerable the doubts raised by it, the deeper and more vital question involved is this: Are we to allow such difficulties in the plane of the flesh—however met, or whether to be met at all—to mar or lower our conception and acceptance of the supernatural in the person and work of Jesus Christ? Certainly it is only the latter, the spiritual so-called miracle, that can give any reason or credibility to the former, the physical or material. God in the person of Jesus Christ may safely dispense with any necessity of our adequate understanding of the *quo modo* of His incarnation on its physical or natural side. It is quite possible, and even actual and not uncommon, that a full, or fuller, knowledge of our Lord's personality on its spiritual and divine side will leave us comparatively and essentially indifferent to questions and difficulties of merely material interest.

Looking at the matter then, at least first, if not altogether, from above and not from below, it is fortunate for us that that is the point of view of the New Testament, outside of the passages we have been considering. It is wholly that of St. John, of St. Paul, of the writer to the Hebrews, and so of all the real construction of the doctrine of the

Incarnation. Still more it is that of the Divine Human, the Incarnate Person Himself: Our Lord's claim upon us is a very human, as well as divine, one—but it is an absolutely and purely spiritual one. He proves it by What He is, not by How He came.

Returning to our Preface, we recall that the "operation" of the Incarnation on its human side is ascribed to the Holy Ghost—evidently meant there (though not in the two Gospels) in the restricted sense of the Third Person. Now, whatever may be the fact, we can form no conception or understanding of how the Holy Ghost *operated* the Incarnation physically or materially, how it changed or affected the *nature* of the assumed humanity mechanically, or otherwise than spiritually. What is the specific function of the Holy Ghost as now differentiated in our thought from those of the other Persons of the Trinity? When it was said originally that "the spirit of God moved (or brooded) upon the face of the waters" of the earth, yet "waste and void"—either we cannot limit the meaning or activity of the Spirit of God then to its functions as now understood, or else we must interpret the words somewhat as follows: The whole-loving, gracious, self-imparting nature and disposition of God was present, immanent and latent, in creation from its beginning. The function of the Holy Ghost in the world is distinctively to impart the holy spirit of God in the creature as the creature is evolved and qualified to receive and share it. Its meaning and operation, so far as now developed, is *God in us—us* as evolved from mere creatures or "things" into children, capable of consciously and freely sharing His nature and disposition, become persons like Himself, and able to fashion ourselves in His image and likeness. This reason and meaning and end of God in creation we are willing and able to find immanent and latent in it from its beginning. All the love, all the grace, all the fellowship with us which we now know in God, and can enter into and share with Him as children partakers of

His being, His Nature, His life and Himself—all this we can carry back and find brooding over and entering into things from the beginning. Under the now more differentiated terms *Word* and *Spirit* we understand God as revealed or expressed alike to our reason or intelligence and to our disposition or affections—in a word, to our mind and our heart, as the supreme End and Object of our faith and our love. Both of these conceptions must be combined in the one term *Spirit* in Genesis. God's heart as well as mind moved and brooded *over creation* from the beginning and out of the waste and void of its formless matter has evolved all its both natural and spiritual order and purpose.

But, as I have said, the term Spirit within the limits of the New Testament itself becomes restricted from *all* divine operation to that specific operation which therefore we now characterize as distinctively *spiritual*—in contrast with natural, material, or mechanical. More plainly, Spirit acts properly only upon spirit, actual or potential, and its function is the production and evolution of spirit. In this sense it may have been evolutionally at work from the beginning in the form of natural affinities, animal instincts and affections, etc., but now, as Holy Ghost, its place and part in Christianity is in the souls and not the bodies, in the personalities rather than in the impersonal nature or natural constitution of men.

We must, however, here and now, emphasize the action of the Holy Ghost as essentially *prevenient:* that is, it is cause of, and not merely consequent upon, the human motions of our own spirits. We must realize that very much apparent recognition and admission of a Holy Ghost does not really mean any operation upon or in us from an objective God, but only the subjective motions of a so-called *divinity* within us. God does operate upon us largely from within—and even, we may say, wholly *through* ourselves; but that His motions come from Him without us and above us, we must distinctly hold in order to be

Christian. And, if His "Spirit" can thus come to us from Himself without and above us in or by any form of inspiration, why not equally may His "Word" come to us from without and above by some other form of self-revelation or self-communication? As I shall ask again, if there is any real inspiration in or through our hearts, why may there not be some equally real revelation to or through our minds?

So, when we consider the operation of the Spirit, or Holy Ghost in the New Testament sense, in the act of the Incarnation, we can understand that operation only along lines which I may illustrate as follows: Some one has replied to the question, when ought the shaping of a child (i.e., its nature, disposition, or spirit) to begin?— "In the third or fourth generation before it is born." I can believe that the shaping of the human spirit of Jesus—in its preparation to become the incarnation of the Word of God—began not only as far back as Abraham, but as far back as Creation, or as God Himself. We must remember that the Advent or Coming of Christ was a process of ages before His birth. And not only so, it has, contrary to primitive (and oft-since repeated) expectation, been and will be a process of ages after His birth. Christ is synonymous with Humanity in its divine meaning, determination, and destination—whether we consider that destination generically and upon earth, or individually and personally in eternity or in heaven.

In a word, the operation of the Holy Ghost, in its proper and distinctive kind, is a work of spiritual and not of material creation; it has to do with the evolution of selfhood in the nature and not with mechanical (or *fiat*) alterations in the nature of the self. The incarnation in Christ was not effected and completed in the act of His conception and birth: those were necessary moments in it, but they were not independent of, or wholly complete without, the entire subsequent process of His perfect human life in the flesh. It was not the mere fact of His being in it, but the consummate act of what He did and was in it that made humanity in His person Son of God. To make it still shorter, the Incarnation was not the mere fact of Christ, it was the entire act of Christ in our flesh or our nature. It was not only *that* God was in our nature in Him—but *what* God was in our nature in Him, and what our nature (in its redemption and completion) became in Him. Now in all our study of the actual part of the Holy Ghost in the incarnation in Christ in the New Testament we can find no trace of any prior change of the flesh, or the nature, for Him, but everything of the complete transformation of it— amounting to re-creation—in Him and by Him.

In the Preface then for Christmas Day, after the words "Who by the operation of the Holy Ghost was made very man"—let not the mind stop upon the physical facts of our Lord's conception and birth, but run on upon the entire act of spiritual new-birth and new-creation which was to ensue upon those facts, and of which they were secondary incidents. The "very manhood" thus assumed and begun and in which the Holy Ghost was chief agent and operant, was not yet consummated, and not to be until Itself could say upon the Cross, "It is finished"—and the Father should raise it up out of even that depth and death, and exalt it to the level with Himself. God was not fully made Man until Man was raised up into actual oneness with God. The "very" manhood, expressed and assumed by our Lord Himself in the title "Son of Man," has more meaning in it than we can realize until we shall "see Him as He is, and be made like Him."

That He was made very man "of the substance of the Virgin Mary" means that He was as very *man* in His humanity as He was also very *God* in the reality of His deity. "And that without spot of sin" does not describe any mere absence of sin from the fact of His inherited nature but freedom from sin in His entire actual and active manhood: He was author and finisher of His own sinlessness.

Finally, "To make us free from sin"—indicates such a truth of Christ in Himself and of His relation to us all, as makes Him divinely inclusive of us in Himself, and makes us potentially and progressively receptive of Him in ourselves—if we will.

But the first point in our Preface, as in any statement of Christianity, is the assumption of a pre-natal or prehuman personality of our Lord, wherein He is "in substance" one with God,—just as in His human nature He is one with our common humanity, or with our personal selves. In speaking of the divine personality of our Lord, I do not presume to interpret God, or to solve the mystery of His method in at-one-ing Himself with His creation in the person of Man as its head. My only effort shall be to assist our apprehension of a truth which in substance we hold together, while in explanation we naturally differ because any explanation, however true, is only an infinitesimal part of a divine fact.

The starting point for us of any knowledge of God must be ourselves: we are the only objects within our experience that in its nature bears the image or is made in the likeness of the personal God. St. Paul says, "When it pleased God to reveal His Son in me—." He was doubtless thinking only of the revelation of Christ, but the revelation *in me* was a very necessary part of the thought. Paul first fully and really "came to" and saw "himself" in the revelation to him of Jesus Christ: and so must we all. I repeat that first of all and most of all Christ is God's revelation to us of ourselves. The end of that revelation to St. Paul was expressed by him in the words: "No longer I—but Christ in Me"! The I was dead, but alive again; was lost, but only then truly found—in Christ. St. Paul was not thinking of himself alone, but of the self, the soul, of humanity, of man: nor of that only, but of all nature, all creation, which here at least, on earth, culminates in man and his destiny. The cosmic, and (before even that) the divine meaning and nature of Jesus Christ was, at least implicitly, all that first revelation of Him to, because in, St. Paul. If we were not in Christ in Eternity, Christ could not be in us in time.

What then was the pre-incarnate personality of Jesus? Its first designation is "Word of God": "In the beginning was the Word, and the Word was with God and Was God"; and "the Word was made flesh and dwelt among us." With us a word is an abstraction—a sign or symbol of something which *itself* is not. A word of God *is* what it means, is all that it stands for. The word of creation was creation itself in the mind or thought or purpose and in the utterance of God. "He spake and it was made," we say; but there was no "and" between the speaking and the making. His speaking is its making. So the Word of God is in general All Things in the eternal mind or thought or utterance of God —or, reversely, The Mind, etc., of God in all things. But the "all things" for us sum themselves up in man and his life and destiny. And so we say that the Word of Christ is man and his destiny as seen in God—*sub specie æternitatis,* as well in its pre-destination as in its post-destination. But this supreme and only Word of God is no divine abstraction like our thoughts and words; it is the "things" themselves eternally with Him and in Him and *His.* So, when we see ourselves in Christ, we see not only ourselves but God in Him. There is no such thing as ourselves in God apart from God in ourselves. If Jesus is one, He is the other: Humanity as seen in God *is* God seen in humanity.

We cannot help continually asking ourselves, *Is* Jesus Christ God or is He Man? The following may not help logic or psychology or dogmatics, but it may help *us* under the difficulties of these. There is no doubt that the same person may in some sense combine in himself different personalities. The only doubt is how far we may stretch that fact. When St. Paul not only recognizes but is awfully conscious in his one self of the co-existence of the I and the Christ, he is stretching a double personality to the limit of two persons within him. He may say, "Not I but Christ"—"I am dead and Christ lives in me." But the wish or will is father to the thought, as he abundantly confesses: they are both there. And St. John who says that "he who is born of God does not sin, cannot sin,"—in another breath has to confess that "if we say that we have no sin, we deceive ourselves and the truth is not in us." The two selves are so potent in even the truly regenerate that either Apostle can claim everything for the self that is Christ in him and nothing for the self that is not Christ. Let us be very careful not to stretch the analogy too far: but Christ's declared oneness with the Father unquestionably identifies Him with God, and He never hesitates in the exercise of His divine office and ministry to speak with all the direct authority of God; and yet, in the humanly personal experiences that lay behind his public functions, how deeply conscious He is that "of Himself" He can say or do nothing. We must even say of His sinlessness—His *posse non peccare* —that it was not His own, His human own. "He prayed with strong crying and tears unto Him that was able to save Him from death; and was heard for His godly fear." But to Him, as to us, there was no death but sin: from what other death was he saved? Sin and death are substantially synonymous. There was a human "self" in Jesus which He was all the time disclaiming—which He disclaimed to the limit of death—the death that is life: and the life which is not only that of God, but that of humanity also, a veritable "resurrection of the flesh." And all the time there was a divine self which He as little fails or hesitates to affirm to its very limit—a divine self that belongs to Him even in His humanity: "There is given me power and authority over all flesh"—"All power is given me in heaven and earth." God's love for us is His Love, God's grace in us is His Grace, God's fellowship and oneness with us is, not only His, it is He Himself in us.

In Christ then, the One Person human and divine, we see the twofold personality: in His assured oneness with the Father we see Him as God incarnating Himself in our veritable and very humanity;—on the other hand, in His temptation, His agonies of prayer and supplication, His forsakings and "conflicts with despair," we see our human- ity, in all its natural and acquired impotence and need, in His person receiving, enacting, completing its redemption and salvation in God. Christ is human redemption as well as divine Redeemer—Man saved as well as God saving. But between the double personality so recognizable in Christ and that of St. Paul or St. John there is this im- measurable difference. In the ever incomplete oneness of the two Pauls—the "he" (or "I") and the Christ whom he is striving to make himself—there is ever visible and evi- dent the individual human subject being saved; in the ever victorious and complete oneness of Christ with the Father that which is always manifest is the universal and divine Subject saving. Paul is each or any man seen as being saved; Christ is all men or every man viewed as saved. Paul may represent the individual or particular element or part in human salvation; Christ is the universal or absolute. If a man says—as any and every man *may* say, if he will believe—"I *am* saved, eternally, infinitely, per- fectly,"—that is Christ in Him. If he is battling for salva- tion in Christ and feeling himself still infinitely far off from it, that is the still only "he"—Paul or John or whosoever —in Christ. The one is the perfectly in Christ, in faith; the other is the very imperfectly in Christ in fact, in personal and actual attainment. But both personalities must be in the evolving Christian on earth, as both God and man are in the consummated Christ in heaven.

I can see plainly enough the shortcomings and failures— if not positive errors—in such attempted analogies as the above. But even if it explain nothing, and yet helps us to conceive and realize the inexplicable facts and realities of God and Man as One in Christ, and Christ and We as One in our true and very selves—it will be something gained. And as mere suggestion, it may move us to further and better attempts to understand and assimilate those essential truths and facts of Christianity.

One more thought: I have alluded to the apparent greater willingness to accept and receive God in inspiration than in revelation. Men who will recognize Christ as Spirit will not believe Him as Word. Is it that the heart of man is more accessible and approachable than his head —his feelings and affections more easily touched and moved than his mind or reason convinced? Or is it that a surreptitious and unreal conception of God can more easily express and impose itself under the guise of spirit than of word? Men will call the Holy Ghost God who will not call Christ God,—and why? Is it because the Spirit is more subjective, and the Word necessarily more objective, in their respective manifestations? It is easy, and sometimes proper, to say "it" and "its" instead of "He" and "His," in speaking of the Spirit. But in doing so may we not too often be evading the question of a really divine personality of the Spirit? We may even confess the "divinity" of the Spirit in Christ and in us, and be meaning only a *quasi* divinity: a divinity, if not of ourselves and not God, yet of God only as immanent in ourselves. The Spirit is subjective and in us—the word is objective and *to* us: the Spirit may be *only* in us after all, only *our* spirit—which we have no objection to calling God's or divine; the Word, as used in Christianity, must be from without, from the objective God. The question is: How much the Spirit called divine in Christ really means the Spirit of the objective and real God. If it is really super-natural, super-sensible, super-human—if it really comes from the Eternal Spirit without and above us and communicates with the finite spirits within us which we call ourselves, in any sort of actual divine motion or influence—then why insist upon the divine communication being only subjective and in no sense or degree objective also? If God speaks to us within, why may He not do so without? Why is not a revelation to our reason as possible as an inspiration in our wills and affections?

Christianity comes to us in strict and perfect accordance with our own nature and receptive organs or faculties. We are compounded of reason and feeling, of judgment and sentiment; from the joint action of these two proceed will, action and all the rest of our complex personality. We must know in order to any rational feeling or wishing,—but equally we must feel in order to any will or action. If Christianity is the perfection of Right Reason and of Free Will—or of Truth and Love; then equally we need Truth as the proper object of love, and love as the proper motive or impulse to Truth. God need not stir or move our affections if He does not provide their proper object— their adequate end and true function. And where that end or object is an eternal and infinite one—one wholly beyond our possible natural or human reach or experience—there must of necessity be something of the nature of revelation, of call and promise and indication from beyond. Thus religion rests within us upon a natural instinct to feel and impulse or intuition to know,—but since these call us to, prophesy and promise to us, things that the natural eye cannot see or ear hear, nor the natural heart of man conceive for himself,—therefore we need not only inspiration from within, but revelation from without "that we might know the things that are freely given to us by God."

And so we say—the Scriptures and the Church say— that Christ—the true Christ, the super-human and supernatural Christ, the eternal and divine Christ—entered into this world not by natural generation, He was "born not of blood, nor of the will of the flesh, nor of the will of man, but of God." It was the function and operation of the

Holy Ghost, not *aptare Deum homini,* but *aptare hominem Deo* in His incarnate person. The "very manhood" assumed, of the substance (the exact nature) of His human Mother, was made *indeed very man*—in the truer and higher sense of Son of Man as Son of God. The Holy Ghost operating in, with and through the spiritual and divine instincts and intuitions of humanity itself, as it comes from and is by nature the child of God, is met by and united with the divine Word and invested with the now revealed and imparted right and title to its inheritance of conscious and free sonship. So inspiration is met and completed only in revelation, the Spirit is fulfilled and satisfied only in the Word. In yet other words, freedom can be given to will and action and personality only in the gift to Reason of Light and Truth.

What, then, is the divine Christ, and what the human Christ? The divine Christ is humanity (and creation) eternally in the mind, will, and purpose of God,—humanity of the divinely right reason and free will, whose expression and utterance is The Word and The Son. The human Christ is humanity brought to self-realization and completion through revelation and incarnation in it of the Word and operation in it and through it of the Spirit. It is creation become Son of God in man through Jesus Christ.

RESURRECTION

The only invincible evidence of the Truth is its own truth: the more we penetrate into the truth of the Resurrection the more we know that it is true. On the contrary, the more we linger among the mere details of the letter of the account of the Resurrection the more we make it impossible to believe it.

The first and deepest note of Christianity has been struck in the one term Incarnation. The perfection of meaning and reality contained in that word has been a matter of gradual and perpetual revelation: God eternally For us, To us, With us, In us—until all connecting particle disappears in the consummated oneness of God and us in Christ. I have wondered whether that is not St. Paul's mind in the unexplained passage Gal. 3:20. The Law was given through the mediation of Angels and of Moses. Now mediation is "between two," it is not "of one"; but God and man in Christ is one. It is true that in this union God is All or All in All, so that man in a sense disappears and "God is One." So even of Christ Himself it is said, that when He shall have put all things under His feet—"then shall the

84

Son Himself be subjected to Him that did subject all things to Him, that God may be all in all." But that God should be All in All in the Unity of All does not efface either the Son or man but only "finds" and exalts them. "Our wills (or selves) are ours, we know not how: they are ours to make them Thine": but when we shall have made our wills God's through His making His ours—*our* very making them so along with His perpetuates us in the all embracing unity of Him.

Incarnation then is the first and most essential note, but Resurrection is the next: and this is as essential in effect as that was as cause. Resurrection is the expression, and the only adequate expression, of the work of Incarnation. Redemption or Salvation are empty terms in comparison; they state the form of a process without giving its substance. Redemption from what? Salvation to what? The answer is, From death unto life—and that is Resurrection. Now in the study of Resurrection, as in that of Incarnation, we are blinded to the truth of the Self-demonstrating Spirit by the apparent contradictions of the physical or material letter. We have to do with a matter which is obliged to be true in the Spirit, and cannot be true in the letter; and yet—so far as we can see—to be true at all, must be true in both.

At present I go only so far as this: The truth of the Spirit may help us to solve the difficulties of the letter; stopping upon the problem of the letter will keep us there forever, not only in doubt but in positive disbelief. We have no right, because we have no honest possibility, of belief in the material accounts of our Lord's Birth and Resurrection, solely upon the plane of the physical and the natural. And yet much so-called faith, or religious assent, and even zeal and activity, rests upon no better basis than the avowed physical and material facts. I do not say, do not believe these, but I do say that a faith that rests only on these is not faith at all, but only belief, —if not indeed only credulity.

The foundation upon which Christianity rests is—on the plane of natural probability—the most incredible and impossible event in human history. It is at the same time one of the best attested: No one can get into the mind of the New Testament without being convinced of the quality as well as the quantity of the evidence for the truth of the Risen Lord of Life. St. Paul and the more than five hundred who had seen Him—the greater part of whom were still alive when the Apostle wrote—are witnesses hard to gainsay. Then Christianity itself—the fact that that incredible event of the Resurrection has also been the most potent, influential, determinative factor in human history and civilization—tells for a great deal: that it has actually given name to the entire era of real history. But the mere testimony of the New Testament and the Christian Church is not our most convincing proof of the Resurrection of Jesus Christ: it is not that that makes us believe it against the unanswerable objections of our most indubitable natural science. The only invincible evidence of the Truth is its own truth: the more we penetrate into the truth of the Resurrection the more we know that it is true. On the contrary, the more we linger among the mere details of the letter of the account of the Resurrection the more we make it impossible to believe it. Even yet we are incredibly far from comprehending or interpreting the full meaning of the Resurrection—and so of the Redemption or Salvation wrought by it. This is no mere fault-finding or depreciation of the Christianity we have got. There is a vast deal of implicit faith in the world whose roots penetrate much more deeply into the Fact of the Resurrection than any of our explicit interpretations or definitions have reached.

Again then I say: Let us look away from the mere natural or contra-natural details of the Resurrection—away from the mere visible to the *not*-invisible features of it, though only spiritual eyes can see them. I will take the Church's Easter Preface for our text:—"But chiefly are we bound to praise Thee for the glorious Resurrection of Thy Son Jesus Christ our Lord: for He is the very Paschal Lamb which was offered for us, and hath taken away the sin of the world: Who by His death hath destroyed death, and by His rising to life again hath restored to us everlasting life. Therefore, etc."

It is remarkable with regard to the simple and beautiful accounts or records that give us what I have called the "letter" of the Birth and the Resurrection of Jesus,—how delicately and exactly they are also true to the spiritual depth and significance of these events: This Child to be born is "Immanuel—God with us"; His Name shall be called Jesus, for "It is He that shall save His people from their sins." St. Mark, who is much less explicit—or rather, does not give the physical birth at all—nevertheless designates Jesus Son of God in the caption of his Gospel and, through John the Baptist, identifies Him with the Remitter of Sin and the Baptizer with the Holy Ghost. I need not dwell upon the wonderful and infallible spiritual instinct and felicity with which St. Luke handles every minutest physical detail of the Birth. St. John gives the Baptist's own impression and interpretation of the Baptism of Jesus and is himself already reached by the fundamental truth expressed in the words: "Behold the Lamb of God that taketh away the sin of the world." In fact when I most wish to divest my mind of the Natural (wherein are the difficulties) and fix it upon the Spiritual that satisfies and convinces me, I find that I get at it best through those very little stories told in terms of the natural, but so breathing all the air and life of the highest and purest spiritual: I don't object to a letter that so utters and expresses the Spirit.

Going then as straight as possible to the gist of the Resurrection, we see that that consists in a doing away with death through the taking away of sin. Now, taking it literally, death has not been done away, and will not be so long as our present nature continues and living beings terminate their existence in it: it certainly is not in that sense that death is done away. Neither is it done away in the sense of the mere fact of the continuance after it of our present natural life in any other form, however supernatural. Christian resurrection, as also a redemption and a salvation, consists exactly in this: It is a removal from life, or an extinction in life, of all that hinders it as life, or that tends to make it not "life." But the extinction of all in life that contradicts or destroys it is equally the extinction of all in death that makes it death in its present "fallen" meaning. What is it then that poisons life and makes even death the evil it now is—in fact, altogether constitutes, and wholly is, death in all its bad sense?

"Then saith He, 'Lo I come to do Thy will, O Lord!'" So the Messiah is represented as proclaiming His Mission. And certainly the key-note of our Lord's life is, "I am come to do the will of Him that sent me": that was His meat and drink. He claims at last to have glorified God, in that "I have accomplished the work Thou gavest me to do." Now what was that will and work of God, for which our Lord came and lived and died? "Lo, I come to do Thy will, O God!"—"By the which will," explains the inspired writer, "we are sanctified." "This is the will of God—even your sanctification," St. Paul impresses upon his disciples. "Be ye holy, for I am holy,"—were God's own words of old—and so our Lord, "For their sakes I sanctify myself, that they also may be sanctified in truth." "Father," He pleads, "sanctify them in the truth; Thy word is Truth." And He Himself was that word and that Truth Incarnate.

To know further what our Lord is, we must enquire further what truth is—the truth that is sanctification, and the sanctification that is life. We must begin with distinguishing truth from merely the actual, "that which is." The truth of any form of life, even a plant, is not whatever it happens to be, but what it ought to be, and must be, in order to be itself. If an insect or any external agency should inject poison or introduce damage of any sort into the plant, producing perversion or deformity,—no one would call that the truth, however it might be the fact or the actual condition of the plant. Now if the plant could —or any higher form or reach of life should—include in itself the thing we know as consciousness of self, and the yet higher power of self-determination or formal freedom, —and so the self-perversion or deformity which is its actual state or condition should be the result of its own will and act,—that would be, and is, what we call sin. That one word covers all that will impede, contradict, impair, or destroy life or that constitutes death—in the bad sense in which it needs to be abolished. All else is in God's hands, and nothing that is not ourself need or will defeat that being or becoming ourself which is our whole and our only truth. When I speak of becoming and being ourself—of course I mean that of which the other side and the necessary condition is the being in full correspondence with one's environment, which means in perfect relation with all the Not-oneself.

Now how did, and does, Christ so take away sin as to destroy death and so perfect life? In order to so take it away, He must (in a sense not to be misunderstood, and if possible to be understood) have "taken sin": and that is what the word and the language of Scripture mean. He must have taken and occupied our place—which means our own actual and full relation to sin: not in our relation to it in obeying it, but in our complete relation to it *except* obeying it. It is in this sense that God "made Him to be sin for us, Who knew no sin, that we might be made the righteousness of God in Him." Christ in our flesh, by taking its sin in so far as sin was—not the truth, but the actual state and condition, of the flesh He assumed,—and by then, under the state and condition, *not* sinning, broke the power and reign of sin over the flesh, and abolished death in its prior sense: the sting of death, the *death* in death, is sin. So again,—"God, sending His Son in the likeness of sinful flesh (or the flesh of sin) and for sin, condemned (or destroyed) sin in the flesh." But before undertaking to explain these extreme texts—let us determine in what sense our Lord "took sin,"—or what was His human relation to sin prior and in order to His breaking its power, and so condemning, and ultimately abolishing and destroying it.

To say that "the flesh," or our human organism, or that "the world" of our humanity is evil,—describes their actual state or condition, but it does not describe their proper nature. It is true to reason and to deepest fact to say that God in the act of creation "saw that they were good." Apart from sin there is no evil: "there is nothing evil but the evil will"—just as "there is nothing good but the good will." If there were no creature or finite "free" will in the world —which means "good *or* evil" will—there would be no such thing as good or evil at all in the world: such moral distinction would not exist. But evil must be possible in order that good may be possible over against it, and so there may be choice and freedom and personality, and so oneness with and likeness to God. At any rate *so it is,* and so alone we could be what we are—rational, free, moral, and spiritual *persons*.

And again—*So it is* that the actual state or condition of our flesh and so of our world is not what it ought to be— what it properly or essentially *is*—good; but it is what *we* have actually made it—and that is evil and hopelessly in subjection to evil. Now when our Lord entered into our flesh and into our world, He entered into them as they are—needing redemption, salvation, resurrection, and for the purpose of being all these in them and for them and to them. In the flesh and in the world He does not judge or condemn or damn them for the fact or actuality of sin. That, as we shall see, had been inevitable; all He ever condemns man for is—*not* being sinners, not knowing that they were sinners, needing and wanting and willing to be saved from their sin. Our Lord had no mission or message or meaning for any but sinners: He turns the very fact and sense and emptiness and poverty, and helplessness and evil and curse of sin into the most potent instrument and argument of divine Love and Grace and Fellowship and Salvation. He makes God one with them as they are in order that He may make them one with God as He is.

The one most essential and emphatic point of Christianity is that it has no condemnation for the universal and inevitable fact of sin. All its judgment and penalty is for those who will not know their sin, whose very sin itself does not drive them to their only deliverance from it. Indeed what we, anthropomorphically, call and look upon as the wrath of God, is something which no one feels against us or inflicts upon us but ourselves. To say, "The soul that sinneth it shall die"—is only warning us of a fact: sin is death, and the only death. God gives us life, which spiritually is as identical with holiness as physically it is with health. He gives us (in Christ) Himself—all His Love, His Grace, His Fellowship—to be our life as it is His own. If that is life, then to be without it—certainly to reject it—is in itself death; and it is a death that none but ourselves can inflict upon us. How, or when, or where this self-inflicted wrath of God shall be visited—and upon whom—I know not. I only know that if holiness is life, sin of itself is death—if one is Heaven, the other in itself is Hell. And it is of this holiness that our Lord speaks: "Thou hast given me power over all flesh—that whomsoever Thou givest me, I shall give to them eternal life." "For their sakes I sanctify myself, that they themselves also may be sanctified in truth."

The chief question yet remains: How may we venture to say that Jesus Christ was under sin, and how did He condemn and abolish it?—And that, not only for Himself but for us? To begin with, Christ in our humanity—considered merely as nature, that is to say, in itself—was as impotent and helpless for holiness, righteousness, and eternal life as we are. When He took our nature He took it with all its natural deficiencies: when He was "born under the law," that law which is none other than God's own, and God's Self, was as impossible for Him as for us. When *Himself* became human, He was as little able "of Himself" to be all His—even human—self as any and every man is. There is nothing of Himself that our Lord so emphasizes as His own utter impotence, "of Himself." "Of myself I can do nothing." Nothing less than the sense and the reality of His utter and absolute oneness with the Father sufficed to enable Him to be Himself. It was in fact this all-essential and necessary dependence upon God as Father that He came to realize for us, to manifest in his own person, to impart to us all. I know nothing of myself, I speak nothing of myself, I am nothing of myself. But I know God, I speak directly from God, and to you I am God. He that heareth me heareth the Father, and he that seeth me seeth the Father. The Word of God *is* God, and the Spirit of God is God. And nowhere else or otherwise has God so revealed, manifested, or imparted These—and Himself in These—to us as in Jesus Christ.

But not only did Jesus Christ embody in Himself these our natural deficiencies, insufficiencies, and impossibilities, in order to bring them into conjunction and union with their predestined supplements and supplies—and so their own self-realization and completeness. There is no question that sin was, at the least, an inevitable and necessary moment or stage in human evolution: it was only over against, in contrast and opposition with, and victory over it, that human holiness could originate. Men can resist this or that sin and practise and cultivate this or that virtue—and so be really responsible within limits for what they do or are. But no man can be wholly sinless or wholly virtuous, or wholly righteous: and there is no doubt that a sense of the universal fact of sin was necessary to the rise of the counter sense of the need and want of holiness. Our Lord in His oneness with us shared, I say, not only our nature as it was naturally deficient, but our nature as it had actually fallen under the universal dominion of sin and death. It was God's purpose to show us in His Person what was its, at once natural and supernatural, redemption and deliverance from that subjection to sin and death. That salvation consisted in the substitution of an all-sufficient Holiness, Righteousness, and Life of God, instead of the impossible and yet necessary—all these—of humanity itself. It had to be that of humanity itself, since humanity was created and constituted for it and predestined to it,—but it could not be, until humanity was lifted to the level of participation in it; could know the reason and meaning and feel the need and want of it. It was the province and function of the *Law* first to awaken and practically to create not only the fact of this necessity, but the sense and experience of this impossibility, and the consequent bitter need. This is what "the knowledge of sin" is, and it was the function of the Law to awaken and impart that knowledge.

Now the perfect act and work of Jesus in His whole life in the flesh was, primarily, to know all the limitations, and yet the limitless distinction and law, of the humanity that was His own and Himself: its at once bitter impossibility and yet absolute necessity of holiness, righteousness, and eternal life. Our Lord was not sinless because—in His (in itself) sinless humanity—He was above the touch or reach or power of sin. He knew He was not, and felt to the very bottom His need of and dependence upon the infinite and eternal Not Himself Who, as the only source of holiness, is the only victory over sin. "With strong crying and tears He made supplication and prayer unto Him that was able to save Him,—and was heard for His godly fear" —and so He mastered the great spiritual science and art of Faith and "learned obedience through the things He suffered." That Jesus Christ was thus humanly, in His own person and in His own life and death, the Author and

Finisher or Perfecter of Faith in God, and of all that Faith makes possible and eventually makes actual in our humanity —is the great truth of Redemption or Salvation,—the Resurrection which as a Fact stands next and second only to that of the Incarnation.

The one real At-one-ment wrought by Christ with God was that of His own perfected human Faith, Hope, and Love,—or in other order, His own perfect Love, Obedience or Service, and Sacrifice. That alone, viewed as a single act, was the extinction of sin, the destruction of death, the restoration of eternal life. Through that Faith, and its perfect work, comes the only true righteousnes—that of which St. Paul speaks when he says: "In it (in the Gospel, which is Christ Himself) is revealed a righteousness of God by (or from) faith unto faith: as it is written, the righteous shall live by faith." And again: "But now apart from the law (which can only call for an impossible obedience, or righteousness of our own) a righteousness of God hath been manifested, even the righteousness of God through faith in Jesus Christ—unto all them that believe."

This is the spiritual reason and meaning, the end and purpose, the actual result of the Resurrection of Christ: in it God has given us a righteousness of His own to take and make our own. We need not hesitate on the one hand to view it as an actual and immediate work, self-revelation or manifestation, of God Himself in our nature and our life: "God was in Christ, reconciling (or at-one-ing) the world unto Himself." Neither, on the other hand, must we hesitate or fail to see humanity or ourselves in Christ— through a victorious faith, hope, and love—in perfect love, faithful obedience and service, complete sacrifice—appropriating and assimilating, converting into itself (that is, into ourselves) the faith, hope and love, the service and sacrifice, the holiness, righteousness and eternal life—so freely given us, so perfectly wrought in us, so divinely

realizing and fulfilling not only God in us, but us too in
God Who is our Life.

An historic issue of explanation or interpretation may
be put into the following form: Did Christ become incarnate that He might stand in the stead of man and endure
the penalty of sin, so that "God might be just and yet
the Justifier of him who believeth in Jesus"?—*Or,* did
Christ become incarnate that He might, in some positive
and real way, take upon Him and take away sin, and so
become the actual holiness, righteousness and eternal life
of man? Was His death the penal and punitive act of
justice upon sin, or was it the consummate act of holiness
and righteousness in conferring and constituting Life? The
fact that for man any birth or life to God or holiness must
be a death to sin,—and *that,* for the deeper than merely
actual reason, that any positive affirmation of good or right
is a negative denial of bad or wrong,—rendered it necessary
that Christ's perfect act of holiness ("I sanctify myself")
should be a complete negation of sin—the life to the one,
a death to the other. But, because it is both, shall we name
the glorious and victorious death of Christ a penalty for
sin rather than a conquest of holiness and eternal life?
"I am come," He said, "that ye might have life": and the
perfect act of life was the perfect negation, extinction, and
death of sin, and so of death itself. For in man all true life
is perpetual death, and death itself with the extraction of
its sting, becomes only life—"a birth and an awaking."
We are saved in the travail or "child-bearing" of the new
birth from above.

There is a truth in the continued use of the terms
"vicarious," "substitutionary," "instead of," etc., but it
needs an immense amount of explaining and transcending.
We do indeed plead—"represent, present, and plead"—
Christ's death and life, His complete satisfaction for sin
as well as His triumphant holiness, righteousness, and

life, *instead of ours*. But it is a temporary truth: the "instead of us or ours" is a qualification for time not eternity, and the life in Christ is "eternal." It is ours now only in faith, in hope, and in love—not yet in all the actuality and reality of complete fact. But God sees us already complete in Christ: time does not for Him defer or obscure His perfect oneness with us: and He gives us—in His love, grace, and fellowship—and through our faith, hope, and love in response—to see ourselves as He sees us, in perfect oneness with Him—complete in Christ. Time, and even practically endless time (which, yet, is not and never eternity) is a necessary factor in relation to us—as the condition of endless evolution and growth Godward. An instantaneous and completed heaven is inconceivable and impossible for us. We ought not to expect, short of eternity, to pass beyond the use and function of anticipatory and proleptic faith, hope, and love—a living ever in the future of perfect self-realization in the Infinite. How deep into that future probation too must extend—or even the formal freedom which is inseparable from possible failure and miscarriage—we cannot know. We do know that the right use and habit of such freedom leads assuredly and progressively to its transition into real freedom which eventually means freedom even from formal freedom—from the possibility of sin and death.

The danger of the terms "vicarious," "substitution," etc.—is that they have led and do lead into the error that redemption, salvation, righteousness, and all that Christianity promises and gives—is expressed in the objective and judicial act and status of acquittal from guilt and condemnation. To separate too widely the "done for us" or the "done instead of our doing" from the "done with and in and through and by us" and so the *our* doing too"— has been the source of no little weakness and failure in our current Christianity. It would not if taken understandingly and faithfully.

Moreover vicarious penalty, or punishment by proxy, is an attempt to safeguard the principle of justice by too severe a strain upon either reason or conscience. I should rather save it by the position: That, if it takes an eternity to be saved, no man is going to be saved or perfected until he knows the death and resurrection of Christ—knows as Christ knows what sin is and what holiness is—what Hell is and what Heaven is.

THE CHURCH

<hr>

The Church was complete in principle in Christ alone; it will be complete in application only in humanity. If our Lord's conquest of the world, His accomplished righteousness, was first an achievement of faith, an attained oneness with God—it was, in the second place, an act and victory of obedience.

What is the Church? The God of Christianity cannot stop short with Himself; He must be God in His world—in all the "not Himself" that proceeds from Him, and that He would fill with Himself. The Christ of Christianity cannot stop short with Himself in heaven. The Christ of our *faith* is there,—because faith must see Him in the consummation and perfection of His part in the world. The Christ of our *hope* must be there, because hope too is of the end of our human participation with Him and in Him. But the Christ of the *process*—of the *all between* us and our faith and our hope—must be infinitely and awfully in the world and in ourselves, if His part is ever to be actually accomplished. In our faith and our hope we want Christ *there*—i.e., crowned and seated; but, for that, we first need Christ *here*—in the present fact, the stress and the strain, of the battle.

And He *is* here: The Church is as much the sacrament of His Presence, as His human Body was of the Presence, the Incarnation, of God in Himself. He is in us, *as* God was in Him: there is no difference in the act and fact of His oneness with us from that of God's oneness with Him —*other* than that which we place there by our want of faith in it. Christ's human oneness with God was an act of perfect human faith under perfectly human conditions: an act of faith consummated in and by an act of perfect faithfulness. In other words He realized or actualized His faith in *fact:* the same faith that made Christ one with God will make us one with Christ; when the faith in oneness is complete, the fact of oneness will be complete.

For the present, and as a mere beginning of further applications which we should all make, let us take these truths more intimately into ourselves and our lives. Christ humanly made Himself one with God only as God divinely made Himself one with Him; it was of faith only as it was by grace. We make ourselves one with Christ only *as* Christ has made Himself one with us. *That* Christ has done in His Church, which is His Body, which is Himself. Until we take the Church for what it is—as *being* all that it means—oneness with Christ, and in Christ with God, and in God with one another and with *all;*—until we learn how to do that, and begin to *do* it, we shall not be either in truth or in earnest in the quest for the unity without which Christianity is a predestined failure.

The principle of the Church we see realized and revealed in the person of Christ as embodying humanity in Himself, —or as exhibiting in human life the conception, process, and completion of divine Incarnation. Christ is human redemption or salvation because He is human righteousness, human self-fulfilment through self-correspondence with reality. But the principle of the Church in Christ ought to be better understood as it comes home to us in its application to our common humanity. Our relation to the righteousness and life of Christ is our relation to the person of Christ: it is described simply as our "being *in* Christ." That can have no other meaning than our being in the Church, as the body of Christ, and as Christ Himself. And that is so far off from our conception only because we are so far beneath God's conception of our humanity as the subject and object and body of His Incarnation.

(The first note (and, if we take it aright, the one all-sufficient note) of the Church is unity.) (The Church originated in Christ, and was fully realized and expressed by Him in the words, "I and my Father are one." That was, of course, true of Him primarily only in His deity. But He came into the world to extend it to, to make it equally true of, His humanity also: and it was in His humanity that He uttered the words. And He came not only to make Himself, as one of us, Son of God and one with God, but to make us all, as one with Him and one in Him, in like manner one with and one in God. He was to be only "the first-born among many brethren"—the leader, captain, author and finisher of a common salvation. It is not being holy that makes us one with God, one in ourselves, or one with one another: it is the being one that makes us holy, that is our holiness. Oneness is the essence and substance of holiness, of righteousness and of eternal life: and the only oneness is that of God—the inherent, essential, and completive oneness of Divine Love.)

The Church was complete in principle in Christ alone; it will be complete in application only in humanity. If our Lord's conquest of the world, His accomplished righteousness, was first an achievement of faith, an attained oneness with God—it was, in the second place, an act and victory of *obedience*.

The tremendous fact of the oneness of God with all, and of the onenes of all—if ever—only in God, and with

53432

God, and through God: which is the reason, and meaning, and end of Christ,—that becomes the essence and substance of Christianity.

The point I wish to make is this: Our Christianity is too far off from us; we think of the Incarnation of God and the presence of Christ as too exclusively in heaven, and not sufficiently on earth and in ourselves. We do not know that in the mind and heart and will of God *we* are the body of Christ and the subject of the Incarnation.

The process of God in His world—or more definitely, in the mode or degree of His relation to the world—cannot but compel our attention and thought, however it may for ever transcend our knowledge. In the first stages of the physical evolution in which we find ourselves to be— viewed now in the light of what it has become and is evermore becoming—we may discover the immanence of Somewhat which we may call Reason, Meaning, End or Purpose,—or God. We believe it to be indeed God, but a God Whom we can know, or know of, only by logical inference. The theory or postulate of God comes to us to account for a somewhat in the movement or direction in things which, we think, the mere things of themselves cannot account for. If this be God, then God so far is apparent to us, not in Himself, but only in the working of the things,—and so far as we know, may *be* only in and of the things.

But we have long since passed out of that world of the mere becoming of things into a higher world of knowing and controlling them. We are not any longer only inside and of, but outside and over the movement and direction of things,—and what is more, of ourselves. What has come in (we know not how) to make the great change, is not the mere appearance in phenomenon of self-consciousness and freedom, but the birth amid things of the *self* as subject of consciousness and freedom.

As ourselves no longer only immanent in but transcendent

above the world of things in which we are—God no longer appears to us as only immanent in things but as infinitely and supremely without and above them: He meets us in the plane of our own transcendence or objectivity—that is, of our reason and freedom. However we may infer or postulate Him, and even worship Him, in the elements, forces, or operations of physical nature, we cannot see or know Him there as separate from these. To worship God in nature is simply to worship nature as God; and that is as far as nature-worship can go. But when we pass out of the world of mere natural and necessary sequence into that of the higher and wholly different calls and claims of reason and freedom, of holiness, righteousness and life, God is ready to come to us—or we are ready that God should come to us—not as mere force or movement, operation or law, no matter how majestic or divine, but as Himself, Person as we are persons, and transcending, as we transcend ours, even all His own presence and part in the world that comes from Him. When we know God not alone as Reason and Will and Purpose, but as Love and Grace and Fellowship, as the Life and Soul and Substance of our own righteousness or personal and social perfection,—then indeed we know Himself, and not some inference or predication about Him.

What we know of God in physical nature is expressed in the terms universality, uniformity, and unity. We know Him only *in* these and not in exceptions, violations, or contradictions of them. So in human nature we know God in the totality of His relations with us, only *in, with* and *through* what He is in ourselves—that is, in the integrity of what *we* become in Him. We know God as Person because we are persons,—as Spirit because we are ourselves finite spirit. If God is anything more than Spirit or Person we are agnostic of it because we do not share it with Him; but we are not agnostic of God in so far as He makes us partakers with, and partakers of, Himself in actual experience. Only we must not expect God to interfere with His own wisdom and love in making us persons, in putting us upon a reason and freedom of our own, any more than to violate the necessary laws and uniformities which He imposes upon nature. Not only nature but human nature must work to its end, in accordance with, and in the integrity of, itself.

It might be said with reverence that if the term, along with the thing, Incarnation, had not been given us, the human instinct of it would not only have created the want but have found the expression. But indeed God could not have given it if men had not so wanted it. When we say that God could not, we mean only that He could not act outside of or counter to His own wisdom and working in the matter. He is as much in the instincts and wants, the purely natural impulses, of His world, as He is in their answer or supply—natural or supernatural. He feeds the raven which He caused to hunger and to seek its food; and He comes in person to meet the soul that hungers and thirsts for nothing less than Himself.

It is amazing how immediately, how definitely, and how perfectly Christianity, or the Incarnation, assumed its cosmic, as well as human aspect. It was the crisis, the turning point, of God's eternal relation with His world. The completion of nature in human nature, of mere sequence and necessity in reason and freedom and personality, is contingent upon and leads up to the further process of the perfection of human nature, the sanctification and glorification of man in God.

If we are seeking the emphasis, or the emphases, which will restore reality and power to our Christianity, we must begin with that upon the personality, what we might call the objectivity, of God Himself. We must lift God above nature and above ourselves, and learn to enter into personal relation with Him: we must be able to say and to mean—"Our Father Who art in heaven." And the heaven we mean must be not one in which God is, but one which is in God—which only God Himself is: the heaven of the love and grace and fellowship of God, of holiness and righteousness and life in God. If we seek *that* first, all the other things that belong to heaven will add themselves.

The Gospel as a mode or process of human salvation—i.e., redemption and completion—is best understood in contrast with law. Law means the fulfilling of nature, the realizing of self, the discharge of obligation and perfection of relation with God and man,—in a word, law means that spiritual as well as natural "correspondence with environment," which is the definition of life and blessedness. It *means* all that, but how far can it go towards effecting or enabling it? Nature by itself, or without *us*, will not do for us what it does for the bee or the beaver; the fact or the knowledge that righteousness *is* life and transgression *is* death will not make us righteous or give us life of ourselves. For that nature and law and self have all to be transcended, and it is wholly with that transcendence that the Gospel has to do: it is not so much the *What* as the *How* of salvation.

"The law," says St. John, "was given by Moses; grace and truth came by Jesus Christ." Grace from God, and truth (realization and reality) in us,—are the Gospel. Is the law then older than the Gospel by so many years as Moses was before Christ? The idea is universally repudiated in the Scriptures. All the Gospel in the New Testament was implicitly contained in the growing promise of the Old Testament. Going backward, in David was the promise of a universal and everlasting Kingdom of God or of Heaven upon earth. In Abraham was promised what was to be the principle and substance of that Kingdom—a righteousness of grace or of God through the human answer and acceptance of faith. Our Lord asked how *He* could be merely Son of David, Whom David himself had called Lord, and affirmed, "Before Abraham was I am." In Adam there was the primitive promise that though the serpent had wounded the heel of his seed, yet that seed should in the end crush the serpent's head. Humanity had fallen under the power of sin and death, but would in time turn by the grace of God and put those enemies under its feet. But the Gospel of Christ, or Christ Who is the Gospel, was older even than Adam or man. He was before the world—the whole process of creation which (here at least) culminates, finds its reason, meaning, and end in man. "Thou lovedst me," our Lord says to the Father, "before the foundation of the world"; and St. Paul adds to this that "God chose us in Him before the foundation of the world . . . having foreordained us unto adoption (rather, unto realization or attainment) of sons through Jesus Christ unto Himself." The Gospel then is as old as the eternal divine thought or purpose of man: it is what God had in mind in his creation, in the planning of his nature and the predetermining of his destiny. Christ was then predestined humanity: man in, not only the mind, but the heart, wish and will, the forethought, provision, and prepared actual inheritance of sonship to God. As thus "Man from (and for) heaven"—Son of God by both origin and destination, Christ is carried back into yet prior and higher identification with God, is seen to be one with the reason, meaning and end or final cause of all creation—the Logos by Whom all things are, and Who eternally is with God, and *is* God.

The essence or substance of the Gospel is thus seen to be: humanity or *we* eternally and infinitely *in God,* and God through Christ, progressively (we might say evolutionally and eventually) *to be* in us. The Church is literally and exactly an *Ecclesia:* "Whom God foreknew He predestined to be conformed to the image of His Son (to the attainment of sonship through participation in the attained or accomplished human sonship of Jesus Christ); whom He predestined He called, whom He called He justified, whom He justified He glorified." The process of glorification or of becoming *de facto* sons is told on God's part, which is un-

failing and invariable. Nothing is said of the multitudes who
are called and do not hear or answer, and are therefore not
justified or glorified,—not that it is not theirs to be, but that
they "will not" be. The gospel of human redemption and
fulfilment is essentially and necessarily a "call," or an invitation: it has no message or meaning save to human freedom, to personal, spiritual, moral distinction, choice and
self-determination. Apart from these *we* are not in it, and
can in no wise be qualified or characterized by it. To make
human quality or character or destiny any other than a
"call" to our own faith, faithfulness and achievement or attainment is to annul and abolish the "us" or "we" in the
matter, and destroy all image or likeness of God in us.
God's parts in the process follow with something more than
mere natural infallibility. He cannot contradict Himself:
He cannot be anything less than the all-loving Self, the all-
sufficient Grace, or the perfect divine Fellowship or Oneness
with us—which are the factors on His part in our glorification or accomplished sonship. But even all that can be de-
feated by our non-concurrence: the human factors of faith
—acceptance and reception of "God with us"; of hope,
which sees and means *us* in the matter as well as God; of
love, which is the only actualized "God with us";—these
human factors are as essential as the divine in the result of
a human salvation. The Church, therefore, may be defined
(as in I Cor. 1, 2) to be "The sanctified in Christ Jesus,
called to be saints." That is to say,—it is humanity—on
God's part already and always included in the love, grace,
and fellowship which alone and perfectly can make it son
of God, partaker of His nature and of Himself: but on
man's part, "called" and waiting "to be," to become by its
own act of acceptance and appropriation, son of God and
partaker of His holiness, righteousness and eternal life.
The eternal Word become flesh, sonship incarnate—the
Love and Grace and Fellowship of God, the Kingdom of

Heaven, placed at our disposal and made "ours to command"—can only give us the right and the power, it cannot force upon us, or dispense with in us, the *will* to become sons of God. There is forever in the heart of God,—would that it could sound ever in our ears—the divine lament, "How would I—and ye would not!"

"One cannot but admire the unhesitating and unqualified manner in which the Church, in all its offices, utters the simple and straightforward language of faith. The trumpet gives forth no uncertain sound. By baptism we are dead with Christ and risen with Christ, and therefore *regenerate*. The only non-regeneration of one whom God has baptized is his own ignorance, or unbelief, or rejection of the fact that he *is* regenerate. But the Church assumes, or suggests, no such doubt or denial, but puts into his mouth only the language of faith, assurance, and fulfilment. As Christ died and rose, so the baptized person is to call and account himself dead to sin and alive to God. He is to *be* regenerate by believing himself regenerate; he is to realize the fact that he *is* regenerate. God has *made* him so; therefore he must account himself, and *be* so. And he will only not be so in fact through not being so in faith. i.e., through not believing that by God's grace and act he is so."

"The Church as a living Church should bring up her children in a living faith to realize their baptism, i.e., to make it real by accepting and treating it as real; to *be* children of God by believing that they *are* children of God, and not that they have to make themselves so by any act of theirs. And if we were born of and into such a living Church, our faith would be such a living faith, and our baptism would be, both to us and in us, such a living fact. At any rate, if it were not, the fault and failure would be, not in it, but in us: not in its not regenerating, but in our rejecting and making naught our regeneration. It would no more make baptism not a divine and a divinely efficacious act, than the fact of our Lord's inability to do His mighty works, on account of man's unbelief, made Him not a divine person." [1]

If we are to follow the transcendent, prehuman Christ in His Incarnation, Resurrection, Ascension, Descent in the Spirit—the next step must follow co-equally and of necessity. If Christ is not as really and as actually present in His Church as in all His previous manifestations, energies, and activities—then Christianity has lapsed. If baptism into Christ does not mean, *is* not, for us, all that it meant and was for Him in His humanity—then by so much has it ceased to be what God made it and gave it. I do not say, as much *in* us as *in* Christ, for there is this immeasurable distance if not difference between Him and us: In Christ God has shown us the completeness of His love, grace, and fellowship working in the perfection of our human faith, hope, and answering love: He has shown us what we would be if we were in perfect response to Himself as Christ was. But even in Christ, however foreshortened, it was a process that required time: Christ, in a few years, *longam expositionem hominis in se recapitulat,* sums up all man's evolution or destiny in Himself. Because our faith, realization, reproduction of Christ in ourselves is a thing of endless growth, or of growth that ends not here,—therefore Christ here cannot be *in us* as God was in Him. But Christ *for* us, as an end, a goal, a destiny, to which we must always be looking and moving, Christ as our faith, our hope and love—is as real, as present and as complete in our baptism as He was in His own. What I mean is that the "given" in my baptism is the same as that in Christ's—however infinitely different the "received": it is my everlasting task, and privilege, and glory to make up that difference. All the love, grace, fellowship was there, and was there, on God's part, made mine; it is for me now, by never-ending growth in faith, hope, and love, to appropriate, assimilate, and convert unto myself all

---

[1] See *Soteriology of the New Testament,* pp. 374, 375.

that is eternally mine in God. We are wholly in Christ by God's grace, it remains for Christ to be wholly in us through our faith. What we need to see is that God's gift to us of eternal life, through His Word to us and by His Spirit in us, is absolute, unlimited, and unconditioned. Baptism receives us into the Kingdom of Heaven and makes it "ours." There is no limitation or condition about it—save the one of our own creation and interposition: viz., the question whether we will take it, and how much we will make it. Whatever of penalty, of death or of hell, of loss or torture to ourselves, there must of necessity be in the rejection, contradiction and consequent opposite of life, blessedness and heaven, is not of God's will or ordaining; it is the result of logical, natural, human consequence. If God says, "Be blessed," and we say "No," the curse of non-blessedness is not of His but of our own infliction. I am speaking only of or to those who have real opportunity and consequent responsibility, or accountability. The Gospel is of course only for those who have it: those who have it not we may safely leave to a God Who is all of love and mercy.

The "in me" of Christ—in Him as eternal Word, Promise and Fulfilment of us, in His Incarnation, Death, and Resurrection, and Eternal Life—is as present and patent in the New Testament as the responsive "in Christ" which became at once the all-inclusive expression of Christianity's relation to Him. "To be in Christ and Christ in us"—as integral parts, continuation and extension, universality, and perpetuity of the Incarnation,—how was this to be effectuated and established as a permanent fact in the world? Was it to be left in the air, or written and left in a book? The Book or Bible was no part of the original institution of Christianity. It arose out of the actual and conscious life of the Church, and was the inspired means of recording and perpetuating that original consciousness for all time. The actual institution of Christianity might be said to have been in the two sacraments—of the new birth and the new life in

Christ. But what were those two sacraments? Divinely given signs and seals or pledges of a deeper fact, parts of a fuller whole than themselves. The fact or whole was achieved, accomplished, realized and fulfilled oneness of humanity with God—its now actually "determined" or effected "sonship in power according to the spirit of holiness, out of or through resurrection from the dead." But of this fact or whole Christ was only the beginning, the first-fruits, the first-born from the dead. God's predestination was of humanity, of us, unto fulfilment and inheritance of "sonship to Himself through Jesus Christ." "Whom He foreknew He foreordained to be conformed to the image of His Son (the end or goal of our creation)—that He might be the first-born among many brethren." The whole process of Incarnation therefore was not terminated, it was only begun, in the Ascension of our Lord. The body of His individual, natural humanity was to grow through all space and time into the all-inclusive body of His corporate, spiritual humanity.

To say that Christ did not institute a Church is on a par with saying that He did not take our flesh, or rise from the dead, or ascend into heaven. It is a break or a halt in the process of His human task and activity just where it begins to apply itself to its real end and purpose. The Church is Christ's one real and whole sacrament to us of Himself—of our being "in Him" and "He in us." Any other sacraments are only acts and parts of that one—"outward and visible signs of the inward and spiritual grace" which is ours only as we are in Him and He in us. It is not our faith, or our conversion, or anything whatever on our part, that places us in Christ or makes us sons of God. It is absolutely and altogether an act of God long before and wholly without us— in our creation, our predestination, and the incarnation in us of His Word and Spirit through our union with Christ. The function of faith is simply to accept, to appropriate, to make our own; true conversion is what will take place in us as the necessary result or fruit of a true faith. Just as in the human Christ the fact and reality of His saying "I and my Father are one," was the legitimate utterance and expression of His perfect acceptance and realization of the baptismal word "Thou art my Son,"—so with us the essence and matter of true conversion is the reality with which we appropriate our baptismal oneness with Him and His with us. To be born anew in the Risen Christ, and to live in Him the ever new life of death to sin and resurrection to God and eternal life is the one simple and all containing truth of the sacraments.

It is not adding a new truth, it is only unfolding the most vital content of the one truth, to say that the Church as the Sacrament of Christ (as Christ Himself is to us the Sacrament of God) is not the medium of relation between "God and the soul, the soul and its God,"—if the soul be taken individually, as though religion were a matter solely between each man and his God. Christianity is distinctly a corporate and social act and life. As Christ, so God says: He that hath done it unto the least of mine hath done it unto Me— and there is no doing unto Me that is not unto all mine. I am willing to extend this so far as to say: There is no whole relation of correspondence and co-operation with God that is not in sympathy and unity with creation, with nature, with humanity, with all things and pre-eminently all persons. In Christ must be the ultimate unity of all these—of science, philosophy, business, politics, personal, social, national and international intercourse and relations—if He is to be unity with God. The divorce and disunity of the various parts of truth, which is one with God, must be overcome before we can be all-one with Him: to be alien from any is to be so far alien from Him Who is All-in-all.

The Church then is in the highest sense the sacrament of unity. Its one mark of unity includes and covers all the others, of holiness, universality and perpetuity. The Church may be defined as organized unity, or as unity incarnate: its earliest expression was, "I believe in the Holy Catholic

Church, the Communion of Saints": i.e., in one Holy and Universal Church, the Unity and Community, the Fellowship or Oneness of all Christians. Now what, again, was that oneness? It was primarily the oneness of each and all with Christ, or with God in Christ. But God in Christ recognizes no oneness with Him that is not oneness of all in Him with one another. There is no common or universal oneness with God that does not abolish between those who share it, I will not say all differences among themselves, but at any rate all differences that deny, contradict, defeat or hinder their oneness together in Him. "As many of us as were baptized into Christ did put on Christ. There is neither Jew nor Greek, there is neither bond nor free, there is neither male nor female,—for we are all one in Christ Jesus." These natural differences and many others, did not actually cease in Christ, but they ceased in so far as anything in them constituted a bar, a hindrance, or a contradiction to their oneness with Christ or with one another in their relation to Christ.

There is no question in any of our minds that the one thing needed, the one condition of all life, is unity—unity in itself and unity with all else, oneness in inward constitution and with outward environment. Nature as such will never of itself bring about that unity. In the wisdom that underlies nature we are passing out of an immeasurable stage of strife and competition in to a yet distant future one of unity, co-operation and order: order among ourselves, though slowly acquired, because rational and free, cooperation with God. Nature of itself will not give us that unity,—nor selfish prudence and experience, nor legislation, nor law, nor outward compulsion of any sort. Only the Spirit of God as new-creative power can accomplish it: "new" only in the sense of ever anew coming into demonstration and action as it can awaken the reason of man to wisdom, and the will of man to true freedom. The Spirit of God has moved upon the waters from the beginning; it begins to move in the sphere and realm of finite created and responsive spirit only as "life becomes light" (attains to consciousness of God and itself) in man. Christ is the incarnation and manifestation of that Spirit not so much in its origin or potential existence in man, as in its historic coming to itself and its complete realization and revelation of itself in His person. And as Christ needed to come in the objective and concrete visibility of a human body at the first, so He needs to come again not in the abstract and suppositious conception of an invisible unity (which if it were true would manifest itself)—but in a visible body as before, the body of all in Him, in which in its unity man may see Him, even as in Himself man could see God.

That the Church, as herein understood, could come into the world only in some concrete and organic form is, I suppose, self-evident. That the Apostolate which Christ invested with His authority was the foundation and source of its future order is, I suppose, equally so. But to the Apostles the Church founded through them was the Body of the Risen Christ within it: *It* was the organ of His "returned," universal and perpetual presence and activity upon earth,— and they were but the members, the parts, to whom were committed the several functions. A permanent ministry to continue these functions after them I assume to have been the first condition of the organized permanent presence of Christ in our humanity. As a matter of fact the constituent elements of a visible Church as the Body of Christ have been and are among all—the faith, the sacraments, the ministry and the worship.

It may be assumed that if unity were—not only of the essence, but the very and sole essence itself of the Incarnation and the Church—one of the earliest provisions that would have to appear and establish itself would be the provision for world-wide and time-long unity.

The question, How to restore and conserve Unity—must go back to a prior one,—What is the Unity in question? Let us recall and repeat it in our Lord's own words: "I will not leave you orphans; yet a little while and the world seeth me no more, but ye see me: because I live, ye shall live also. In that day ye shall know that I am in my Father, and ye in me, and I in you." And in His last prayer: "Father, the glory Thou hast given me, I have given unto them: that they may be one, even as We are one; I in them and Thou in me, that they may be perfected into one; that the world may know that Thou didst send me, and lovedst them, even as Thou lovedst me."

The Church, as we have seen, is the Body, Incarnation, or Sacrament of that Unity. In such a Union or Unity of two, there is the inevitable danger of holding one, either one, at the cost—even to the extreme of the denial—of the other. In the transcendent person of Jesus Christ Himself there have been from the beginning those who have held His divinity to the practical annihilation of any real humanity in Him; and on the other hand, those who have seen Him only human, to the practical exclusion of any real divinity. It is not surprising that in what we might call the corporate personality of our Lord—that which He shares with and in which He includes *us*—there should be similar extremes of contradiction, some denying and others exaggerating and distorting the real divinity of the Church. But all the way between these widest and even outside extremes there are few who call themselves Christians that would not resent the thought of being "out of Christ," that would not acknowledge the necessity of being "in Christ" and "one with Him" in all that "Unity" means or involves. And also,—all the way between these widest extremes there is no one point at which we can say that Christ is all *there*—to the exclusion of every, or of any, other point.

If then, in all our differences we are thus able to concentrate and agree upon the one necessity of being in Christ and of being one in Him, we must not despair of some ultimate Way to it. If we will cultivate and prepare the disposition, the will, and the purpose—God will make the Way. The curse of the present state of Christendom is that our differences have erected such barriers and entrenchments that intercommunication, exchange, and mutual understanding are well-nigh impossible. Let us once begin in very reality to reverse this spirit, attitude, and policy—to bring together, compare, and contribute to the common good of the One End, the End of Oneness;—let us, I say, once begin on that line, and the differences that do not eliminate themselves will be turned into the higher service of deepening, broadening, and heightening the resultant Unity.

CHRIST THE SOLUTION
OF HUMAN LIFE

―――――――――

He has put us in the only relation, disposition or attitude to the law and its righteousness now and here possible for us. He has given us the obedience to it not of law but of faith. To understand at once the difference and the essential relation between these two obediences is the gist and matter of the Gospel.

There is nothing more necessary than the continual revision of ourselves and our religion, and certainly never was the need greater than at present. *Is* Christianity the solution of human life? And if so, are we Christians? In answering— or rather in proposing—these two questions, I may be pardoned, in order to get back to the root of the matter, for recalling a little of the A B C of thought and conclusion upon it.

It was Socrates who first, in our western world, brought down human speculation from the air or the clouds to fix it upon ourselves. His "Know thyself" was the beginning for us of true reflection. Plato developed the common sense intuitions of Socrates into a finished philosophy, and Aristotle formulated the whole into a science. From each of these I will select an indisputable principle which underlies all subsequent thought or conclusion. In our reflection upon and knowledge of ourself, the very first fact we encounter is that of *want*. Want is, if not the origin, yet the inception of all life. It is the impulse not only to action but to knowledge. Feeling is before knowing; the "feeling after" what we want is the beginning of knowing as well as of acting. In the process of evolution through feeling into knowing, want becomes *wish* with the growth of consciousness, and *wish*, with the evolution of freedom, becomes *will*. Now it is with *wish* (Plato's βούλησις) in its very simplest and most elementary form—as utterance of want, and substance of will —that I wish first briefly to speak. Plato's dictum of it is, absolutely expressed: "Wish is of the good." Wish is, as a matter of fact, the most primary, universal, and necessary principle of human life. It is in itself—absolutely, as Plato says—"of the good." It is absurd to say that any man wishes, not his good, but his evil. There is of course very much of what we call "wish" of evil; but it is a perversion of the term: it is not wish but *lust* or something else. Plato, in his great idealism, or intuition of the true, the beautiful and the good, thought that all vice was ignorance, the fatal "mistake" as to the good. Aristotle saw and said that evil was not all ignorance, but much of it conscious or "knowing" choice: "Men know the better yet the worse pursue." But in substance they agreed: There is only one real want, and there is only one real wish: and that is of the good; there is only one real good.

Aristotle's great treatise—once pronounced the greatest, not only on that but on any subject, in the world—is an extended definition of the good. It is first a formal definition, which may be and is complete and conclusive; nothing else or more can be said about it. It is then a real definition, rather an exposition, of the good: which may be, or can be, final or conclusive only so far as it goes, for the good is infinite and eternal.

"The good," says Aristotle, "is that which all things aim at"—"feel after if haply they may find," "wish for"; and going farther, it is the one object of rational knowledge, and the one end of free action. If human nature and human life be considered and described only positively and constructively, "the good" is the sole and supreme motive, process, and end of human thought, affection, will, conduct, character, life or destiny. It is in this last aspect, of human good as summing up and giving reason, meaning and end to all other earthly good, that Aristotle further defines it, and to that we will limit ourselves. All lower good, inorganic, vegetable or animal, is indeed included in and necessary to composite man—but only as means, not as end. It is only the ultimate and real human end that gives to good its meaning.

The good of any being, says Aristotle substantially, is that which completes its nature, and perfects its functions—brings all its potentialities into actuality. Thus, again, the good is identical with the end of a being. That, however, is not a complete definition: it does not cover the whole meaning of good. We may conceive of a thing and a very highly organized and complex thing coming to the end of its nature and perfected in all its functions, to which all this is not a good. There must be conscious want, intelligent or understanding wish, and rational and free will of the end to make it altogether a good. Good, to be so, must be a gratification and satisfaction of wish, as well as a fulfilling of nature and perfection of function. The element of feeling which came first must go on to the last in its successive stages and heights of pleasure, happiness, blessedness. There is no question that the final and highest expression of good is joy. No philosopher has found a further definition of the end or good of life than the identification of perfection and blessedness.

Passing on now from the formal definition to the real exposition of good, we often hear of the distinction between *personal*, in the sense of individual, and *social* good. Admitting the propriety of such a distinction, I should not begin but end with the personal. There is no worse confusion in thought or life than the confounding the term personal with individual or particular. In fact they are at opposite extremes: the truly personal is the end and perfection of the social. No man is perfectly himself, attains full personality, elsewhere or otherwise than in the completest and truest and rightest relations with all others. The good of an individual no more exists apart from that of society, than the good of a hand or eye apart from the body, or of a branch apart from the vine. The man at last is what he has become in living with his manifold natural and spiritual relations.

Good then is a social fact: it is a matter of relation and relations. Those relations are concrete realities; they exist between actual entities, and *are* just what they are. They are succinctly expressed in our duty toward God and toward our neighbour. We will not waste our time in refuting the ancient moral heresy which would deny the primacy and divineness of the natural social instincts and affections. We are by nature children, and partakers of the nature, of a God who is Love. As God, so nature, and so *our* nature is that universal "wish of the good" for all, which is—not the impossible absurdity of an abstract impersonal love as the principle of the universe, but—the personal, living and loving God of the universe.

It is not strange that in process of evolution the universal wish of the good should have attained successively to higher —not merely heights, but even—transformations and new creations of form and meaning. The first momentous revolution or transition was the newbirth of mere natural into moral good—the passage from mere wanting, getting, and having good into doing, giving and being good. With the genesis of even the beginnings of reason and freedom there loomed into being the great fact of the moral law. The recognition of the demand (the "categorical imperative") to do good and be good implies that of the possibility or freedom (within whatever limits) of obedience to it. And there is no possibility of a real obedience which does not carry with it and in it that of an actual disobedience. The first task of the right reason is to interpret the fact and possibility of evil—the "what" of the fact, and the "why" of the possibility. I venture to put the solution of the mystery in a single word: God wills and means—it is His "good will" or "will of the good"—to make His world a partaker of and sharer in its good. To enter ourselves into its joy—we must ourselves have been makers of its peace; and to do that, we must be full sharers with Him in its righteousness. "The Kingdom of God is righteousness, and peace, and joy": the reason and meaning and end of the world we live in is not that these three things should exist as empty abstractions or as impossible ideals. Nor is it that they should be actualized here by omnipotent fiat. God does not want the kingdom of heaven—its righteousness or peace or joy: He has it, and wants *us* to have it, and we can have it only by having them; and we can have them and it only by ourselves making them our own. The Kingdom of God is within *us*—only in *our* righteousness and peace and joy. And there is only one way of getting them.

In spite of itself the world cannot but in its heart want and wish and worship Christ. There is nothing else to worship: He is the only expression of its want, the only real object therefore of its wish;—unfortunately before the wish that is "of the good" strengthens and realizes itself in the *will* of the good, a thousand attractions, inclinations, lusts and concupiscences divert it from "the way"—from its true and real self, and it is lost. What the Way, the Truth and the Life is—we are not left in doubt. Christ stands before us first of all as the Resolver of doubt, the Winner and Revealer of certitude, the achievement and embodiment of human knowledge of self. He reached beyond the fundamental prayer: "Noverim Te, Domine, noverim me!" He spoke not out of the wish for knowledge, but out of the knowledge attained: "No man knoweth the Father but the Son, and he to whom the Son shall reveal Him." He could say thereafter: "He that believeth in me believeth not in me but in Him that sent me; and he that seeth me, seeth Him that sent me." In the clear faith of Jesus Christ the truth of God stood revealed; in the accomplished obedience of the Son, the holiness, righteousness, and eternal life of the Father were made manifest.

If God will or can reveal or manifest Himself, make Himself in any way known—where and how *must* it be? Can the heavens really declare Him? What possible image or likeness to Himself can He find in which we may see Him or know Him! There is only one that we can conceive or imagine—the knowing mind, the loving heart, the wanting, wishing, obedient will of man. There and there only can God make Himself known, or possibly *be* known, in all the range at least of our human experience. If God is good— there is nothing here that can share the goodness, nothing that can *be* good with Him, but the good will, the consentient, concurrent, co-operative *free* will of man. If God is wise—with that infinite "rightness of reason" which *knows* the good that it wishes and wills—who or what can partake of that wisdom, but the human heart that with Him loves the good and so the human mind or reason that with Him is open to know it? If God is righteous, if righteousness (along with its necessary antecedents of love and wisdom) is God,—for whom is the problem and its ultimate solution of the mighty mystery of life's warfare of good and evil? No—there is no other answer: only man can interpret God, —or God man. And the solution can be found, because it exists, only in their unity: if we look at the actual process— in their primal unity, temporal disunion, ultimate and eternal re-union.

That neither the reason, meaning, nor end of humanity is

soluble nor solvable save in terms of incarnation becomes more and more patent as we more and more take in what may be called "the other side" of incarnation. Christ has been too one-sidedly interpreted as the revelation of God: He is equally the revelation of man. We have not thought enough of Him as (1) the forethought or fore-purpose, and (2) the realization and fulfilment ultimately—of man. What humanity was to be in the end actually, it was from the beginning potentially. In every rational act or process the end is the first thing and determines all the rest; the last in execution was the first in conception; final cause was first cause. When we think of our Lord's humanity at all we think of Him too much as a man, and too little as man or humanity. He was only "once" on earth, and now He is, actually, altogether, in heaven. It is a strained figure, as we use it, to think of ourselves as His Body—or the Church as the Incarnation. For most of us all reality has evaporated out of the great fact: How much are "we in Christ"? And consequently we may well ask, How far—how deeply or widely or highly—is He in us?

What was intended for and given to man, or humanity, as the revelation or manifestation at once of God in us and us in God was given of course in the person of a man—*The* Man Christ Jesus. The universality of that Man had been historically prefigured in the assumed personality of a predecessor as universal as Himself. Permit me to give a little turn of punctuation, and so of interpretation, to an important passage (Rom. 5:12): "As through one man, sin entered into the world, and death through sin; and so death passed unto all men, for that all sinned." I do not otherwise justify the change, but it brings out an unquestionable truth, an indisputable fact: *As one man* mankind sinned and sins; in Adam all sin and all die. The "one man" expresses the solidarity of our humanity: we speak without hesitation of our all being "in Adam," and of the "Adam in us." So far from its being a strained or difficult conception, it is a natural and inevitable one: in our common nature and under our natural conditions we all sin and all die. Now there is in us not only a "temporal" but an "eternal"—an organ and function of the infinite: our "finite spirits are not products of nature but children of God." As the former (the temporal, or products of nature) we are "living souls," as the latter (children of God) we are "life giving spirit." Jesus Christ is the revelation and manifestation, as also He is the realization and fulfilment, of the eternal and the divine in us: in Him we see as clearly and definitely ourselves in God as God in ourselves. When St. Paul says, "Not I but Christ: *I* live no longer, Christ lives in me," he means that the natural and temporal self in him had given place to the spiritual and eternal. It was not the true and real "he" that still sinned and fell short of the glory alike of his primal destiny and his final realization. He had forever given up, disclaimed and repudiated the old man of sin in him, and identified himself with the new Man who, as Son of God, could not sin. Those two men are in every man, and the choice and decision between them is the matter of our probation.

That there should be the old man to be judged, overcome, and crucified in order to the attainment of the new manhood in Jesus Christ ought to be to us the most solvable and solved of mysteries. Christ presents to us the most comprehensible character and career in human history. *There* is the whole reason, meaning, and end of ourselves portrayed before our eyes. How true it is that in believing in Him we are simply believing God's Word of ourselves, in seeing Him we are seeing God in us. In deference to the principle of agnosticism in us all, let us drop the question as to *Who,* and take it up as to *What* it was that Jesus Christ as the universally accepted embodiment (if we prefer that to Incarnation) of human faith, obedience, and self-devotion, believed in, was obedient to, and sacrificed Himself for.

First, Jesus Christ is to us the embodiment of human

faith. Faith in *what,* we ask. And I answer, faith in what alone is its proper or possible substance or object: faith in reality—in the sole and universal fact and principle of existence or life as we know them. If want of the good is the one only principle and end of actuality, then good as the one fact or reality of the universe is the one substance and satisfaction of faith. If the question recurs as to the meaning and truth, or as to the indefiniteness and uncertainty, of good, I answer as before: our goods and our good are not mere ideas and abstraction, they are concrete and actual. We know sufficiently well what is the good of the body— and no less of the soul, or of the self as a whole. We know that the body and the bodily life exist as organs and instruments of the higher life and whole of the soul, and must be amenable and subordinate to its interests. We know that the highest good of the soul is its *goodness,* and that that consists in its freedom from the trammels and hindrances of sloth and sensualism and selfishness. We know that so-called individual or personal good and social good are not two but one and the same, and can only be had together. We know that the so defined right life of right persons in right relations possesses a good which in its highest expression we may call joy; that the necessary precondition of joy is peace, peace in oneself and peace with all selves; and moreover that the precondition of peace is righteousness, right thought, right feeling, and right dealing among all the sharers of the common life. Good, therefore, human good, is so far sufficiently knowable and definable to be the natural, rational, and free want, wish, and will of all. And it *is,* at bottom, in the underlying real soul and self of every man. Yet, even so far as this, it is unquestionably hard in this world as it is—to believe in the good; so to believe in it as to live for it and die for it, to give one's life and self to it.

Yet just this our Lord did. First of all, He *believed* in it —and believed in it in spite of all His experience of all the opposite, in the wilderness, in the garden, and upon the cross. What else could have led and enabled Him to endure and survive all these? Again then, what was it that our Lord so believed in, and that His triumphant faith so manifests and reveals to us that to see and know Him is to know *It?* It was, behind and before all the poverty and sorrow and want—the deep-down divine *wish*—of the world, the infinite and eternal will of the good as the principle, potency and promise of its ultimate destination. That mind and will and purpose of the good so underlies and indwells all being and all life, that we must perforce conceive it as before them, principle, final and first cause of them: in other words as the reason, meaning, end and purpose of the universe as we know it. Whether such a first principle and cause could have pre-existed abstractly and unconsciously, itself without all by which it was to manifest and reveal itself in its own creation or evolution, we need not pause to consider. However properly agnostic we are or ought to be, we are not assuming too much or venturing too far in knowing and addressing it in terms of ourselves, attributing to it the reason and the freedom which from it we have ourselves received.

At any rate our Lord, speaking out of "what (in the perfection of the faith of which He was Author and Finisher) Himself saw and knew," speaks of and speaks from the manifest principle of this world as it is, not as abstract reason, meaning, promise, or potentiality; but as His and our Father, whose children we are, bearing His image and called to share the glory of His likeness. But the faith of Jesus was only the beginning of His self-revelation. He embodies to us something yet more difficult or in itself impossible than human faith, that is, human *obedience*. Obedience must not only know its truth, but live its knowledge: "If ye know those things, blessed are ye if ye do them." There is no doubt, in the mind not only of the Church, but of the world, that Jesus lived His faith, *was* what He believed. There may be some question as to how, or in what sense, He realized His faith in Himself, but as to the utter and complete

faithfulness as well as faith of Jesus Christ there is practically no question. His baptism of profession, in water,
went on unhesitatingly to the baptism of performance, in
blood. Human life in its totality must be not only profession
but performance, not only faith but obedience, not only the
water of repentance, but the blood of death and resurrection.

Why should human faith and human obedience, human
life, be so hard, so painful and humiliating, so impossible for
flesh and blood? If we really knew and really lived our
Christianity, we would ask no such question; we should
know for ourselves that it could not and ought not to be
otherwise. Take the utmost limit of all that our Lord un-
derwent;—how else could we express or measure the perfection of His faith or of His obedience? Why?—Because not
otherwise could there have *been*—could there have originated, or developed, or been attained—such a human faith
or obedience. In other words, not otherwise could our humanity have achieved such a reason and freedom and personality of its own—have so transcended itself as to realize
the height of selfless selfhood that makes it like unto God.
"Perfected through suffering"—"made perfect by the things
He suffered!" And when at last our Lord prays to be
glorified with the Father in heaven as He had Himself
glorified the Father upon earth,—what was the glory He
sought, as had been that He had achieved? It was the one
and only possible glorification of our humanity—the finding
of faith, the doing of obedience or righteousness, in, through,
and by just such conditions as environ us—all their hardness, all their painfulness, all their hopelessness, all their
impossibility. It is a high glory that God calls us to, "to be
perfect even as He Himself is perfect," to be righteous with
a righteousness not lower or less than His own. If we want
to be sons of God, bearing God's nature and doing God's
work, we must not stop at impossibilities, we must not stagger under a faith that can remove mountains, nor faint in an

obedience that can not only believe all things, but do all things, bear all things, and *be* all things.

Faith and obedience do not complete the manifestation of our Lord's glory in our humanity. There is another element necessary to their completion, as indeed to their existence. We said somewhere above, in speaking of the successive, not merely stages, but revolutions and transformations in the very meaning of good, that the first of these was when natural good passed over into moral good: when in the appearance of reason and freedom good became *our* good, and we rose from mere objects or receivers into doers and subjects of good. When the Law came in, righteousness came with it in the form of the demand upon *us* for righteousness. Righteousness is *our* doing good and being good: good passes from all lower senses into the higher sense of the "good will." There is nothing good now in the full meaning of the term but the good will: men are become as God knowing good and evil. But the high call to conformity to the good will, the glory of a righteousness like unto God's, the privilege of sharing the holiness and attaining the perfection of our Father in heaven,—in a word, the Law (for that is what the Law means and requires of us as the ultimate condition of human life: "Do this, be this, and ye shall live")—the Law, I say, how could it end, how did it end, but in the demonstration of its impossibility! The Law could only bring us so near to righteousness as to give us the experience of unrighteousness, prepare us to know obedience by awakening us to the sense and fact of disobedience. "By the Law was and is (only) the knowledge of sin." For that purpose only was "the Law given, that sin might abound and become exceeding sinful"—make itself felt in all its evil, that man might know the want, the need, the necessity of holiness in all its good.

And so comes in the paradox of the next and final transformation or transcendence of good: Good must be *our* good or goodness, the good will *our* wills, righteousness *our* right thinking and feeling and acting and essential *being*. That is the Law, and the Law cannot be annulled, for the Law is the life: it is simply the expression, definition, declaration of what life is and how it must be lived. What then, if the Law is impossible, and if its claims and requirements, instead of producing holiness, only convict and convince of sin, instead of giving life only inflict death? The answer to this is in what I have called the paradox: Righteousness must be *ours,* and *not ours,* life must be "ours" and "not ours." "Not ours" because a higher and larger than ours—a higher and larger which includes not only ours but all others', of which ours is only receptive and participant and co-operant. And yet necessarily "ours" too, because unless "ours" is of the all, and the all is ours, by our own consenting and co-operating act, it is impossible and non-existent. My righteousness and my life—in the sense in which I shall further expound them—will not be equally, but will equally *be,* both God's and mine in order to be mine at all. "Our wills are ours, we know not how,"—but they *are* ours, and we must take them so and make them so, if anything soever is to be "ours" in the true sense. For not only "what a man thinks in his heart," but even more what he wills in his life—that, and that alone, is *he:* righteousness and life are ours if we will, and only if we will. We may not know the *how* our wills are ours, but we have no excuse for not knowing the *why:* "Our wills are ours, we know not how,—our wills are ours to make them Thine." We are free—that we may of ourselves take part in and make our own the good will that is the reason and meaning and end of our universe. The righteousness which is the precondition of the peace and joy that are the kingdom of God, for the coming of which we pray—itself has its precondition.

Righteousness is indeed a necessity to any and all goods of life—to any kind of peace or joy in it, to any satisfaction or even endurance of it. But no selfish necessity, no earthly prudence or wisdom, no merely rational law or compulsory legislation or moral sanction or consent will ever beget or create the righteousness we want. Even the deepest thinkers have sought something before it, behind it, and within it to give it worth enough, life enough, and power enough to conquer all obstacles and survive all trials. If the actual righteousness of the world is needed for conquest of the world, reversely it needed all that resistance and opposition of the world for its own perfection through conquest of it. The world of sin and death and hell was necessary to the making of the righteousness which abolishes them all. So Aristotle sought a *prius,* an antecedent ground and root and principle of righteousness in *philia.* More recently some have sought it in *endokia,* a natural good will antedating, pervading, and preserving all existence as source and condition of it. So naturally are we assured of and accustomed to the *fact* that all things in their essential being and function are aiming at and seeking the good, that philosophy, science, and empirical ethics simply start at that point, without questioning the why or how.

Religion alone raises, or at any rate answers that question. The *prius* of so-called natural, abstract, ideal *philia* or *endokia* or what not, necessary to account for it (it says) could never have originated, and become efficient and actual of *itself:* the mere abstract cannot concrete itself or the impersonal become or make the personal. It must have existed as pre-creative reality and efficiency, as eternal personal divine Wish and Will ("good pleasure" in Scriptural phrase) —in order so to have become and to be the universal actual principle of all creation. We cannot worship the patently necessary *prius* (not temporal but logical), the precondition and cause of a universe whose manifest reason and meaning and end is universal, rational, free, and personal righteousness, peace, and joy—as abstract potentiality or immanent necessity. We can but worship the *Who of it* as God, and the What of it as Love,—because that is what it is—whatever more it be. Whatever of actual agnosticism or boundless ignorance the words or terms in and by their limitation may to higher or further intelligence express, we know they are true so far as our knowledge goes.

So to return at length to our third element of our Lord's manifestation of the divinely human life,—faith and obedience complete, realize, and fulfil, become *all* themselves only in and through the essential culmination of sacrifice. Even from our inchoate point of view there is no possibility of denying this as the culminating principle and fact of creation, of nature, as finally evinced in human life. The principle of sacrifice, as that of good, has been subject to the process of evolution: it has had to make itself, rising from the purely natural and unconscious into the conscious and moral, from the involuntary into the voluntary, from the necessary into the rational and free, from the impersonal into the personal. I need not say how far sacrifice is still from having become the law of human life, the discovered and applied essence and principle of human righteousness, peace, and blessedness; but at least we have got as far on the way as the following: There is in the long run nothing human so recognized, so convincing, and so worshipped as genuine and real *heroism*. And we have come practically to admit that where the element of sacrifice is not merely lacking, but is not the gist and essence and matter of an act or a character, there is no real heroism. Already the meek are beginning to possess the earth, and they are destined to do so completely under "the Name that is above every name"— the name of humanity's Lord. What as yet stands in the way of His more universal kingdom is our lowering, if not perversion and degradation, of the truth and meaning of *meekness*. We do not see that it is, in the person of our Lord, the supreme and absolute human heroism: man's complete victory over *self*, as the last and greatest and most obstinate of obstacles not only to God's kingdom and righteousness, but to man's own greatness and blessedness and self-realization. He that gives himself gets himself, he that loses finds himself, he that serves God and man, in the act of self-transcendence attains self-fulfilment.

Taking the Cross of Christ as the necessary culmination and limit of His human faith and obedience,—among the thousand points of view from which it may be seen and described, I select the following: There is a point in the human approach to God, or at-one-ment with God, at which we say (in scientific theology) that "formal freedom" passes, is transformed, into "real freedom." Men can sin; if they could not, they could not be holy, for holiness is the free and *voluntary* not-sinning, it is *choice* between holiness and sin. In the process of sanctification, of becoming holy as God is holy, there is (so to speak) a moment, a crisis, in which one "dies to sin," surrenders all sinning to the limit of the loss of the *posse peccare,* the power of sinning. That is the transmutation of formal freedom, the *posse peccare,* into real freedom, the *non posse peccare.* Real freedom is eternal life, it is the highest heaven. When our Lord's faith and obedience approached its final and completive act upon the Cross, He spoke of it as the "crisis" of this world—the end of sin and death and hell in humanity as represented in His person—in humanity at large so far as it should be ultimately included in His person. Then was the beginning of the new creation, the restitution: the conquest of sin, casting out of Satan, and abolition of death.

The so-called "work" of Christ, of which so much is made, of which too much cannot be made, cannot be interpreted apart from Himself. It can be seen of course only in what He did; but what He did is visible only in what He was. He brought humanity in faith, obedience, and sacrifice up to God and into God, by the surmounting, overcoming and abolishing in these all that stood between and separated humanity and God. In Christ, the individual spiritual Man, we see the natural limitations, hindrances, and impasses of our humanity all transcended. These may be reduced in

principle to three, sloth, sense, and self—the fundamental
obstacles divinely and designedly put in our way, that in
and by overcoming them we may evolve, find, and fulfil ourselves. The first obstacle, as the natural principle of *inertia,*
is as essential in the moral and spiritual world as it is in the
physical. The primary virtue of effort, exertion, energy
could not come into being except over against and in overcoming the hard, the painful, the impossible and yet necessary and obligatory, in human action, activity, and actuality.
Life is not static or passive, it is active—in all that is positive, real, and constitutive in it: all that is *actual* in it is act,
action, activity. To complain that life is hard in any sense,
kind, or degree of hardness, is to complain that life is *life.*
To say that effort or energy is for the most part natural or
constitutional and not acquired or therefore a virtue, may
be true of some lower forms of energy. But the higher or
real energies of real life do not come that way. The energy
of a faith, or an obedience, or a self-sacrifice like Christ's is
a height, an extreme, a limit of human actualization and personal achievement and attainment that nothing else in the
world but itself could or can be.

The second natural obstacle to oneness with God is sense
or sensualism. If we were meant and called to be spiritual
beings, why were we made first to be beings of flesh and
blood, with bodies, parts and passions, with the powerful
incentives to the things and interests and pleasures of this
life? To beings predestined not merely to action but to freedom of action, *choice* was as necessary as effort and energy,
and even more vital. As a matter of fact energy is only a
formal not a real virtue. It is as necessary in a bad action
as in a good action, in a devil as in God: it has nothing to
do with the moral or spiritual *quality* of the act, but only
with its efficiency. The function of choice is to discriminate
qualitatively among acts, to distinguish good and evil, to
approve the things that are excellent. The true exercise,
trial, and test of choice is not bluntly between good and

bad: no one will wish or choose the bad simply as bad. Wish of the good, as we have seen, is the universal instinct, impulse and aim of all things, as well as the right reason and true freedom of those most highly endowed. Choice is rather between or among goods than between good as such and evil as such. We learn in lower goods how to compare, contrast, and value them, how to elect among them, to prefer the better and ourselves to arise to the higher. The quality and worth of ourselves depend upon and are determined by these insights, judgments, decisions, choices. The end divinely in sight for us is the cultivation and attainment of the right reason or judgment, to know and value goods according to their worth, and the freedom in pursuit, acquisition, or accomplishment of them. The man who loves eating and drinking, or money-making, or empty pride or ostentation or applause, more than righteousness and peace and joy in the holiness of God—is not consciously choosing between a good and an evil as such; he is choosing between vastly discrepant but not in all cases or necessarily contradictory goods, and making a very foolish as well as fatal choice. It is the folly that is the essence of the sin: a man's true value and worth, his choice, pursuit, and attainment of the highest and the best, is an obligation, a debt, a duty, which he owes to himself, to others, and to God. It is an obligation which carries its own sanction, its own reward or punishment, its own heaven or hell with it. God does not have to work these things, He has so ordained and made them that they work themselves. "Do these things and ye shall live; do them not and ye shall die": the so living or so dying are not mere matters or incidents of fact; they carry in them and with them all the accompaniments of glory or shame, of joy or pain, of height or depth, that human experience has invested them with. The natural life then of sense—or of sensationalism, from its lowest form of appetite to the highest of empirical reason and natural understanding—is not an evil to be renounced;

it is a stage or a plane to be transcended, to be passed through and above, and to be used to the uttermost as the necessary stepping stone to higher things. St. Paul (Rom. 6) represents the bodies, parts, and passions which we make the instruments of our sins as being so far from sinful in themselves as equally to be the necessary instruments and conditions of our human holiness, righteousness and life. The essence of sin is the using the lower *for* the lower, instead of for the higher and the highest, not using it as a stepping stone to the higher things. I like to think of our Lord as having passed *through all the heavens* into the very Heaven of heavens.

It is instructive to remember that, in the general tenor of our Scriptures, there is a sin beyond and above those of sloth and sense. When inertia (the root of the negative in us, the voice of simply not-being, the bottomless sin of omission) has been overcome by energy, of which it was the occasion and counter-cause; when sense or sensualism has given place and given rise to spirit and spirituality, which comes in and through and by its—not so much conquest and effacement—as by its conversion and sanctification; there still survives an obstacle and enemy which may be found even in the energetic and the spiritual, or in the most energetically spiritual and spiritually energetic. What do we mean by "spiritual pride"? Do we not read of a revolt or rebellion in heaven itself—among angels who are not creatures of sense, and certainly are not devoid of energy? In our Lord's typical temptations, after He had repelled and disposed of all assaults or attempts upon His faith or His faithfulness, there came the farther, subtler, more intimate and personal temptation—of setting up Himself in setting up His kingdom. Our Lord knew instantly that the most secret remembrance or thought or seeking or conscious presence and part of self in the supreme conception of His Kingdom was treason to the Divine, was a worship of Satan instead of God: "Get thee behind me, Satan!" The last touch, the touch of perfection, to be put to the kingdom of Christ is this: "And when all things shall have been subjected unto Him, then shall the Son Himself also be subjected unto Him that did subject all things unto Him, that God may be all in all." The all-in-all-ness of God is the end of religion: when Christ died upon the Cross the human self of possible sin, because of possible separation or otherness from God, died with Him. That death is the goal of us all: "In that He died He died unto sin, in that He liveth He liveth unto God. Likewise reckon ye also yourselves to be dead unto sin and alive unto God!"

How can we so reckon ourselves? Our Lord tells us *how* He Himself is the way: "He that believeth in me, believeth not in me but in Him that sent me, and he that seeth me seeth Him that sent me." We persist in, we insist upon, seeing in Him not the one Man Jesus, but God Incarnate, God in our common humanity; the glory of our manhood, not only as it was with God before the world was, in conception and predestination, but as it is with Him now in consummation and fulfilment.

But Christ is not only the first and the last, the divine end in purpose and fulfilment, the final cause of creation. He is the revelation to us not so much of these as of the divine process between these. If we were son of God in the beginning, in potence and promise, by natural creation, the question remained, how we were to be so in the end, in act and fact, or in realization and fulfilment. Between these two extremes emerges and is to be determined the whole question of the *we* and of our part in the process, and our minds and our wills in the matter. God will make us, will we make ourselves?—Both the makings are essential to the making;—and we shall be made only when the two wills are *one*. Whose will shall it be? God's, of course, we say; but then,—God's will in the matter will not *be,* unless *we* make it ours.

In the light of the human faith, obedience, and sacrifice

of Christ, I can see every question of religion answered, every phrase or term of Christianity explained. Such ideas or expressions as incarnation, salvation, redemption, completion so patently interpret themselves that we need not further consider them. Atonement in its original and proper sense of at-one-ment, of reconciliation, the making peace between God and man—is sufficiently plain. So too with the word propitiation, in its simpler sense of bringing near or conciliating. But there is no question that in such words as atonement, propitiation, satisfaction, Christianity has intensified the meaning and emphasized an element that must be reckoned with. Certainly no human being has of himself or in himself *satisfied* even himself—the law of his own being, of his own perfection and blessedness. That man is a finite being under an infinite law, no man who lives and thinks can question. That perfection, as not an individual but a social act and fact, is a debt, a duty, an obligation— to oneself, to society, to the world, and (in all these and above them) to God—is indeed a "categorical imperative," the ultimate test and standard of moral, spiritual and personal worth. Now it is not that God sovereignly and autocratically imposes upon and exacts of man categorical obedience to that absolute law, or conformity to that perfect standard: "Be ye perfect as I am perfect!" But it is that God has endowed us, purposed us, called or invited us to share His own perfection and blessedness. In Christ He has shown us how, has promised us that we shall, and has given us demonstration not only of His will and purpose but of His power,—if we will. "Do this and ye shall live, do it not and ye shall die"—is neither a promise nor a threat: it is simply a fact, this is life, and that is death; and only *you* will either acquire the one or inflict the other.

It is necessary for life and blessedness, it is the absolute condition of the kingdom of righteousness and peace and joy, that the law of them all shall be respected, obeyed, and satisfied. Christ has made Himself to us the Way, the

Truth, and the Life of that obedience and satisfaction. He has put us in the only relation, disposition or attitude to the law and its righteousness now and here possible for us. He has given us the obedience to it not of law but of faith. To understand at once the difference and the essential relation between these two obediences is the gist and matter of the Gospel.

We cannot be saved except by obedience to the Law, and we cannot be saved by obedience to the Law—expresses the fact of the situation. To exact of us an obedience of "works" or acts, of *actual* or complete conformity, the "righteousness" which the Law expresses and requires, could have only one of several effects. Either it will be immediate condemnation and death to us: or else it will be ignored as impossible and irrelevant to us; or finally, as has been the case, we will lower it to an easily possible and average level, and render it a practicable or plausible service. The essence of real righteousness is that it must be God's or none, all or none: its only end, aim, or measure is the divine perfection. To say that this shall be the standard of all human conduct, of all personal human relation, family, community, state, nation, world,—is to say a great deal, but what less or other is there to say? Ought any man to be less than perfectly good or true or right? And supposing he were that at *any* point of less or lower, ought he not to go on to more and higher? Could he possibly attain any height at which he should not and would not feel the eternal obligation to the best, the highest, the All?

Christ shows us in Himself the necessity, the possibility, and the final realization or actuality of the perfect law of liberty or righteousness. He makes it ours, not in *fact* (that would be bringing it all the way down to ourselves, to our possible present level of achievement or attainment) but in *faith;* that makes it our infinite and eternal end and aim, our everlasting standard and measure. That is what evermore we should be bringing ourself, our family, our community, our country, our world more and more, nearer and nearer, up to. If the process were really always going on, it could never stop, inasmuch as infinity or eternity could never be reached. Faith, hope, love are principles of never ending movement, action, progress. There is need for their presence and operation in the one only direction of glory to God, peace on earth, good-will in all to all, in every spot of our hearts and of the earth today.

CHRIST THE REVELATION OF GOD

God is as much in creation and in nature as He is in Incarnation. The Word that was in the beginning with God and was One with Himself, by which He made the heaven and the earth and all that are in them, Which took flesh and dwelt among us, and Whose glory we beheld, as of the Only-Begotten of the Father—is all one Word.

When we speak of Christ in absolute terms as the Revelation of God, in order positively to define what we mean we must of necessity begin with a process of delimitation, or even seeming contradiction. Not only cannot God Himself be wholly revealed to us, but actually there are many things in God's relation to ourselves, both in our constitution and in our condition, upon which He has made no immediate or direct revelation in Christ. There is nothing in our Science proper that is matter of divine revelation or that we are under obligation to take "on faith." As little is there anything of technical revelation in our Philosophy—or even in our Morality. All these are distinctively human tasks and accomplishments, upon which I will not say that our Lord has thrown no light from without or from above, but which

He has in no wise lifted from the shoulders of humanity itself.

And the revelation to us in Christ would be less truly divine than it is, if it were, what to our foolish eyes might seem, *more* so—that is, if it relieved us of any whatsoever of our own human part in the fellowship of God and man. Indeed, to bring out and vindicate the true and real divinity of Christ, it becomes necessary to rid our minds of much of the spurious deity too popularly ascribed to Him.

It may seem to be going far towards extremes to say that the habitual and characteristic miracles of our Lord were distinctly and distinctively human acts: that is to say, they were the things that humanity should do and could do and would do if it were raised to that fellowship with God which it attained in Christ. And as our Lord's works on earth were wrought in and by His humanity and were human works, so His knowledge upon earth was a human knowledge, a human knowledge whether of God, of man, or of things—a knowledge which we ourselves shall share, if in imperfection here, yet unto perfection as we are more and more conformed to His divine image and likeness.

How else are we to interpret our Lord's own teaching: "The works that the Father hath given me to accomplish, the very works that I do, bear witness of me, that the Father hath sent me" (St. John 5:36). "Believe me that I am in the Father, and the Father in me: or else believe me for the very works' sake. Verily, verily, I say unto you, He that believeth on me, the works that I do shall he do also, and greater works than these shall he do." And, why? Because He is going to the Father, but will return to consummate in them all that He has accomplished and attained for them in Himself: the Incarnation in Christ is complete only in humanity. Are there not in every age indications and assertions, more or less irregular and futile, but always significant of what the life of faith, the life in Christ and of Christ, should be and might be if only we had faith? What stronger language could our Lord have employed to express and declare the possibilities of faith? I will anticipate now so far as to say, that the positive and definite revelation in Christ is sufficiently expressed in the primitive statement: *Totam expositionem hominis in se recapitulat.* Christ is the eternal divine Foreknowledge, Predestination, Process and Fulfilment of humanity. He is not merely the How but also the What of human evolution.

Jesus Christ had a spiritual as well as a physical human genealogy and descent: He was by faith as well as by blood the Son of Abraham and of David. However far He transcended it, He was in the direct line of human spiritual evolution and progress. If Abraham was His precursor— with others before and after him—in that life in God through faith of which He was to be pre-eminently and finally "the Author and Finisher," so too David and the Prophets after him were already at work upon the Kingdom of God of which only He could be the ultimate Founder. Jesus was filled to overflowing with the piety of His ancestry, whose very language He appropriated while fulfilling their thoughts, realizing their hopes and embodying their aspirations and expectations.

There are two absolute correlatives that can in no wise exist apart: there is no true or real natural instinct, intimation, or intuition that has not its proper object or objective. And in such a case the object is as dependent upon the receptivity and potency of the instinct or intuition as the latter is upon the fact and satisfying reality of its object. The infant would have no instinct of the breast if there were no breast, but neither could the breast draw the infant if there were no infant impulse and impulsion to it. Any possible drawing of God to man must have its natural correlate in the drawing of man to God: there is no imparting where there is no receiving. Jesus Christ was just as much the coming of man to God as He was the coming of

God to man, and He could have been neither without the other. He is absolutely the revelation to us, because the fulfilment for us and in us, of both; and whatever difficulty or confusion we find in doing so, we must know Him in unhesitating terms of both.

God is as much in creation and in nature as He is in Incarnation. The Word that was in the beginning with God and was One with Himself, by which He made the heaven and the earth and all that are in them, Which took flesh and dwelt among us, and Whose glory we beheld, as of the Only-Begotten of the Father—is all one Word. But He speaks in different tongues and addresses Himself to different organs of reception in the different spheres which we distinguish as the natural and the spiritual. The function of Nature is the development or evolution of man's part in the life and work of the world. This consists in the right exercise and use of his own reason, the right disposition and ordering of his own affections, the right direction and employment of his own will or freedom. All these are concerned primarily with conditions and matters lying within his natural observation and experience. What he has to do with them is to make the most of them, and to make himself in doing so: in other words, to more and more realize or fulfil himself through the perfecting of his relation and correspondence with his nature and his environment. Revelation is out of place here; man is purposely thrown upon his own resources for the bringing out all *himself*. So I repeat that the intrusion or assertion of revelation in the legitimate spheres of science or philosophy or of what we call natural morality or ethics is an impertinence. God is in these things but His plan here is to work them out in, with, through and by the intelligence, affections and will of men: these are the means and methods of all distinctively *human* evolution.

So all that we know, or properly call by the name, of *Law* is outside of revelation, except in so far as we say that all nature too is in a lower sense a revelation of God. How we distinguish the higher or proper revelation will appear further on. Law lies wholly within the sphere of the lower revelation of nature; the higher revelation of Spirit does not abolish, but lifts it into something higher and infinitely more effective than itself. In its higher form and spirit law is, or becomes, identical with (simply the fact and expression of) holiness, righteousness, life. Below or outside of these it remains itself, and as such can no otherwise be either evaded and escaped or compromised with— law is simply and absolutely the demand for righteousness, and righteousness is no mere imposition or requirement of even eternal or divine authority: it is an inexorable and irreducible *Fact*. "He that doeth" the thing that we call righteousness "shall live,"—because righteousness *is,* and is nothing else, and nothing else is, *life*. Because it is, and nothing else is, life, therefore it carries with it and in it *all there is* of worth or value, of peace or joy, of merit or reward, to be found in life. By natural necessity or logical consequence, "He that doeth it not shall die," for what is death but the negation of all that is life? All that is *of God* is so *in itself:* there is no question of "vindicating" either Him or it.

There is only one way then either of evading the necessity or of escaping the consequences of law—and that way lies neither below nor beside, but only above it: we must find it in something higher and stronger than law.

For what hope is there in mere law, in the mere fact that righteousness is life and unrighteousness is death, and that always and inevitably we shall find it so? That is a natural, not a revealed fact; is natural morality able to cope with it? For that matter, it may be replied, has revealed morality or religion been able to deal with it? Has it made the world, or any elect portion of it righteous? Has it produced the fruits of righteousness in the peace and joy of human life? This brings us to the attempt to state positively *What is* new or revealed and efficacious in Christianity. Taking it very gradually and step by step, it is not enough to say that Christ reveals God as Love, and love as the soul and life of righteousness. That in principle may be discovered in the devotional life and worship which our Lord inherited and to which He largely conformed—as for example when He says, "Thus it behoveth us to fulfil all righteousness." Our Lord was indeed the absolute revealer of Love, but we shall have to say a great deal more about love before we can say just How He was so.

Again, it is not enough to say that Jesus revealed God to us as Our Father. Did not St. Paul at Athens recognize and acknowledge the natural intuition and intimation of that fact even among the Gentiles? Our Lord did indeed in the very highest sense, and in a way unknown before, reveal to us the Fatherhood of God; but it will require much to be said upon the nature and mode of the Fatherhood of God and the consequent sonship of man, before we can undertake to answer the question How He did so.

The point to keep constantly in mind is that Jesus Himself came to, arrived at, these truths or facts—God as Love and God as Father—humanly as well as divinely. The human way to God is—through faith, by obedience, and in sacrifice: there is no other approach for man to God. Even in these acts and processes which constitute what we call "man's part" in our life in God, it is God Who is drawing us to Him; but He draws us "with the cords of a man." That is to say, it is only through our own needs, wants and susceptibilities, in this case our spiritual instincts, intuitions and affections—in a word through the spiritual selves that He has made us—that God can draw or take us into Himself. Our part, whatever it is, is the necessary condition of any inclusion of *us* in any relation or co-operation with God. So when we say that love or fatherhood or any goodness whatever on God's part towards us is conditional or conditioned in any way, the condition is wholly and only in us and on our part and not with Him. He absolutely "would"—it is only whether "we will."

Our Lord said, "No man cometh to me except God the Father draw him." What is true of us was true of Him: God perfectly came to Him because in response to the drawing He perfectly came to God. He humanly took to Himself *all* the truth and fact that God is Love, God is Father, and God is Life eternal. He realized in Himself all that God "would be" in Him and through Him in all humanity. We shall see this more plainly if we dwell a moment upon the distinctly human drawings of our Lord to the Father through which the divine Sonship became so completely incarnated in Him. No one can read understandingly the earthly life of Jesus without seeing how utterly it was a life of faith, and how human that faith was in all its conditions and manifestations. It is only in temptation or under trial that faith is really called for or occasioned, and so is evolved or can be brought to perfection: faith is and lives and becomes all itself only through the difficulties it encounters and overcomes, the things it suffers and survives. There is not only no other measure or manifestation of it, but also no other reason or meaning or cause of it. The divine in us needs to pass through all the necessary process of evolution, and this process is furnished by the conditions to which it is actually subjected. Under what other conditions could Jesus have been or become just what we worship and all that we worship in Him? In what other sense and for what other reason was He "perfected by the things He suffered," and what were the things He suffered but, to its utmost limit, the common lot of our common humanity. If human conditions were necessary to make, and make perfect, the human Jesus, they are necessary to make us: we need no other theodicy, nor vindication of our human lot. Jesus as the Author and Finisher, the completer and perfecter of human faith has opened up and become to us all the process and the way, through and over and *by* all that confronts us here, to God and eternal life. The only way truly to believe in Jesus is so to believe in as to share with Him the faith in God that made Him Conqueror of the world.

Not only was our Lord's faith a human faith, but equally His obedience was a human obedience. By obedience we mean the absolute conformity of His human life and self to His faith or to God the Object of His faith. Obedience is too low a term for that conformity, except that it brings it down into touch with our own so incomplete subjection to God. The obedience that transcends all mere law and rises into the love that is God, raises itself and the law with it into the closer relation of oneness with God. The perfection of our Lord's faith and obedience manifests itself in a wonderful contrast in His own attitude respectively towards God and towards man. Towards God in His hours and agonies of doubt and fear (which were not these to Him only in so far as He met them in faith in God and willingness in Himself) He is all weakness and dependence: He is all in God just because He is nothing in Himself. "In the days of His flesh, having offered up prayers and supplications with strong crying and tears unto Him that was able to save Him—and having been heard for His godly fear, though He was a son, yet learned He obedience by the things which He suffered; and having been made perfect, He became unto all them that obey Him (i.e., that enter into the spirit and life of His own obedience) the author of eternal salvation."

On the other hand, when Jesus turns His face from Godward to manward there is no trace of doubt or fear or weakness, or even of suffering or sorrow. He speaks and acts with all the certitude, authority and calmness of God Himself. He whom God has sent to manifest and express Himself *in* (and not merely *to*) man, must come as man, not in appearance only but in fact; but He must come in each act and stage in the perfection of God in man. And so Jesus unhesitatingly and unflinchingly turns towards man the aspect of the victor and conqueror of and over sin, sorrow, death and hell in the name and power of God.

As to the matter and form of our Lord's human obedience, they are expressed in the three intimately and inseparably connected terms, love, service, sacrifice. That "love is what love does" is a commonplace or axiom of thought and feeling. And what does love do? Is there any possible answer but that of our Lord's life? "The Son of Man is come into the world not to be served but to serve." And what in turn is service, what is the essence of it and what is the measure and limit of it? Again, is there any other answer than this, "The Son of Man is come not to be ministered unto but to minister, *and to give His life*." There is much more in the giving of life in sacrifice than the mere suffering of bodily death, but let that appear as we proceed further. For the present let us try to take in the extent of the truth that even in the commonest judgment and sentiment of the world we value a gift or an offering or a service (as such) just in proportion to what it cost the offerer to render it: that is in proportion to what and how much not only of his own but of himself he has put into it. All the real worth of a gift as a gift, and not merely as a thing, is in what the giver has put into it of thought, of affection and goodwill, of his own and of himself. In a word, the instinct even of the unthinking world teaches it to attach no real and abiding value to any act or character or person in which or in whom self-sacrifice is not, or was not, the distinguishing and essential element and principle.

We approach now to the all-important question, just where and how comes in the distinctive and proper fact of *revelation* in the work and in the person of Jesus Christ. I mean revelation in the sense of divinely communicated and not humanly discovered knowledge, of which we are in possession—which we never ourselves could have attained, but to which we can "set our seals" as eternally true when in any way communicated or revealed to us.

Men have been found to compare and even confuse John the Baptist and Jesus as founder or founders of the Kingdom of God, and again St. Paul and our Lord as Author or Authors the Gospel of salvation. It is sufficient to refer to John's and Paul's own testimony and attitude in that matter: as well as to every page of the New Testament as the record and report of the actual impression made by Jesus upon the world. We do not hesitate to speak of the work of John the Baptist and St. Paul as ministries, acts, or works of God, for we believe that God was in them and even did them. In the life of grace in any and every true believer, as described by such a witness as St. Augustine, the true Doer and Worker is God, however it must be also the believer himself,—and so we say of the ultimate and highest in Christ that He must (for the end in view) be man, and yet—before this and above this and *for* this—must be God. Between Him as thus absolutely Man as well as God and all others there is this vast difference, which we must as we can try to depict to ourselves.

In the case of the holiest, most righteous, and divinest man other than our Lord there is this anomaly: just in proportion to his actual holiness does he feel himself a sinner; just in proportion to his righteousness does he know himself a transgressor. The explanation is this: the further he proceeds in the life of faith and obedience, of love and grace, the more he realizes and appreciates the eternity of his quest and the infinitude of his task of righteousness. Its only limit is—to be perfect as his Father in heaven is perfect, its only end and aim is to be son of God in the plentitude of the divine image and likeness. Think of St. Paul proclaiming, I have already attained, I am already perfect! Or St. John asserting, I have no sin! And then look from them to the self-assertion and personal claim of

Jesus. Was He either less humble or less truthful than they? His faith, His obedience were not different in kind from theirs, yet how infinitely beyond them in attainment and in degree! Think of it—to be able to say in utter certitude and manifest truth—and in as utter selflessness and humility —"My Father worketh and I work; I and my Father are one." "He that seeth me seeth the Father!"

Those are none the less divine utterances because they were equally human utterances. The Son of Man was not here to voice God in His infinite aloofness from humanity but in His even more divine oneness with humanity. How could God make Himself really one with a humanity that was not thereby itself—in all the constituents and factors of its selfhood—one with Him? When we look at Jesus Christ in all the perfection of His human divinity and divine humanity, the question inevitably arises, Which was He, God or man? If we say as we must—Both;—then it comes back to us: But which *first*, and as ground and cause of the other? Is God human in Him because or by act of man? Or is man divine in Him because and by act of God? Does man or God originate and consummate the unity?

In seeing (as it has) in Christ, primarily God in man and only secondarily man in God, Christianity has done its best to express the Incarnation in human language; but whether or not it has successfully done so, or makes itself intelligible and understood in doing so, the fact (implicit if not explicit) remains and will remain, that God was in Christ, reconciling the world unto Himself, and that by consequence *in Christ* man is at one and is one with God, is *de facto* reconciled and saved—if he will receive and know it.

The two extreme and supreme affirmations of Christianity, the Incarnation of God and the Resurrection of man rest upon the claim and the fact that Jesus humanly accomplished oneness with God through faith, realized sonship with God through obedience, and consummated both these through the progressive holiness and righteousness of His entire life, but supremely and conclusively in the act in which He Himself said, "It is finished!"—the act in which "through the eternal Spirit He offered up Himself without spot to God."

It is impossible to express Christianity otherwise than in the extremest terms, even as it could be enacted "to its finish" only in the extremest acts. Nothing less than death and life will adequately or even at all express it: human evolution must of necessity pass through such crises. As the brute or animal in man must wholly die in him (as such) to give place to the rational and free, the human;— so the rational and free as the merely rational in him, the *self* in him, must undergo nothing less than death in order to live again in the spiritual or the divine. I spoke of the death of the animal *as such* in order to the life of the rational or human: the animal dies in the human only *as animal*. It does not become extinct, but is taken up into the human and made the instrument and material of its rationality and freedom. A man is not temperate or pure or virtuous outside of his animal needs and instincts and appetites and affections: he must mortify and extinguish them only as *mere* such—i.e., as lusts or passions. As we are constituted, we can be pure only *in* our flesh, but that only by taking it up into the sphere of reason and freedom and making it the instrument of ourselves, not as animals or brutes but as men.

So when we speak again of our dying even in our higher human selves of natural reason and freedom, of mere legal or ethical or moral righteousness and life, we do not mean that our own use of our reason or our will, that our natural wisdom or morality, is to be abandoned and become extinct. What we do mean is this: That, just as instinct or appetite or passion—*as* mere such—must be wholly transcended and superseded by and in the subjection and exercise of them in conformity with reason and freedom,—so our natural

reason and freedom themselves must in turn, and in the
process of their yet higher evolution, be transcended and
superseded by subjection to and conformity with the
higher power of the spiritual and divine that lie above them
—that are, as we say, supernatural and superrational: superrational because they are the eternal and divine reason itself,
of which our finite reason is but an adumbration, and our
wisdom and morality only our own attempt at conformity to
it.

How clearly now, from the higher standpoint of the
spiritual, can we see the necessity of that stage or dispensa-
tion in our human evolution to which is given the name
of The Law. It was essential that, through it and by it,
humanity should be made to do its part in the predestined
oneness and fellowship of God and His world. Let science
and art, ethics and politics, philosophy and divinity do their
natural part, elicit, discipline and prove man's natural
powers. What is law but fact or reality in process—or
rather the mere process itself of inexorable and inevitable
fact or reality. And the ultimate and necessary fact to which
all things, and above all, all persons—all hearts and minds
and souls and selves—must come in this world, is expressed
in the words Right and Righteousness. The lowest intelligence can recognize the fact that "nothing is settled until
it is settled right." The consensus of reason and experience,
of wisdom and prudence, of ethics and religion is the fact,
the imperative and uncompromising condition of human
life. It is impossible to lower the end and aim of human
existence below the claim and demand of universal and
absolute Righteousness. The Law then in its extremest
expression is only the statement of an absolute fact, that
cannot be compromised or modified.

There is an address in the Prayer Book to one under
sentence of death for crime, which begins in these words:
"Dearly beloved, it hath pleased Almighty God in His
justice to bring you under the sentence and condemnation

of the law!" We are all criminals and must all come under the sentence and condemnation of the law; can it be true, both, that we are "Dearly beloved," and that it "pleases God" to bring us "under the sentence and condemnation of the Law"? How can He Who is Love and Father take pleasure in bringing His children under the awful penalties of the Law? Let us try to put ourselves into the highest and truest attitude of the criminal in response to such an address coming to him in the name of Almighty God Himself. It will involve all possible comprehension and understanding on his part at once of the justice and of the love of God towards him. From that highest and truest standpoint, if he should attain it, let me endeavour to speak for him.

God "in His justice" has brought me into this condemnation; what do I understand by "His Justice"? It means that He upholds His law, that He will not compromise its claims or lower its demands upon me: the sentence holds, Do it and live by it, or do it not and die by it. I will not attempt to say what is due to God Himself in this assertion and enforcement of His divine authority and right,—but let me look at it as it concerns myself. What is this law which I have transgressed and under whose sentence and condemnation I stand? Is it not my own law as well as God's? That is to say, the law of my own life, and of all the life that interests or concerns me. We call it the law of righteousness—well, what is righteousness, but the establishment and maintenance and inviolability of eternal and universal *Good*—physical good, moral good, spiritual good! We need not go now into a distinction of these successive and ascending goods—their relation, connection and dependence. It is enough to know that our law—or God's law as concerns us—would unify and identify us with the good of things, the good of our kith and kind, the good of God. How, in the very nature—the reason, meaning, intent and actual operation—of such a law, can its claims be compromised or its penalties averted? They follow by natural and inevitable consequence; to ask for exemption or relief from them is to ask that things and their consequences shall not be what they are. The one thing in the universe we should love and not pray to be saved from is God's Law, for it is the sole condition and expression of our own, as of all, completion, perfection, and blessedness: all prayers should be addressed to being saved *to* it, not from it.

But this goes only half way; it is only saying that to annul the natural consequences of law is not only to contradict the nature of things but to overthrow the whole scheme and process of good in the world. There is a nearer need that the transgressor should be brought under the sentence and even execution of the law. As matters are, we shall never be brought to know what holiness, righteousness, life (and these are the names of spiritual, moral, and natural Good) are, until we learn to see what their opposites are. We may well thank God that He brings us up face to face with all the inherent and inseparable penalties of sin—the inevitable judgment, sentence, yes—and actual execution of the law. We must all die,—not merely in the body, but in the soul and in the spirit. We must realize that we have crucified the Lord of Life—the divine in ourselves—the sonship to God in which and for which we were created. It is not until we know the death and the hell of the sin in which we are, that we can know the life and the blessedness of being in the love and the grace and the fellowship of God in Christ. God does not spare us the death that is the condition, the cost and the price of the life. His justice is the perfection of His love. It is because we are His well-beloved that it is His pleasure to subject us to the poverty that is the condition of our wealth, the death in ourselves which is necessary to, and but the obverse of, life in Him.

What, then, finally, is the revelation of God to us in Christ? To state it first superficially: It is the Object Lesson of the Eternal Divine Intent and Meaning of humanity, the predestination, spiritual re-creation, and ultimate destiny of man. So far I have spoken mainly if not wholly of God in the human life-struggle or life-process of Jesus Christ—the faith that sees and knows God, the obedience that identifies itself with and manifests God, the self-sacrifice that crowns and completes the at-one-ment. But we do not thus see God only in man: it is contrary to reason to try to divorce the meaning of man from that of his environment—to find in his outcome a reason and a meaning for himself and not also for the process and conditions by which he has realized himself. The Logos of man is the Logos of nature, for it is nature that has produced and includes all that is natural in man—even all his natural potentiality and affinity for the spiritual or the divine, his instincts or intuitions of God. What is distinction after must have been predestination before; what produces ends must have been means. And that all has come as it were automatically, by a process of seeming self-evolution, only reveals as more perfect the reason and meaning of it all.

So the divine in Christ reveals itself as the divine no less in nature and in creation—and no less also as the eternal and infinite divine in God. But as we identify, so also must we distinguish between the Logos as universal and co-equal with God and the Logos as Christ. Christ, as such, is the same Logos, but the same distinctively *as in man,* that is to say, as Incarnate, as the eternal reason and realization of man.

The representation of the historical Christ, or Jesus, as an object lesson of Incarnation and Resurrection is—as I premised—a superficial statement of the reality or actual fact. That could indeed only stand for a "salvation by sample": it could make our Lord nothing more than an example to us of what should be true of us all. There would of course be a certain amount of revelation to us even in that: it would show us in absolute effect or result the full fact of God's answer to faith, God's real presence in human obedience or righteousness, the consummated union and unity of God and man. But such a so-called revelation to us of the thing is not necessarily to us The Thing Itself.

The Thing Itself, the True Christ, and The Real Christ, is not A Man, not even Jesus in heaven—regarded by us only *as such*. Until we see Him as humanity, as ourselves, —as God in us and us in God—until we see Him *here*, and *so*, not only in faith but in fact,—we may have something, and even much, of a revelation about Him, but we have not the revelation of Himself. For that we must have *The Real Presence* not only in His Body in heaven, but in His Body upon earth.

THE SUBJECTIVE

AND

OBJECTIVE IN RELIGION

Truly our God is an impotent God—so long as He persists in being Himself only in and with and through and by us—*for our sakes, or the sakes of* us.

My aim in this paper is very much a present and a practical one. But the question of the subjective and objective in religion goes back into and is part of the prior one of the immanence and transcendence of what we call *The Divine* in the universe. I assume that no serious mind will deny the fact or existence of a "divine" in the character or person of Jesus Christ,—if it be allowed its own conception or intention of the Divine. And in large part the conception would be about this: the recognition of a so-called divine order or aim in "things"—in nature, and pre-eminently in the mind and will of man, as manifested in exceptional Man. Socrates felt and reverenced the divine in himself, and in great measure conformed himself and his life to it. In a way he objectified and even personified it, but he knew it only as a monitor to himself. Plato in his philosophy,—but so too no less Aristotle in his more exact and scientific view of the world—includes *God* (thus meaning fully to personify the "divine") in the order of the universe and especially in the higher reason, meaning, and end of human life.

Modern free thought need be considered only in its culmination in the discovery of the great truth of evolution. I do not see that evolution, however true a fact it may be, and whatever be the final statement of its law or process, can interfere with or impair—indeed can do other than strengthen and confirm the (deeper than merely rational) conviction of a divine in nature as seen in nature's highest product, man.

Let us begin with the two terms that perhaps best express what we call the divine in ourselves—Reason and Freedom. Reason to perceive or know *What?* Freedom to do and be *What?* However we may indeed be only at the beginning of either the intellectual comprehension or the practical realization of the answers to those questions, or objects of those quests, yet already and once for all we know that we *are* at the beginning of an eternal and infinite adventure. And though we cannot define the great objective further than by such predicates as the Good, the True, or the Beautiful—yet the fact that we call, and have always called, the subject and substance of them "The Divine," is in itself an evidence of our cognition or conviction of a *Somewhat* which exacts of us the application to it of the ultimate and highest name.

There is a sense in which the word *Agnostic* is a real modern contribution to a right understanding. All merely natural, or merely human, or merely rational and practical questionings of ultimate truth are necessarily agnostic as regards it. By ultimate truth I mean the eternal and divine reason and meaning, process and end, of human life. And I do not underrate the part and the necessity of the merely natural or merely human in human life. If man does not do all his own part in his life, God cannot do His part in it. It is only so that man discovers his need of God and so his relation to God, his divine oneness with Him, and so comes to realize in Him all the reality of *himself*.

Even where merely natural or merely human knowledge goes beyond its immediate field—of, say, science, philosophy, psychology, or ethics—and undertakes to investigate or explain religion, it is there, and there most of all, properly agnostic. For how far can this purely natural investigation of religion really go? Suppose it goes so far as a correct and thorough discovery and report of the universality and the various forms and expressions of the religious instincts—the human "feelings after God if haply they may find Him." Still the instinct, intimation, or intuition of any real object is in its very nature a very fragmentary part or condition of knowledge. It never of itself actually "gets there." It comes or amounts to nothing if it is not met, or except in so far as it is met, from the other side. And "the other side," and its meetings or respondings, are not visible or tangible or in any way cognizable to the natural faculties of human observation and experience.

I will not undertake to go into the matter of the meetings from the other side to the drawings of humanity to God prior to Christianity—or in other religions. We may take the story up at this point: "God Who at sundry times and in divers measures spake in time past to our fathers through the prophets, hath in these latter days spoken to us in a Son." If Jesus Christ is indeed God's final and full Word to us of Himself and ourselves, we can know it only by an observation and experience outside of and beyond and above the criteria of natural knowledge. There is a spiritual discernment for spiritual things which needs no less than natural observation to be made the fullest use of. The instincts and intuitions themselves must be kept pure enough and directed wisely enough to be able to recognize their proper object when presented to them. Reason itself is not solely a natural or human faculty: if in its human limitations it cannot discover what is as yet beyond human observation or experience, it nevertheless only comes to itself and comes to its own when that which is beyond is revealed to it. For reason is that which in our measure—but in ever growing measure—we share with God. The reason whose function, within the reach of nature only, it is to see natural things aright, or "as they are," is the same as that which can discern spiritual things when, beyond the reach of nature, they are revealed to it. Its higher function then is to perceive and appprehend the correspondence between the natural instincts, intimations, or drawings, and their spiritual or revealed ends, objects, or supplies. Looking forward boldly along a direction which has been amply determined, we may affirm that what the spiritualized, or spiritually enlightened, human reason can and will in the end establish, is—the absolute correspondence between all the truths of creation or of nature and the ends and destiny of man as predestined, accomplished and revealed in the person of Jesus Christ. More explicitly—it is matter of fact to the spiritual reason that the truth as we see it in Jesus Christ, from beginning to end (in human predestination or intention, human evolution or actualization, and human fulfilment or glorification) is, is alone, and is completely, the truth of God and man which man needed to know (and could not know otherwise) in order to know, or even to be, *himself*. This being so, it becomes self-evident to reason itself that the end of human function is to see man its subject at one and one with God—through the eternal and perfect act of God, one and at one with man.

More than that—the spiritual reason sees in the human part of Christ on earth a full understanding and justification of the ordeal through which humanity came to its divine self in the person of Jesus Christ. It sees how, as the animal must die in and *into* the man, through the conquest in it and over it of reason and freedom;—so, in turn and in order to that, the man must die in and to himself—*into* his divine and true self—in God. The natural man must die into the spiritual, just as before it or with it the animal into the rational and free. We need to apprehend more clearly *why* Christ could be made perfect only through the things He suffered, how eternal life could come only through mortal death. The ordeal of doubt, pain, and sacrifice was the only means of making and perfecting the faith, obedience, and true selfhood or manhood in God that constitute and are eternal life.

More still, the spiritual reason sees in the story of man as it is told in Jesus Christ, a complete, or completer, revelation of the meaning of creation in general, and of nature in particular. The more we see that all the mineral or material, all the vegetable or animal, all the mere natural in the universe, exists only for the end and sake of the spiritual, or, limiting ourselves to our own experience, that the only "end in itself" on earth is man, and that he lives ultimately only for and in his spiritual part,—the better, I repeat, do we understand creation or nature or both together. They are in fact all that they are only for us and in us, or other spiritual whom we know not.

All the natural thus becomes only the instrument and the environment of the spiritual—that in correspondence or in reaction with which the spiritual both is made and makes itself. Only One in this universe is entitled to know how, or how best, finite spirits—finite personalities in His image or like Himself (at however infinite an interval)—can both be made and make themselves; and He has constituted things and persons "as they are." What the spiritual is to come to, and how it comes to it, we see in Christ; and we can know no better and do no better than to come to it in that way and in Him.

We are prepared now to pass to the practical uses and

applications which I avowed at the beginning. No one will accuse me of making too little of the human in Christ, or of the human side and part of ourselves in our relation with Christ; of faith and conversion, of hope and progressive holiness, of love as actual participation and manifestation of God. All these are terms which describe what I call the *subjective*—or the "ourselves" or "our part"—in our religion; though of course no Christian denies God's prior "Self" and part in them. In anything I may say on the other part I speak not against but in behalf of all the foregoing. It is indeed in behalf of myself, and because of the constant danger of an over-subjectivity, that I bring myself to magnify against it the counter truth of the objective in our common Christianity.

To touch in passing what would require a separate treatment all of its own—there is plausible excuse, if not full reason, for the disposition and effort to make a severance between the God of humanity as represented in Christ, and the Author or Power of creation and nature. To God in Christ "things," outside of humanity and its (in different senses) free acts, "are what they are, and their consequences will be what they will be." There is no changing creation or nature except through the minds and wills, the reason and freedom, of man. God works, and can work, only through the consent and co-operation of man, against alternately the powers and weaknesses of nature—the powers of objective and the weaknesses of subjective nature. Apart from that special form of it which we call grace, and which is at once divine and human, a combination of God's will and man's willingness, nothing whatever is or can be changed, produced, or accomplished in the relation and reaction between man and his environment which we call life. All that Jesus Christ Himself was, or could be and do, on earth, or in heaven, was through the union and unity, the necessary consent and co-operation, of the divine and the human in Him: only that could or did achieve the needed victory over sin and death and hell, and so accomplish the conditions and constituents of eternal life.

Under this point of view the God of humanity and of Christianity is not in any true sense the God of creation or of nature. He is only, in infinite love and sympathy and co-operation, striving with humanity against the inflexible and unchangeable outside and inside conditions that would hinder, overthrow or destroy it. This may be enough to suggest the case on the side of the plausible objection before referred to: that the God of Jesus Christ is the God only of human life, as against conditions of objective creation or nature over which He has no control.

The matter may be studied under the form of a careful analysis of the scriptural statement, "God spared not His own Son, but delivered Him up for us all." The Son stands here, as always, as the exponent or representative of humanity and the implication is that He could not be spared because humanity cannot be spared the necessary conditions or process of its salvation. There are two possible reasons why it could not, and cannot, be spared. The one already given is: that the conditions are such, in facts of environment, in obstacles of creation and nature, as the God of humanity Himself cannot remove or evade, and can only be in us and with us to overcome and survive. God spared not His own Son—as Undertaker, Captain or Leader, Author and Finisher, of human salvation—any whatsoever of the circumstances—the weaknesses or impossibilities, the labour or pain, the doubts and fears and failures, the sufferings and death—to which humanity is subject,—simply because all these are prior and inevitable to both it and Him. All that He can and will and does do, is to give to humanity "a heart for any fate," a will to do and be in spite of all, patience and strength to endure, to survive, and outlive sin and evil and death itself.

Let us admit that our God cannot spare His Son, because

He cannot spare humanity any more than the previous view allows. Is there not another explanation of the inability or impossibility? Is it not that the God Who determines all ends knows best the ways to those ends, and imposes upon Himself the best ways and means to His best ends? If creation as it is, nature as it is, and human nature as it is —with all their possibilities and actualities of good and evil, physical, moral, and spiritual—constitute the best ordeal, crucible, or what-not, for the evolution of (the occasioning, quickening, testing and proving, making or creating) finite spirit in the image and likeness of Himself, through its own rational and free participation of His own divine and eternal holiness, righteousness and life;—is not that sufficient justification and explanation of things as they are? Does it not become easier to believe that the divine Father of finite free spirit should not only not have spared His Son the experience of all the evils of nature and creation, but should have, of His own will and wisdom, subjected Him to them?

If God could not have prevented the possibility and existence of evil in all its forms, for the simple reason that the permission of them was necessary to the evolution and perfection of the highest good; yet God can and will see that that highest good shall—for all who will—be the final end of all the ill. But the present result is the fact that our God, the God and Father of our Lord Jesus Christ, does present to us in this world of ours the aspect of One Who infinitely *would*, and finitely, constantly, *cannot*. God is always and infinitely seeking and striving to make the world of spirit His own and Himself; and the world is weakly and effectively rejecting and defeating His efforts. Nevertheless, He will not and cannot be Himself in the world without *us*, because His whole end in this world of *selves*, or of free spirits or persons, is not to be, to realize or fulfil, Himself, but Himself *in us*—and so us in Himself. Our Lord perfectly voiced His and Our Father when He cried from the depths of His heart: "Oh Jerusalem, Jerusalem—How *would* I, and ye *will not!*" Truly our God is an impotent God—so long as He persists in being Himself only in and with and through and by *us*—for our sakes, or the sakes of *us*.

But time counts not, and is not, in God's calculations. The task is before us not only individually and socially, to make ourselves, in and with and through, and by Him, as He gives Himself to us in Christ,—but to make ourselves in and with and by remaking this world for Him. How infinitely, at our best, we *would,* and *cannot!* The world hears not, heeds not, and goes on in its own way. But Jesus Christ despaired not—upon the Cross; and we cannot lower nor defeat forever God's power and promise through our weakness and unwillingness: Time is long, and eternity is longer; and God is in heaven—yes, and on earth.

If we have succeeded, however little, in relating (for ourselves) our God to all His world;—let us come down now to the task of placing Him in our own little world upon this earth. God's special Word to this world and His Spirit in it are by no means to be dissevered from His Word and Spirit to and in all worlds. The Logos of one is the Logos of all, and the Spirit here is His Spirit everywhere. We know that there is one Reason and one Will in all the universe, and that all the parts work together in conformity to the one end of good to all. Nevertheless the way or mode of working is adapted to each part and to the particular character of each several process. God in relation with the finite spirit, with the personal reason and the free will of man, does not reveal or present Himself as He does as the God of material creation or of physical nature. It is indeed the God of humanity that we want to know—the God of all else only as the environment and condition of ourselves.

How Jesus Christ, *as such*—not as eternal and universal Logos or Word of all, but as Incarnate God and Divine Man —is the sole and all-inclusive object of human realization and fulfilment, is now as always the question before us. That He was the pre-eternal divine meaning or intention of us, or that He will be the post-eternal fulfilment and perfection of us, are not facts that so immediately concern us, as *how*, here and now, in the actual and vital process of being or becoming ourselves, we shall avail ourselves of, appropriate, and make Him ourselves, and make ourselves *Him*. This may be not the best way of saying it, but it is not too strong or extreme an expression of the fact; it is not stronger than eating and drinking, and so converting into ourselves, the body and blood, the life and death and life again, the divine humanity and human divinity of Jesus Christ. And it is just that, and all that, that our Christianity must mean to us and be to us—and be to us and in us here and now—or else it will be to us much less than nothing: if it is not our justification, it will be our condemnation; if not our salvation, then our damnation (however we may dislike the word).

To realize Christ! That and nothing else or less! How shall we do it? For only so shall Christianity ever be a reality or a power either in a human soul or in the world of humanity. As in others, so in that most vital and essential of all processes, there are apparently two ways, which in fact are only two parts or sides of the only One Way. And yet in our world of actual or practical these two parts or sides of the One and the Same Way are liable to be set in mutual not only exclusion but contradiction of each other. We may roughly express the two paths to the realization of Christ as the subjective and the objective ways,—though they are constantly and unconsciously running athwart and into each other.

Just as a true—or truer (true as possible)—subjective knowledge of God in general must rest predominantly upon what *we* have in common with Him, upon *our* part in Him; that is to say, upon God as immanent rather than as transcendent; just so the more subjective relation to Christ, appropriation of and oneness with Christ, will rest upon, predominantly, *our* part in Him, our faith, hope, and love, or our holiness, righteousness, and life. On the other hand, the more objective knowledge of God will dwell more upon God's part in the world and with ourselves, God as transcendent, as outside of and before, as the reason, meaning, cause and end of all things and of ourselves. And so too, the more objective sense and mode of relation to Christ will dwell more upon the objective or external facts or truth of Christ—*His* part with and in us, God incarnate, our regeneration, redemption, resurrection, and eternal life.

I have said enough upon the subjective, human side of Christ and of Christianity. I need in the interest, and for the better conservation of that subjectivity itself, to look away from it to the opposite, corresponding, and equally essential objectivity. And I shall try to do it by a series of practical illustrations in our Lord's life and our own. The youthful Jesus in His first recorded utterance struck a note which resounds throughout His earthly career, and which we would interpret and apply to ourselves. When for the first time the oft-since question arose, Where is He? His own answer was—and always is, Wist ye not that I must be in my Father's House? He may have meant then only the great and beautiful temple in Jerusalem which filled His mind and heart as His Father's Home. At either the beginning or end, or both, of His later ministry He abundantly manifested His sense of its sanctity: "The zeal of Thine house shall eat me up." But already the word and meaning of the temple had outgrown its earlier significance: "Destroy this temple and in three days I will raise it up." He was the Temple, the Temple was His Body, and in His person "The Lord was come to His Temple." He was in the deeper sense where He "must be"—in His Father's House, and that house and home was henceforth the "Flesh" in which God was incarnate, the Humanity in which He would dwell and be at home. The question shall come up again:

Where is He now—after these two thousand years since then? And the answer must forever remain the same: Wist ye not that I must be in my Father's House? Again,— when "He spake of the temple of His body" which He should raise from the dead, He may immediately have meant only His natural body. But again too, as of the temple, so of the body, the word and meaning have outgrown its earlier significance. The temple of Christ's body is His Church, it is the "All of humanity that will"—into which He has entered and which enters with Him into the oneness of the life of God.

Suppose that—instead of "in my Father's house," as before—we take the other translation, "in the things of my Father," or "about my Father's business." In that, as in the other, we may trace a single persistent note running through the life. What was His Father's business to which already He was giving Himself with singleness of heart and mind and will? We see Him not until eighteen years after publicly and officially entering upon it; and in the circumstances and the meaning to Himself of His own Baptism we may undertake to interpret what it was He was called and undertook to do—and in all His life and death and resurrection *did*. We may adopt His own words: "Thus it behooveth us to fulfill all righteousness."

"To fulfil all righteousness" expresses precisely what humanity *must* do for itself and *cannot* do of itself;—and also precisely what Jesus Christ did for it and does in it. And equally baptism reveals and confers the precise *Quo Modo*. The heavens were opened, the Spirit descended, the voice of God uttered the word, "This is my beloved Son, in Whom I am well pleased!" It makes not one particle of difference how much this account of the event is either literal or symbolical: the fact or matter is eternally true. And what I say of this, I say of other events in our Lord's transaction of His Father's business. In the person of Jesus Christ the heavens opened, the Spirit descended, the words

were spoken to Humanity on that occasion. He was there
not merely in its stead, or in its behalf, but as Itself. The
incarnation which our Lord, both humanly and divinely,
was enacting and accomplishing (for the act of incarnation
did not end in His birth but proceeded through regeneration, redemption, and resurrection into eternal life), was not
to be into a bit, or an individual, of our race or nature—as
Jesus alone—but into humanity as Christ and Christ as humanity. The words "This is my beloved Son in Whom I am
well pleased" were not spoken of God but of man in our
Lord, and they were not intended to express a love or a good
pleasure of the Father to Him which was the consequence,
so much as one which was the source and cause, of what He
was. Even our Lord was only secondarily Beloved Son
because of what He was in Himself in the flesh, and primarily and causally was what He was because He was beloved Son.

Let us trace the order of our Lord's own mind in the matter. In all His previous thirty years, no doubt, in due
measure and growth,—but now decisively and practically,
in this culmination and crisis of His baptism,—the *Thing*
faced Him in the form—which we may also define or express as the *objective truth* or fact—of Baptism in general.
Baptism is God's word of His Fatherhood in terms (or in
the term) of our, of human, sonship. What was the business, the task, the work, imposed upon the human Jesus—
implicitly, of course, by and from His birth, but now explicitly and formally by His baptism? It was, first, individually and personally, to realize or make good the objective fact of the Divine Fatherhood in the subjective fact of
His human Sonship—it was to *be* Son of God subjectively
through *knowing* Himself Son of God objectively—or
through knowing God as His Father. That the Sonship of
God was the question as to fact of baptism becomes evident
at once. Our Lord goes into the wilderness, there to face
and assume. His task, incipiently to *realize* it: i.e. to realize
it in faith as "The Way" of realizing it in fact, the way to

make the objective subjective, to make the divine human. And instantly the inevitable temptation, the universal question, assails Him: Am I, are we, is humanity—Son of God? If so, why only these stones in the wilderness, this hunger and drought in the desert, these wild beasts and savage enemies in the way to the promised land? When humanity asks of its Father a loaf, does He give it a stone, when it asks an egg, a scorpion, or a fish, a serpent?—I fear He does: but He knows why He does: and we by now ought to know it. Only so can we learn not to live by bread alone, but by the Word of God: the Word that calls us away from sight and sense to higher ends and aims of spirit. "The kingdom of God is not meat and drink." Our Lord's one word of response to all temptation was: "My meat and drink is to do the will of Him that sent Me!"—until He could say with His last breath, that His work was "finished," His Father's business accomplished. Not that that business was simply to accomplish in His own person, as Jesus of Nazareth, the Fatherhood of God in the sonship of man. It was not alone to reveal and manifest that sonship in Himself; it was not only to reveal but to communicate and to impart. He was to baptize with the baptism wherewith He was baptized. He was Himself the Baptism of the world, and was to baptize "all us the rest" with and into Himself, so that all that baptism was in Him it should mean in and be to us—death in the flesh and eternal life in the spirit. The temptation is still with us—as it was with Him: How can God be in a Man—how can be, and *is,* God in the world of man—in the face of everything that contradicts and makes it impossible to be so: How can we all with the One Man say in truth, "Our Father Who art in heaven!" In a sense we may say, and say truly: When we all like Him will *take* it so, we all shall *make* it so. But in a sense that is higher, or highest, that is only true because on God's part, as seen in Christ, it essentially and eternally *is so,* and only waits on us, by knowing and taking, to make it so on our part also.

In the earthly person of Jesus Christ, all the subjective

human elements of our relation with God, in the form of
Faith, Obedience, and Sacrifice, are clearly visible to us in
all their perfection. But His own human eyes are not upon
these in Himself; they are all upon the objects, or Object,
of these in God, or The Father,—the objective grounds,
causes, and conditions of these subjective responses and affections in Himself. We see supremely in Him that the Way
to be, in ourselves, and to be ourselves,—is to be out of ourselves in Him.

Turning from the life of our Lord to that of His Apostles
and disciples, St. Paul above all others might have been
expected to interpret and apply *subjectively* the truth as
he saw it in and received it from Jesus. And certainly in
none is the subjective or human side of the life in Christ
more clearly developed and exhibited; but also in none is
the need and fact of the objective *being in Christ* more
recognized and insisted upon. The objective being in Christ
by baptism is on a par with him with the transcendent being
of God in Christ, or the Father in the Son, by incarnation:
they are equally essential parts of one divine human act or
operation. Baptism was with St. Paul as divine an act or
fact as the human birth or resurrection of Jesus Christ: by
it he saw himself not only *de jure* and *de facto* no longer "in
himself" but "in Christ,"—but, in Christ, "dead to sin and
alive to God." To do that on his part was simply to do
what Christ had done (only unto a perfection impossible
for St. Paul)—namely, *take God at His word,* and, by so
taking, make it a truth or fact to himself.

There is a passage in St. Paul (Eph. 4:9) which I hold
to be susceptible of two modes of translation—not both
intended, but both possible and both not only true but
necessary to each other—I will give these, freely, in succession. *First*—speaking of our Lord's *Ascension*—"that He
ascended, what is it but that He (first) descended," etc.
The meaning would be sufficiently suggested by St. John's
similar saying (St. John 3:13): "No man hath ascended

into heaven but He Who descended out of heaven," etc. The
second translation is: "That He ascended, what is it, if He
did not also descend. He that descended is the same also
that ascended in order that He might (return and) fill all
things (with Himself)." All that Christ did in and through
His first coming—life, death, resurrection, and ascension—
was in preparation for His coming again to be in His Body
of humanity or the Church—all that He had done and been
for it in the natural body of His flesh on earth. "*I* baptized
with water," said John the Baptist,—"*This* is He that shall
baptize with the Holy Ghost." That baptism of God and
into God, by His Word and Spirit, is just the function of
Christ and of Christianity. To stop short of it is to cut off
the Incarnation at the very beginning of its work. To make
baptism a mere *opus operatum* in the void and empty sense
so often applied to it is of course not only an insult to God
but the greatest robbery and injury we can possibly inflict
upon ourselves. But now let us look at the matter on the
other side. When Jesus was baptized, was not the act per-
formed upon Him—in the descent and abiding upon Him of
the Holy Ghost—and the Word spoken to Him from heaven,
Thou art my Son,—was not all this, both to Him and in
fact, an *opus operatum?* And when St. Paul was baptized,
was it not to him *what* it meant—the real and actual being
in Christ, and in all that Christ means, the death to himself
and to sin and the life in God and holiness? Why was baptism an *opus operatum* to them? Because, we say, they saw
it so, because to them what God *says, is,* because God's
words are not signs, grammatical vocables, but *things*—
they *are* precisely what they say. We say, I repeat, that it
was so to them *because* they believed; well, ought we not
all to believe in the same way?—And that "because" needs
a good deal of explanation and discrimination.

There are two senses of "because": there is a real or
causal cause, and a medial or conditional cause. God is not
God because even Jesus, with His perfect faith, believed in

Him; Jesus believed because God *is* God. Christ was not all that He was, either to St. Paul or as St. Paul, because St. Paul believed in Him—but *vice versa*. Baptism is not *only* what *we* see in it or believe in it, *how* we take it or *what* we make it. Baptism is a Word, an Act, of God—which *in us* depends infinitely and eternally upon how we take or what we make it; but which in itself is what it says—God in Christ to us, and we in Christ to God—the free gift of God's own self to us, to be by us eternally accepted or rejected.

I am not just now concerned with the no doubt immense danger and evil of losing the *opus operatum*—trusting to a mere baptism in the letter or the sign. I am concerned about the equal opposite danger and evil of our being blind to and losing the right *opus operatum:* the not seeing and receiving baptism in the spirit, the not seeing and knowing it as on a par with, part of the same process with, *one* with Incarnation itself: Christ in the great body of our common humanity as of even greater truth than in the individual body of His flesh; because the latter was but the preparation and the means, the former is the real accomplishment and end.

But the most immediate point of all is this: transcendental or immanental in our philosophy or theology, subjective or objective in our faith and religion, Protestant or Catholic in our bent or facing,—let us realize that we are looking in opposite directions for the same thing; and that The Thing is in fact on both sides and on all sides of us. Let us turn from emphasizing and embittering our differences to recognizing and cultivating and enlarging our agreements. Let us fight a false objectivity only with a truer objectivity, or a false subjectivity with only a truer subjectivity. Let us aim only to *give* what is true in our greater freedom—individualism, liberalism, or protestantism—to the great Fact and Truth of Catholicity;—or, on the other hand, what we know and feel to be true and necessary in Catholicism to those who in the One only Christ are taking liberties inconsistent with the unity of His Person and His Church.

THE DEMAND FOR THE
SIMPLE GOSPEL

———

*As God is with us only in Christ, so is Christ with
us only in the earthly Body of His Church. What
God wants done, what He means to do, what He is
doing and will do—He is going to do in, with,
through and by man. He will never do it until we
do it in, with, through and by Him.*

I was recently consulted upon the subject of a proposed
plea and plan for a simpler Gospel—in fact The Simple
Gospel. The proposer claimed to represent a great many,
indeed the great body, of those who are willing to be saved,
but find the doubts and differences and contradictions of
current Christianity in the way. Men, he said, were ready
to believe in God, in Christ, and in the need of human salvation; but the moment we go beyond these primary and
sufficient elements of the Gospel, differences and divisions
begin and religion is lost among them. His plan to stop short
of these and confine ourselves to the unifying and saving
principles of simple Christianity he puts into the conclusion
and proposition of one who, represented as having every
personal qualification, and having had every experience and

opportunity for testing the present possibilities of the Christian ministry, comes to a halt and seeks a new beginning in a simpler Gospel and a less entangled ministry of it. Men, he says, will believe in God, will accept Christ as the revelation and manifestation of God, and will be saved in Him— without more ado. He wishes then to begin afresh with the distinct understanding and engagement that he is to preach only these essential elements of the Gospel.

If it be true that men are willing to accept the Gospel so far as that, I should wish to meet them at that point, and discuss the question of anything further from their own point of view, with the feeling of a great deal already in common between us. It is very far on the way to be able to say, I believe in God, in Christ, and in human salvation through Christ. I ventured, when asked my judgment on the proposition, to say: Let this concession be made to your position, that nothing more need be added to your Gospel that is not already included or contained in it—that is not deducible from or is not reducible to the three terms of your statement of it.

I am not speaking to scientists, experts, or critics—nor to theologians, but to the many said to occupy the position described above; and I wish between them and myself to test the validity and the value of this concession. Of course it is necessary first to see that we accept the three terms of our starting point in a sufficiently identical sense. We cannot go very far in the definition of any one of them, but we can go far enough for an initial agreement as to our "Simple Gospel." And, first, as to our meaning of "God." That God is everywhere and in all things, including all our natural selves, we will raise no question; but as to *our* knowledge or understanding of God, I think we will agree this far: In terms of our own highest faculties of relation with Him and consequently our highest conceptions of Him, God stands to us for all that is True in thought or reason, all that is Good in feeling or affection, all that is Right in will and action;

in a word God is to us the perfection of Wisdom, Goodness, and Righteousness. That is defining God in the terms of our own (potential) selves; but that God is That *to us,* is no detraction from whatever more He is in Himself.

By "God in Christ" we mean precisely the same as "God Incarnate"; only that in the latter we emphasize more the Godhead in humanity, and in the former humanity in God. For *Christ* means *the Anointed* rather than *the Anointer,* the Baptized rather than the Baptizer; in fact He is the two in one.

The third term "Human Salvation" is wholly included in the first two and actually expressed in the second: that will be seen more and more as we proceed.

Now is Christianity wholly completed in the earthly story of Jesus—including in it His Resurrection and Ascension? Or is it only then ready to begin? Let us assume the second position and put it to the test; and let us take it first objectively and historically. The Christian account of the matter is that on the night in which He was betrayed Jesus instituted and ordained for all time a Sacrament of Union and Communion with Himself. After He was risen He appeared again and gave further instructions, finally giving commandment to His Apostles to go into all the world and make disciples of all nations, baptizing them into the Name, etc.,— and promising to be with them to the end of the world. Ten days after His final disappearance in the body He returns in the Spirit; several thousand persons are baptized, and the Church begins. So the first so-called additions to the Simple Gospel may be expressed in three terms, the Church, Baptism as union with the Church, the Eucharist as Communion with or in the Church. Now there is no denying that each, and all together, of these additions (so-called) have been the occasion of endless difference and division among Christians and the source and cause of much obstruction and injury to the Truth and the Life of God among us. What are we going to do—What is best to be done—about it? I say—and will show—that it is impossible within the Simple Gospel (as we have agreed upon it) to abolish the *Thing*— Church, or Baptism, or Communion. Can we get rid of the name, or change the mode, or do anything else with "the Thing"—that will solve the manifest present difficulty about it? No! nothing can be done with the Thing,—that is all in God's part of the matter: what is needed is all in ourselves; there is no end of what is to be done in our part of the matter.

But, *first*,—let us see why it is that in the Simple Gospel it is impossible to get rid of Baptism, Sacrament, or Church. These three are really one, and that one is the Church: Baptism is *into* the Church, the door or entrance, and communion is the Life *within*. Why cannot the Church be either abolished or ignored?—Because the Church is Christ, and Christ is the Church. The baptism that added three thousand on the first day to the Church was the true beginning of the being *"in Christ,"* which is the essence and sum of the Christianity of the New Testament. It was the beginning for the Apostles themselves, for prior to that day the Holy Ghost was not given, because Christ was not yet ascended —*and descended:* He had not gone in the perfection of our life in Him,—and then returned to be forever the perfecting of His Life in us. So I say that the Apostles themselves, when the Lord left them in the body, were bidden to await His return in the Spirit—the Baptism with the Holy Ghost which was to be the Regeneration, the Redemption, and the Resurrection of the world. But what was that Baptism? It was *into Him*. And what was that Spirit or Holy Ghost? It was Oneness with Him, participation with and in His own regenerate, redeemed, and risen human life. Every possible exactness, fulness, and delicacy of human expression is employed in the New Testament to tell us how intimately and completely God in Christ has united and identified Himself with humanity and humanity with Himself in the Church which is His Body and Himself. We do not do justice to the marvel of the change in the Apostles after that pentecostal birth of the Church—that second and fuller birth of God in Christ into and in our humanity:—for when the words, "Thou art my Son, this day have I begotten Thee," are applied to the human Christ, they are applied not to the birth but to the resurrection of our Lord, and of humanity in His person. That resurrection was not in the Head alone but in the whole Body that was baptized into and lived in participation with His (I repeat) regenerate, redeemed, risen and eternal Life. From the moment the Apostles ceased to speak merely *of* Christ and began to speak *in Him,* and He in them, they speak with a new knowledge and a new authority: The Spirit had taken of the things of Jesus and shown them unto them. Their Master was *with* them no longer, and how bereaved they had felt themselves! But lo! now He was *in* them, and how infinitely more near, intimate, and real was His presence, not only in their midst but in themselves.

The New Testament in calling the Church the Body of Christ means to identify it with Him;—and all the weakness and failure of Christianity is due to lack of appreciation and appropriation of that fact. We can see the fact first established and manifested in the person and work of Jesus Christ, and then accepted, appropriated, and applied in such instances as St. John and St. Paul.

I will repeat—and go on doing so—that the work and ministry of Christ's life in our nature was the realizing or "making good" of the definition of Himself given by word and sign from Heaven in the act of His Baptism. That he could and did know Himself Son of God in our nature and in this world—against all appearances to the contrary and contradictions of the fact; that He could be and was human Son of God over all the deficiencies, impossibilities, and depravities of our condition,—was an act of faith and an act of achievement or accomplishment, both of which transcended all that our humanity is in itself and lifted it up into unity and fellowship with God. Of course the human in Jesus could not have so lifted Him but for the divine in Him,—but then neither could the divine have *so* lifted Him without the act of the human expressed by faith, obedience, and sacrifice. Again, it may be said: How was that such an act of faith in Jesus, when God had told it Him in so many words from Heaven? We must remember, that voice and that sign from Heaven were audible and visible only to such faith as Jesus had. If we had the same faith we should hear and see the same things. What we see and hear of spiritual and transcendent things is measured by our faith, and that by our obedience—we cannot believe beyond what at least we are wanting and willing to be and do. And then again, obedience is measured by the principle and spirit of sacrifice. Jesus believed and obeyed to the limit of being— "*Nothing* of Himself and *all* of God."

Now Jesus as the Christ, the Anointed, Humanity baptized with God, and so the Transcendent or Divine Man, becomes the Baptizer with the Holy Ghost. The Holy Ghost, as differentiated from (though One with) the Universal Spirit of God, is that Spirit *as* "become human,"—just as our Lord Himself is the Universal Wisdom or Word of God *as* Incarnate or "Become Man." The Incarnation was not completed in the physical birth of Jesus into humanity, but only in the spiritual birth of humanity into God in the resurrection of Jesus—when humanity in the person of Jesus had, in the perfection of its faith, obedience, and sacrifice, transcended itself and risen into God—become *de facto* as well as *de jure, actû* as well as *potentiâ,* Son of God.

Now just as Jesus, by complete human reception and appropriation of the Word spoken and of the Thing signified to Him in His Baptism, throughout a human life of accomplished faith, obedience, and sacrifice, *made Himself* (even as God made Him) *Son of God* in all its meaning and reality of personal fellowship and oneness;—so St. Paul (or St. John, or any one who like them enters into the full reality of baptism), when baptized into Christ (as Christ into God), took to himself, not merely a word and a sign, but the Word and the Sign of God, and therefore The Thing in all its divine reality of Oneness with Christ and Sonship to God.

The difference between Christ's baptism and St. Paul's or ours may be described as that between a first and all the others of a kind. In *Him* humanity came into immediate touch and relation with the Father and consummated the *de facto* personal Sonship to Him which was from eternity its predestination. How that was extended from Him to humanity at large, let our two Apostles, from very different points of view, unite in telling us. "The Word," says St. John, "became flesh and tabernacled" (not only "among," but) "in us." The tabernacle grows into the temple, the temple into "His Body the Church," the abiding and permanent place of His presence upon earth. "In Him," says St. Paul, "dwelt the fulness of the Godhead bodily." That is, in Him, first, was completed God's gift of Himself to man, the Incarnation, or Unification of God and man, Father in Son. And then St. John takes it up again: "And of His fulness have we all received." So our Lord's oneness is at once with the Father, ours is with Him, and (only "in Him") with the Father. But precisely as Jesus assumes and asserts, because He realizes and actualizes, His Sonship and Oneness with the Father, so does St. Paul, if in lower degree, yet in the same way and for the same reason, affirm and assert his oneness and identity with Christ. And that not only for himself, but for all the baptized: "As many of us as have been baptized into Christ have put on Christ." He does not mean of course that all have *actû* put on Christ as much as he has; but why not?—Only because they have not seen and taken in baptism all that he had, and (infinitely more) all that Christ did. The Word and the Sign to them were word and sign only—not The Thing: the letter that killeth and not the Spirit that giveth life.

A letter that so killeth needs to be and must be done away. But *how* done away? There is a false and a true way, and the question is wholly with *us: Which* shall we choose?—The one way is to give up the Church and Sacrament. I might freely concede that this is better than to hold and treat them as multitudes among us do—keep them only to make nothing of them, or what is much worse than nothing, to desecrate them by neglect and contempt.

The true way of doing away with the letter that killeth, the "mere forms" that stand between us and the "Simple Gospel," is to use God's appointed words and signs of the Things of the Spirit as we use our eyes and ears: not as things in themselves to stop upon, but to see through and hear with. The so-called "mere" letter or sign or form will best disappear, not by abolishing them, but by assigning to them their proper and modest place and part—as things not to be looked at or seen, but to look through and see by.

I invite therefore the seekers after the pure and simple Gospel, instead of discarding the accessories of Church and Sacraments, in view of the fact that these are as old and come from the same source as the Gospel itself (in fact that the Gospel was given not simple or pure but actually embodied and expressed in them), that they unite in an attempt to find the proper part and use of these accessories—as not human additions but as divine ordinances and institutions.

Instead of Baptism as joining the Church, let us take it as Grafting or Incorporation into Christ. In other words, let us take the Church as Christ. But why then—not simply and solely Christ and not the Church?—For this reason: Because just at that point Christ ceased to be *only* Himself and became the Church: He passed out of the individual body into a Collective Body. In the flesh He was Jesus, in the Spirit He is the Church—Regenerate, Redeemed, Risen Humanity. Why then is not Christ or the Church the whole body but only a part of humanity? Because in the very essence of the thing to be accomplished in Christ—the at-one-ing of God and man—the process is necessarily one of *election* or selection. The product or result is not limited or conditioned by anything in God: "He would have all men to be saved." But in the very nature of it, it has to be conditioned or conditional upon the will of man: it cannot be *his* without his part in it. In this way it comes that it is equally true that Christ's redemption includes all, and that it only includes some—all *potentiâ*, but only some *actû*. Now the *potentia* is with God and is absolute and universal; the *actus* is with us and, even by God, cannot be exercised without us: whatever our freedom, it is the essence of our selfhood, and to extinguish it would be the extinction of *us*. Christ then in Christianity is humanity *as* potentially regenerate, redeemed and risen in Him. By potentially we mean in the eternal "good pleasure" (*eudokia*), purpose and promise of God, subject to our freedom of action in the matter.

Now then, as to our action in relation to the fact of Christ in the world, Christ in humanity—in other words, Christ *as* the Church: for as I am in the world and of it only in my body and through it, so Christ is practically and actually in this world of ours only in and with and through His Body the Church. We have yet to realize the fact that "God in Christ" does nothing whatever in or for the world that is not done in, with, through, and by us who are the members and organs of His bodily presence and operation upon each. God is and acts in creation, in nature, and in all the purely natural or human life of man, according to the fixed and uniform laws of these. These are not the Church, which is restricted to that aspect or part of the life of man which we call regeneration and whose operation is redemption and resurrection. Regeneration reacts upon all the natural in human life, and not only awakens or quickens in it something of itself or of its own, but brings and breathes into it something of the Infinite and Eternal Not-itself—in Which alone man can ever become all himself. For we are made for

—and are potential of—more than Nature and our merely natural selves,—for marriage with and new birth from the Life that is God. "Except a man be born again of water and the Holy Ghost"—of repentance and faith—*out of* a proper sense of himself and his needs and condition and *into* a saving knowledge of God and His Grace in Christ— "he cannot see the Kingdom of God."

What is the regeneration which in its completeness and reality we see first in Christ Himself, not only distinctly manifested but (we might even say) clearly defined? Suppose we call it life in the Spirit, as contrasted with life in the flesh; "flesh" here must not be taken as in itself evil. *We* are universally sinful "in the flesh": because, only *in it,* which means *in ourselves alone,* we cannot be otherwise. But our Lord was "in the flesh" and raised it with Himself into God and Holiness. How then shall we attempt to describe regeneration or being in the Spirit—by which we mean not only the Spirit of God but the spirit potential in us all as part of our personal endowment?—For it is in our spiritual part or faculty that we come to our true selves in Christ, to the things of God in us, to our *actû* or *de facto* sonship.

I once knew the very strong mother of eight very strong sons, who afterwards spoke to me very interestingly of her experience in their rearing. I shall not give her account but only my own impression of herself and of her task and its results. Those boys were not saints by nature; there was no badness natural to boys with which they were not acquainted. Describing it she said: "I did not treat them as liars when they 'told stories,' or as thieves when they stole sugar or sweetmeats." Yet she reared them every one up to the highest standard of her own true nobility. How did she do it? She did not hesitate to lay down the law to her boys when it was helpful; she did not spare punishment when it was needed; she did not neglect to point out to them the natural consequences of evil doing in this world. But was it by any or all of these or of such incidental means that, in reality or at bottom, her great task was so happily accomplished at last? No, the true and efficient cause was something more spiritual and invisible than these. During all the years of their growing up she was friend and companion—sister as well as mother—to her boys. She continuously revealed and manifested to them *herself*— her own temper, attitude, and disposition in all those endless and varied matters of conduct, character, and manners. What does all this mean but that insensibly and by degrees she imbued them with her own *spirit,* she communicated to them her own spiritual *self?* And she did it by living with them in that personal relation, intercourse, and communion in which such a mother communicates to her children something other and more than their physical being or mere nature—nothing less than her own spiritual self. Among the forces and causes of nature is there anything comparable with what we call *personal influence?* It touches springs, awakens responses, quickens and moves impulses, and fires motives beyond the reach or touch of any other agency. Only spirit can beget, affect, or inspire spirit. The father and mother who are the begetter and bearer only of their child's body and not of its soul in the highest and widest sense have not earned their title to the names.

And shall God limit His relation to us to that of mere source or cause of our natural being, and leave us at that, to make of ourselves among ourselves what we may? Is there no spirit of fatherhood or motherhood in Him to touch, quicken, and inspire the spirit potential and responsive in us? Our spirits cry out for the Living God to come and show Himself in us—that we may find and possess ourselves in Him. It was needful for us that we should make this cry. In the higher birth of the spirit, unlike that of the flesh, the want or need must sensibly and consciously antedate and condition the supply. Not only is it that man must know that he cannot do or be without God before he will want Him,—but, more than that, man must be and do all that he can of himself before he reaches, and in order to reach, the height of wanting and being able to receive and unite himself with God. The son (by nature)—"though he is heir—is under tutors and stewards (of this earth) until the time appointed of the father": that is, until he is of age to assume and exercise his sonship. Until then he "differs in nothing from a servant." He is under training and trial for the development and use of his own reason and freedom, his own selfhood and manhood—which are in no sense to be lost, but rather truly to be found when he comes into his spiritual majority. In this prior state, his minority, he is *under the law*—under the demand of that law of personal and social righteousness, obedience to which is life, and disobedience death. The function and end of this law is not to give him life, but to bring him death: "It cannot give or produce righteousness; it can only convict and convince of sin." But that is just the preparation needed: first to have tried and known ourselves for all we are or can be, and then to want and receive God for all we are not, and only in Him can be. So the Law was the schoolmaster to bring us to God. When we are ready God comes to us in person—and reveals Himself to us as our Father, and ourselves to us as His children. He throws away the Law, which could never make us perfect. He does not call us liars or thieves or what not, but, whatever we are and just as we are, publicans and sinners and all, He takes us into His arms and into His heart—and tells us that we are *His*, and He is *ours* forever. And so the Spirit of Eternal Love and Grace and Fellowship does, or ought to do, in a moment what the Law could never have done.

In the fulness of the time—at the proper moment of human history—God came into the world in the person of His Son to communicate and fulfil in it the fact and reality of His Fatherhood and of our Sonship. His coming was in itself human regeneration, redemption, and resurrection, because it accomplished the human righteousness which alone is all these, and which the law of our nature and our natural selves commands and cannot produce or enable, convicts us of not having, but cannot empower us to have. St. Paul (Romans 3:18) defines the Gospel as the power of God unto salvation in every one who believes; and adds that it is a salvation of God because it is a righteousness of God. Righteousness is the only salvation from sin and death, just as health is the only salvation from sickness and natural death. Now God's Gospel is Christ, because God's righteousness (for us) is Christ. It is no mere tidings of a thing, or law or doctrine or definition of a thing, but it is The Thing itself. How does God go about, not merely giving us, but *being* our righteousness and so our salvation in Christ? The wisest, most loving, and most righteous father and mother in the world have but one supreme gift or blessing they can confer on their son —and that is to make him what they are, to transfer to him all their own love, wisdom, and goodness; and we have agreed upon their best way of doing that—by imparting to him their own spirit or selves.

Now God is the Father from Whom all fatherhood or motherhood is named. When He sent His Son into the world, He sent sonship into the world—"that we might receive" —not "the adoption of sons," as our versions have it—but the inheritance, or coming into our own, of sonship. And what is the rationale or mode of this imparting of sonship? "Because ye are sons God sent forth the spirit of His Son into our hearts, crying, 'Abba, Father.' " Jesus Christ, we may venture to say, came into the world from the Father—not as the inception of sonship, an act of "adoption" into sonship, from God: humanity is son of God by nature. Christ is, as it were, our second birth, out of the natural into spiritual sonship, out of "infancy," or non-age, or minority, into maturity, manhood, or majority.

There comes a time in Divine as well as human fathership and sonship when the son passes from wholly or merely *under* the father into quite another relation, which we may safely characterize as *in* and *with* the father. The father's, not only heart or affection, but reason, meaning, end or purpose, have penetrated and begun to communicate themselves to him. God is giving him to have—shall I say His life, God's life, *or* his own life, *"in himself"*? The life so consummated is God's life in the man, but it is no less the man's own life in God. The two are become, or becoming *one*. Just as the wise son of the wise father, from being wholly under, passes into the relation of in and with, and finally takes the place of the father over himself and over the family business and interests;—just so,—only how much more so?—God's Son, as seen in Christ, enters into the Father's heart and mind and will, loses no time in being "about His Father's business," has a "zeal for His Father's house," wants "no meat or drink but to do His Father's will," offers up His Soul or Self or Life (the terms are all synonymous in that passage) in His Father's service and ceases not until all "is finished," His work is done. There the Father has passed into the Son, the Son has taken His place and is Lord and God of this earth. God is just as much God and Father as ever, but all that He is in this world of ours He is in the person of His Son: all we know or have of the One we know and have through the Other.

And all that is true not only of God in Christ but of Christ in His Church. As God is with us only in Christ, so is Christ with us only in the earthly Body of His Church. What God wants done, what He means to do, what He is doing and will do—He is going to do *in, with, through* and *by* man. He will never do it until *we* do it in, with, *through* and *by* Him. That is what this present, or this part of, creation is for: it is for the making of *man* in, with, through and by his making himself. And he will never do that until he and God are one in the making. As Christ is God, so we have to be Christ—or we shall never be ourselves. We have to die in our present selves and rise and live in the selves that are *He*.

So I come back to those with whom I began—and from whom I fear I have too far departed—with this (*not* counter-) plea: Let us find together our Simple Gospel, not away from, but where and as God placed and gave it. And that is: not alone in a personal presence of our Lord for us in heaven, but in His bodily presence with us here on earth. When one talks about being a "naturalized citizen" he is not thinking of the *mere*-ness of the act of naturalization; or, when one calls himself a married man, of that of the marriage ceremony. So let our baptism be to us, *indeed, into,* and for ever *in,* Christ; and our eating and drinking Him, in reality, a partaking of Himself and sharing His life; let the Church be the real presence and activity of our Lord in humanity and on earth, and our membership in it our *living* part in Him and His work;— let our souls, ourselves, and our lives be *so* in our Real Gospel of God and Christ and Human Salvation—and we shall all agree, and laugh at differences about the *mere* anything of the necessary instrumentalities and concomitants.

The more we deal with Living Realities, the less shall we quarrel over the mere forms or expressions of them. But where these forms or expressions have been divinely given us along with the Things—the best way to make neither too much nor too little of them, to give them their proper use and function is, as I have said, to look, and to see, *through* them, to the Diviner Things of which they are the Divine expression. Even such divinely selected signs or expressions will naturally be objects of the utmost reverence; in a sense they will *be* to us the things they signify;—but that only because the vision of faith absorbs and obscures that of sense—we cannot see the light of the letter in the glory of the spirit.

EVANGELICAL AND CATHOLIC

*Each Needs The Other: Both Need The Church
And The Church Needs Both.*

———————

An able article in the December, 1916, number of *The Constructive Quarterly* terminates in the following, not so much general conclusion, as special application: "The whole future of the Church of England is dependent upon whether the two 'extremes' can learn to understand one another better, to recognize the true religion of the grace of God which is the source of the strength of both, and, passing beyond mere tolerance, and even the higher sentiment of good will, to work together for the good of the whole Church." (J. K. Mozley) The words need not be limited to the Church of England, they are true of the whole Church and Christianity of our time, and possible of all time. They go down to the root of the chief source of all the genuine, conscientious, and really religious difference

188

and division among Christians. We need not consider any Christianity that does not fully recognize both the divine and the human in Christ—whether in His person or in His Church. The Extremes spoken of here are those expressed by the two terms *Evangelical* and *Catholic*. As a matter of fact, each of these terms—over and above its profoundly universal signification in which both sides would claim and really hold it—has become the designation of a "party" in the Church, almost synonymous with Catholic and Protestant in the wider field of Christianity. The fact that neither party or extreme in this controversy, while arrogating to itself one of these terms, as against the other, could afford, or would consent, wholly to surrender that other (and its content) to its opponent—indicates how much they are one in substance, and two only in attitude or emphasis. And indeed the truly Evangelical as necessarily presupposes all the real Catholic, as the latter necessarily issues in the former.

There is a parallelism if not identity in certain institutions which we cannot but make, because they actually exist, and yet cannot make without securing oppositions which look to us like contradictions. Those who hold the transcendence of God look upon those who teach His immanence as enemies. It is almost impossible to express the real humanity of our Lord without bitter offence to those who would vindicate His divinity. So in the corporate Christ, Christ in the Church which is His Body, Christ in the world, in humanity—in *us* in whom and to whom alone He is personally present, and does things, and fulfils His promises and Himself on this earth—it is inevitable that there will arise oppositions that will look like contradictions and set us who are really brethren in opposition to one another as enemies.

Suppose I say (as I do)—that every man must be his own saviour, that only *himself* can save him—that "what he thinks in his heart (not only in his head) that *is he*": and who can think it, in head and heart, in will and act and life, but only he? Suppose I say of the remission or "putting away" of sin, which is the distinctive act and grace of Christ, that none can put away one's sin but oneself. If it is to be done only by repentance and faith—who can do his repenting or his believing for him but himself? So there is a tremendous human part in our salvation which even God cannot absolve us from or do for us. If, then, I reverse my speech and say, with equal positiveness and assurance, that the whole of what constitutes man's salvation, his redemption and completion, is the act and operation of God,—first or objectively of God in Christ, and then, subjectively, of Christ in us,—am I contradicting myself? Just that seeming contradiction in the wholeness and thoroughness of both sides of it is the absolute and necessary demand of Christianity. It appears and reappears in the transcendence and immanence of God, in the deity and humanity of Christ, and in all there is or shall be of reality in our own Spiritual lives or selves. God does it all, but He does it only with and in and through and by our own doing it; we must do it all, but we can and will do it only in union and co-operation with His doing it in us. There is no contradiction in God's oneness with everything in creation, in nature, or in human life and destiny except sin,—i.e., with the one exception, the possibility of which is essential to any real oneness on their part with Himself. When God endowed our finite *selves* with reason and freedom, He called us thereby to become *Doers, Be-ers,* and *Sharers* with Him in not only what He does but what He *is.* He gives us *our* part with Him in what He does and is, and lays upon us the task of doing and being it. We can see only in the light, we can breathe only in an atmosphere, we can know or love or live in our finite spirits or spiritual selves only in God. It is He that lives in us—but only as we too live in Him. Now Christ perfectly realizes and exemplifies that life of God in man and of man in God—of

God and Man in One—which is the Eternal Reason and Meaning and End of us all. *That* or *He,* is the Eternal Life which God has given, and gives us in Him.

The Divine-Human Eternal Life, which is in Christ and which is Christ, is primarily, of necessity, objective to us. We can make it subjectively ours only as God has first made it objectively ours. If God did not make it outwardly ours by His word to us, He could not make it inwardly ours by His Spirit in us. Only as the Object first of our faith, hope, and love, could Christ or God become secondarily the Subject and Substance in us of all these. A rational, free, or personal finite spirit like ours can be or become only what he knows, loves, wishes or wills, and himself does and is.

The *Objective* then in Christianity is, first, God Himself; —then God *as in Man,* or (actually) God in man, Christ; and so, conversely, Man in God, or God Man; and finally God, in and through that One Man, in humanity—the Church.

Now the true "Evangelical," whom alone we consider, cannot be said not to be wholly alive to all that objective fact and system of Christianity. If he is a party-man or a partisan, it certainly is not because he holds *only* to the subjective in his religion. On the other hand, the sincere and religious "Catholic," however he may cling to and make much of what we may call the "externals" of his religion, cannot be assumed to be not as much alive to all the subjective implications of it—faith, conversion, personal piety, etc.,—as the earnest Evangelical is to all the objective presuppositions and grounds of his own subjectivity. The ground taken by the article quoted from in the beginning is that the genuine Evangelical and Catholic partisans are emphasizing opposite aspects of one and the same thing, and that, not only is that one thing the very substance and reality of Christianity, but that both the aspects need all the emphasis that can be given them,—and only err, each in its misunderstanding and need of the balance of the other. The subjective really presupposes and involves all that the objective seeks to emphasize and express, and the objective is only going back to the means and source and ground of all that the subjective would emphasize in feeling and experience.

I would anticipate my own conviction with regard to the matter by saying that, so far from any Church having anything either to regret or to fear in the existence of such extremes within it, no Church, not even the ideal and hoped-for One Body and Bride of Christ, can fulfil itself in this world of ours without the ability to contain, not only extremes, but just those extremes. For extremes there will be in this world of probation, and these particular extremes are extremes of truth—and of equally necessary truths. Such extremes may err in their misunderstanding or defective use of other truths, but they can make no mistake in over-valuing their own truths. There is no exaggeration of either the objective or the subjective realities or values of Christianity—either as to ends or means.

In any further discussion of the relative and respective aspects or attitudes of objectivity and subjectivity in practical religion—which give such diverse colouring and appearance to our outward practices and professions, I wish to limit my observations to the matter of Sacraments; and further—in order to be as concrete and explicit as possible —I shall not go outside of my own experience in relation to them. Having occasion quite late in life—in a reunion of my old students of many years, and of various attitudes towards life—to take a retrospective view of my own relations with them, I undertook to define my attitude to the several extremes with which we were all more or less familiar. After the self-revelation, which generally was not new to them, I subsequently heard myself "placed" or classified somewhat as follows, by one of the most acute of my hearers and critics. As I have to confess to a little suggestive enlightenment to myself in it, I shall expand a little the somewhat pithy judgment actually expressed. In effect, or actual experience, fundamentally and primarily, I was "Evangelical." What more or also I was of Catholic or "High Church" was—he did say "put-on"—but subsequent accretion, more of outward persuasion or conviction than inward conversion. It is very true that at first and for a long time in my student life what I had of real religion was of the type of my time and place,—that is to say, a mild and rather indefinite Evangelicalism. With it too I very much more thought myself, than actually was, a High Churchman. After a very distinct and sincere "awakening," which I do not hesitate to call a "conversion," at the age of eighteen, there was nothing more than the most ordinary and occasional connection of what religious experience I maintained with the external functions of Church and Sacrament. Theoretically I valued them, but practically I cannot say that I kept up any intimate use of them or life by them. Personally I was wholly inclined to cultivate and nurse my religion within me, to make it a matter of my own thought, feeling and interest. When I passed from secular to theological and distinctively spiritual studies, I did so as a student and an incipient thinker: the intellectual and spiritual in myself were fired and interested.

In a word, my life on the whole has been very much more disposed to be subjective than objective. I have thought more of myself to Godward than of God to meward—of my faith than of God's love, my hope than of God's grace, my love for God than of God's fellowship with me—in a word more of the human Me than of the Divine Christ. More and more, as I have discovered this, I have come around to lay more stress, to be more positive and emphatic upon the things I feel I *am not* than upon what I am. Instead of entrenching and defending myself in my subjectivity—my Evangelicalism or Protestantism—I feel the need of balancing, supplementing, and even correcting it with something of the other side, with more of High-Churchism or

Catholicity. In doing so I am in no danger of making a
surrender of one side to the other. The modern outbreaks
of Protestantism and the ensuing higher and higher waves
of Evangelicalism were inevitable in the evolution of Christianity. As the universal human mind more and more
opened and human freedom upon all planes, mental, moral,
social, and spiritual, asserted itself, necessary consequences
followed resistless causes. These are now history and fact,
all questions and judgments of their happening are of the
past. Our present business is to discover and reap the fruits
that are worthy and needful of preserving. The conservative
and the progressive in history are never essentially or wholly
contradictory; they are never to be sacrificed or done away,
either both or one to the other. There is always a reaping
and reconciling the good of both. The time is come to perform this office for the conflicting claims of the Subjective
and the Objective, the Evangelical and the Catholic in our
common Christianity. Each really means all the truth of
the other, and is only afraid of it as seeming to deny, obscure, or mutilate the truth of itself. At the risk of exhibiting myself as neither a thoroughgoing Evangelical nor a
true Catholic—and with the consciousness and confession of
going only a short way in either direction as a beginning—
let me, as a pronounced Evangelical, expose some of my
tendencies to Catholicity.

First—I am more and more turning away from myself to
the Church. A woman truly in love does not think of her
love but of her lover. Marriage is out of herself, into *him*.
It gives her his name because it takes her into oneness with
himself. You may say, spiritual marriage is with Christ, not
the Church. That is just where I begin to take issue: I am
not as yet one with Christ in heaven—which means completeness, perfection, blessedness; I am one with Him here,
where He is one with me in all the little I am in Him, in all
my own wildernesses, Gethsemanes, and Calvarys. The life
I am trying to live is not my life but His life here upon

earth. It is not so much in me as without me, about me, everywhere and always. My little faith, hope, love, my little love, service, sacrifice, my little holiness, righteousness, life (however you analyze, characterize, or express it) is an infinitesimal moment in the real presence and work of Christ Himself, and of God through Him in this world. We complain of God's *not* being in His world, or else of His being in it so feebly, strangely, and ineffectually. "They know not my Ways!"—says God: We sit down, or stand aside—and are amazed or horrified that God does not do things Himself —without us. We do not see that, as in Creation and in Nature, God's purpose and "way" is to fulfil Himself in, with, through, and by *us*. The "us" or *we* are His end and purpose in the matter. He is not here to do Himself, but to be, to reproduce and find Himself anew, in our doing. God no more violates, or substitutes His separate action for, the proper reason, meaning, end or purpose of human reason and human freedom and responsibility, than He interferes with or takes the place of evolution or the laws of nature. All these are "His ways," and to violate them is to contradict Himself. No, "God is in His world"—but He is so *in us* who are the proper head and heart and soul of it; and all He does in it *we* are to do in Him. Our Christ is God in us in His world, and what is the matter with it is that we do not recognize and know Him where He is, and are standing by asking why He does not do in a way in which it is not His eternal will and purpose to do. What this world is going to be—*we* have got to make: if we will, He will make it all it ought to be. And only in the making it as not ourselves, shall we make ourselves.

My life in Christ then is not in myself, my faith, my hope or my love and service. It is true that all these must be in me, in order to live the life; but every one of these looks to, is wholly concerned with, Something, a Life, and a Living that is not mine—but God's, Christ's, the world's. The "Saving of One's Soul" is an old Evangelical end, that is not

the end of Christ's Gospel. As an incident, as a blessed result and reward of life, we cannot but regard and value it,
—but we must remember that our Lord's last word and act
meant this and *was this:* "He that seeketh his life, his soul,
his self, shall lose it; and that loseth it—for God, for me,
for the world—shall find it."

Now God in Christ in the world is the Church,—and so
I say I am more and more turning away from myself to the
Church for my religion and my life. I want to be more in
the Body and less in the one member that is myself. I emphasize this direction, not because it is my way, but because
it is not my way. I am a subjectivist, a personal religionist:
I want to stop looking at, or looking for, *my* faith, hope, or
love, my conversion, service or sacrifice, my holiness, righteousness, or life;—even though I have long known and
sought these only in Christ. I am beginning to see Christ,
not in God, or Heaven, or me—but in the Church, in the
world, where is His business, and where He is at work—so
far as He can awake and arouse and inspire His slow and
dead members to do His work. God knows, as I have said,
how I am condemning myself in this tardy longing! If I had
known from the beginning and all along that I was baptized,
not my individual self into the individual personal Christ in
heaven, but into the corporate Christ of the New Humanity,
as a member into a Body which is His Body—the sole organ
and instrument of all His presence and all His love and
sacrifice and work in and for the world! For God works in
His ways—because His all-wise purposes are subserved by
these rather than other ways.

It is into the Church then, and not outside of it, that we
are baptized into Christ—into His Body and not into any
conception of Himself apart from that. The Church is the
only Christ in which we are, or can do anything either by
Him or for Him. We are by faith in His perfection in
heaven—only as in fact He is in all our imperfect love,

service and sacrifice for Him here. Here is His and our life and business.

As I would be more and more disposed to take the Church as Christ Himself—the Sacrament of His spiritual presence and operation on earth, even as Christ is the Sacrament of God, the outward and visible sign and symbol of His real presence and operation to usward,—so I would more and more take the several specific sacraments as direct and immediate acts of Christ Himself. Each Sacrament, with its definite meaning and positive statement, is a word to me straight from Him, and through Him from God. Baptism receives me into Christ, as with Him Son of God and heir of heaven. That word is both declarative and creative or constitutive. It both declares me what I am and makes me what I am not. From eternity, by creation, and in nature, I am child of God: that was God's meaning of man from the beginning; we are out of, or *of* Him by nature, and thus constituted to *become* so in a higher sense and state by grace. His word as *dictum*—mere creation or nature—could make me His son in the former (potential) sense; only His Word as "Call" or invitation can make me His Son in the latter (or actual) sense. We were made sons by nature, we are "called to be" sons by grace. But it is one and the same Word of God that made and that calls and it is as able in the call as it was in the making. Only the call is to *us*—and to our necessary part in the making: This is a making of God— which He has made dependent and conditioned upon our making. He cannot make *us* without *us*: and so His Word here is not a *fiat* but a Call: "Whom He foreknew He predestined, whom He predestined He calls"—what follows depends upon us—"Whom He calls He justifies and whom He justifies He glorifies."

God's Word, I repeat, is as able and creative in Call or invitation as in *fiat*: If we hear it, if we receive it, if we obey it—*now* through grace, i.e., through God *and* us, as before *only* through the good will of God—we *are* sons of God indeed and heirs of heaven. And now that we know ourselves sons of God in entirety, what has made us so? It was my faith in the Word of God, says the Evangelical. No, says the Catholic, it was the Word of God spoken to faith in Baptism. And that, as we shall see, is about the amount of difference in principle between them. One dwells upon man's part, and the other upon God's, in the joint act of our making or becoming children of God. One (the latter) says, "In baptism I was made a member of Christ, the child of God, and an inheritor of the Kingdom of Heaven." The other says, "No, in my Conversion, by my act of faith, etc., I became all that." Or, if the issue is not made right there or in those terms, it turns upon the meaning and moment of *regeneration*. Are we regenerate in baptism or in conversion? That is in reality the rift that widens into the extremes we are considering: how minute a beginning of how wide a chasm! One side sees regeneration in God, in Christ, in the Church, in Baptism and all it means and involves. The other side sees it in the human awaking, seeing, hearing, believing, appropriating, conversion and assimilation in holiness, righteousness, and eternal life. I am instancing in the very rightest representatives of each type. Each side claims, of course, that it holds all the others also, and holds it the better (if not *only*) by holding and insisting upon its own. Why then, and what the difference, the recrimination and opposition? Because each is convinced the other is ignoring or neglecting its side in insistence upon the other. Evangelicalism is pure subjectivism to the Catholic; Catholicism, or "making everything" of the Church, is pure objectivism (which is near to idolatry) to the Evangelical. Of course I am using the terms in their "party" force, if not sense. Well, is there not all the objective truth possible in the divine act of human regeneration? And is there not all the subjective truth possible in the human act, the human realization and experience, of regeneration? Is there any possibility of exaggerating either? If there *is*—the natural cure for too much objectivism is more Evangelicalism, and for too much subjectivism is more Catholicity. The two sides *may* go to the extreme of self-exclusion from the Church, but within it they are so far from contradicting that they need to be constantly correcting and balancing themselves by each other. The outward and general point to be made, as stated in the text with which we began, is this: That instead of its being an inconsistency and self-contradiction in a particular Church to contain within its not only tolerant but willing embrace the widest types and expressions of both Evangelicalism and Catholicism (however we may regret the "ism" of both),—on the contrary, seeing that each is standing for one of the two essential parts of the One Truth of Christ, and not only so, but must and does for its own sake claim and possess all the other part also, it follows that any Church not wide enough to hold both is too narrow for the whole of Christianity.

I was taking the position of one who, both by constitution and circumstance, disposed to and practicing Evangelicalism, has nevertheless (or perhaps therefore) the more felt the call and the claim of Catholicity. Let not what I shall say in illustration be taken too literally as my own individual personal experience. Either as all of *it* my own, or as *all* of my own, I only use it for the sake of certain contrasts of attitude.

The act or moment of my youthful conversion was not taken up with thoughts or consciousness of myself. It would not have stood examination or analysis. It knew nothing of sin or forgiveness, of death and resurrection, of Church or Sacrament, or even of Christ and Holy Ghost. There was nothing there, in consciousness, but God and myself; but that was a new light, a new world, a new life, and a new self. Of course I can see now how much there was implicit in it—how much of the previous letter of early instruction or of the general Christian conception of God; but to me then it was only "God and the soul, the soul and its God." It was long before all the implicit in that early experience became explicit in the later; it has not become so yet; it is still in process of becoming so, and the process feels itself separated by infinity from completion. And between eighteen and eighty a long series of changes or transitions have been very gradually and slowly taking place in the relation between God and myself in the joint transaction of our common life—mainly in the direction of from my part to His in it.

God knows I do not ignore or underrate the absolute necessity of my human part in the joint life with God. But what is that part, as it has grown and is ever growing upon me? The answer is to be found only in that to another question which includes it: what was that "work" of Jesus of which He was ever saying that He was sent into the world to do it; that He must do it while it was day, before the night should come in which no man can work; that it was His meat and drink to do it; and, at the last, that it was done, "I have done the work Thou gavest me to do"?—Was it not simply to live human life, *to the finish*—to be divinely human, and humanly divine, God in Man and Man in God. And His task was to be, and is, humanity's task: "Where I am, *there* shall my disciple be." He did not die instead of us, but *for* us, that we might die: His death is, and must be, our death in precisely the sense and extent that His risen life is our life. Why is it that the holier the Christian, the better he knows what sin and death and hell are? Because the more he knows of holiness, life, and heaven, the better he knows what any and all lack of these *are*. Christianity does not whittle the divine immanent in humanity, man's immortal right and heritage, down to what he may become in a day. Our Lord's one standard, the level and measure up to which He lifted us all in His own person, was, "Be ye perfect as your Father in heaven is perfect!"

Now the first great reach of our Christianity as it begins

to comprehend and define itself, to become explicit, is a deep sense of the gracious, the divine provision which brings us at once, "just as we are," to God—God so infinitely far and yet so equally infinitely near! At the very first breath of my awakened spiritual consciousness, I am right there with Him, as when an infant awakens and opens its eyes straight into those of its mother. There is nothing between Him and me but love and blessedness. Not long does this last, of course; there *is* something between. But, graciously, the sense of sin that separates comes not all at once but gradually. We think we know, and more and more do know of sin, but never perhaps until the Great Day of the all-opening of all eyes shall we know all that sin is. And then—when we look upon Him Whom we pierced—the greatness of the remedy will reveal to us the depth of the disease.

The essence of grace is that *pari passu* with the sense of sin comes to us the revelation and assurance of faith. The more we look at ourselves in ourselves, in confession and contrition, the more we are shown and can see ourselves in Christ and in God, in faith and in hope. There is the disease, but here is the remedy and the cure. God can and does turn sin itself and its consequences into conditions and means of holiness. Without going into the metaphysical question of the necessity of evil to the existence of good, and describing things simply as they have been and are, we see that the genesis and growth of the sense and consciousness of sin bespoke and prepared the possibility, the awakening and coming, of the principle and power or holiness. The Law was given—that is, it came in due course of evolution—for the sake of sin, to awaken the sense of sin: "By or through law is the knowledge of sin." And through the sense and consciousness of sin came the want, need, necessity of holiness. So, further, through the death and hell that sin essentially and inevitably is, God brings us to the knowledge of the life and heaven that holiness is.

When we truly see Christ as the victor over all the evils—

sin, death, hell, as the Author and Finisher of Holiness, the Prince and Lord of Life, the Finder and Founder of Heaven, —the dark mystery of all ills is cleared up in the use God makes of them for the production of all good. Here, indeed, is a Holiness, a Righteousness, an Eternal Life of God for and in man, brought about in ways that baffle us but are known unto Himself. The point I wish now to emphasize— as offset to my petty subjectivity—is the infinite objectivity of all that! Herein, indeed, is revealed a Holiness, a Right- eousness, a Life *of God*—which cannot be spoken in lesser terms than Revelation, Incarnation, Regeneration and Res- urrection!

Catholicity thinks of and deals with all these things in the infinite and awful objective. Baptism is not *my* act of faith or fact of conversion; it is Christ's death and resurrection, and humanity's in Him. In that and not in my infinitesimal modicum of as yet uncomprehending faith am I regenerate. I am surely not making *my* faith and conversion any the less in their necessity—through exposing their littleness in real- ity;—but in the interest of the faith itself, how is that interest best subserved? If an earthly father begets or adopts me, it is all important to myself to believe and know him as my father; but does my faith "generate" me or make me his son? Can I better acquire the necessary faith by seeking it in myself in order to become his son, *or* by accept- ing *his* having made me his in order to my believing and knowing myself so? Baptism both attests our being sons of God by nature (i.e., *potentiâ*) and makes us so (*actû*) by the Word of *Grace* spoken to us in it.

God's Word of Grace creates spiritually, as His Word of Power or of *Fiat* creates naturally. Grace can work and fulfil itself only through faith—assent and consent of free finite spirits; but faith cannot generate grace, and *only* grace can generate faith. The general object of human faith is God's Word; the specific object of regenerating faith is God's Word spoken in baptism. God's Word in general is all expressed to us in the one word *Jesus Christ*. God's Word in baptism is—I, or we, humanity in Christ, the Church. In the Church, in Christ, in God, *we are regenerate*. Of course, if we do not believe it, it will be nothing *to us;* but that does not make it so *in itself*. We are not in Christ because we believe it, we believe it because God says so, His Word of Baptism makes it so.

It is in this way that I have long taken Luther's saying: "To be a Christian is to realize one's baptism"—to take God at His word, and *be* what He makes us—i.e., *"in Christ."* Not to be *in Christ* by baptism is to contradict and neutralize God's Word, which will fulfil itself in us—in, with, through, and by our faith, but cannot otherwise. The door into Christ is open to all—absolutely and unconditionally—on God's part. If I invite a whole community and throw open my house to all without exception, those who decline or fail to enter, or entering to partake of the entertainment, cannot say that I have imposed any condition. Of course their entering or partaking is conditioned and conditional, but by whom and upon what—but themselves. So God imposes no conditions upon His call in Christ: it is to "whosoever will"—and to come "just as he is." It is true there is the "wedding garment"—without which, etc., but that is not to be brought by the guest, it is provided for him by the host.

I go back thus behind *anything* on my part, even my faith, to God's Word. In the person of Jesus Christ, acting alike on God's part and man's part, God opened His heaven, and came down, and said to the humanity He had taken into Himself—to *all* humanity, for He took all—"This is my beloved son in whom I am well pleased!" The good pleasure that saves us in Christ, that would "give us the kingdom," is all in God, not in us: "the mystery of His Will" is "of His own good pleasure, which He purposed in Himself." I am God's son—by generation and by regeneration—by God's Word, not by my faith. Faith accepts, it does not make: all faith means "by grace through faith," God's will operative through my will.

So also with the other Sacrament: God takes me into and gives me His Son, not only in new birth but in continuous new life. My faith does not put Christ into the Sacrament: God puts Him there for and to my faith. Neither does my lack of faith take Christ out of the Sacrament: He is there, if not for my acceptance, then for my rejection, or at least non-acceptance. The best way to put Him there in faith is to know that He is there in fact. Formerly I came to the Table or the Altar, or both in one, saying, "Lord, I come with nothing in me but faith, and hope, and love." Now I come *with* nothing, and only *to* God's love and grace and fellowship or oneness with me. I seek to sink all my pitiful subjective into the all-embracing and inclusive Divine Objective.

It was not only the Divine Objective that I was putting at the mercy of my pitiful subjectivity. It was equally the universal, or Catholic, human objective. I have to confess that the largest part of my Evangelicalism was the immense concern of my personal salvation. Christianity, it comes to me too late, is not alone "my soul and its God": it is "myself and humanity." There is no such thing as a relation to God "in Christ," that is not a relation also to humanity "in Christ." Christ is as truly Manhood and Mankind, as He is Godhead. If I am not in the Church which is the Body or the Whole of our Lord's humanity, if I cannot say that in Him *nihil humanum mihi alienum est*—assuredly in no mere individual (or, in that sense, "personal") way am I in Him. Not apart from, but only as a part in the Body of Christ, are we "in Him" at all.

All that I have been trying to say is only a glance in the opposite directions or at the opposite sides of a common truth; or rather, a glance from one side at the other. I could have spoken with much more ease upon the subjective, the personal, or the human side,—I might even say the Protestant side; for it is to this I have given most of my thinking. The point is, that not for any particular Church, but for Christianity as a whole, there has to be, not alone a consent "to live and let live," but a deeper understanding, a truer union, and a more real sense of oneness between Evangelical and Catholic. Each side needs all the true emphasis of the other for more than correction—for completion of itself. And as long as we are in all stages of the process of enlightenment and sanctification, of spiritual reason and freedom —while corporately striving to keep Christianity as true and pure as possible, we shall have individually to put up with much weakness, folly, and diversity in Christians.

There are, of course, excesses, travesties, caricatures of religion at both the extremes we have been considering, but short of these there is also much of earnest sincerity and deep truth on both sides. And how much more of healing and edification there is in magnifying and manifesting the good we have in common than in fighting and striving over the counter evil that more and more separates and divides us!

THE FAITH OF A CHRISTIAN TODAY [1]

My Faith in the Presence of Doubts;
not Doubts that have Arisen in my Faith.

---

*So in all my spiritual dealings with myself or others
I recognize this fact: that in the real things of the
spirit the issue at last, and the decision, lie between
the "things" and the spirit. Be Spiritual and you
will know the essential things. Receive, believe, do
—and you shall know; the spiritual things verify
themselves to the spiritual man.*

As I myself date back eighty-two years, I may represent my
Christian faith as having been taken over from an even
earlier period. It began, let us say, in the widespread Evangelicalism of the time, passed through and was enriched by
the more Catholic stage of the Oxford Movement, was
deeply affected by the new and youthful Liberalism of
Maurice and Frederick Robertson,—and so passed on into
the more troublous questionings and doubts of the century.
But up to that point there was nothing of the faith and
doubt of which I am to speak. I was too wholly concerned
with the matter and substance of the faith itself to pay
sufficient attention to the gathering difficulties in its rela-

---

[1] This last article by Dr. DuBose was written in February and revised a
short time before his death at Sewanee, August 18, 1918.

tions with the environment of other truths, scientific, historical, etc. So that when in turn these surrounding and conflicting claims presented themselves and demanded attention I was already settled in my religious convictions.

I believe the spirit of man, in its deepest dignity and highest prerogative of inherent relationship and actual relation with God, has rights of its own, which no other truth is entitled to violate or ignore,—nor can be in any real conflict with or contradiction to. The Spirit cannot verify its truths or its true conclusions by any kind or amount of spiritual observation or experience, agreement or consent, which the purely natural investigator may not reject or ignore as excluded from *his* observation and experience. When then enquiry is carried on exclusively on the natural plane, which of necessity excludes "the things"—The Deep Things, and High Things, and Eternal Things—of the Spirit, those who represent the wisdom and even truth of this earth should not be surprised at the slowness of religion to accept its manifest and demonstrated facts which *seem to it* to contradict precious spiritual truth. Many a humble good man will prefer to surrender his senses or his reason rather than his faith. And however ignorant he may be in thinking the contradiction between them, he is less despicable for sacrificing sense for spirit, ignorantly, than the very many more who practise the reverse knowingly.

It came about through rather peculiar circumstances that my faith at the time—so far as it was not merely received, but made my own—was almost exclusively that of the Greek New Testament. The principle that most worked itself to the front with me was this: That if there was spiritual truth for the spiritual man, the truth would have its way of coming to the man—and coming to him with some power in itself of self-verification. I was not blind to the door that this opened to illusions and delusions of all sorts, but that did not weaken my conviction of the truth of the principle. Where are we not subject to illusion and delusion in our choice or pursuit of any good? Discernment and election between the true and the false, the good and the bad, the right and the wrong, is the essential principle of all probation, all self-determination, or spiritual evolution. Shall we forego *all* good because of the difficulties and dangers of determining it?—Or shall we forego the highest and ultimate *only,* because of the tests and the proofs to which it subjects, and by which alone it determines us?

I early began to think and to teach upon the line of the following principle: In the long run, and in the end, we know things because they are true, we love things because they are good, we do things because they are right; not for any of the intermediate and incidental reasons that we give for knowing, loving, or doing. Anything short of this, or other than this, is illusion or delusion. The mind for truth, and truth for the mind, the heart for love, and love for the heart; right for the will, and the will for the right. Each of these pairs are in the world to find each other and come together. The reciprocal things are all here seeking, testing, proving each other; and when they find the other they will find themselves, for they are themselves only in unity with their other. It is only in these unions and unities that our world of the spirit comes into being, and the tests, trials, proofs, the temptations, doubts and fears, all the hard and painful experiences by the way, even our failures, faults and sins, are (by love, grace and fellowship of God) made the means and instrumentalities of our spiritual making.

So in all my spiritual dealings with myself or others I recognize this fact: that in the real things of the spirit the issue at last, and the decision, lie between the "things" and the spirit. *Be* spiritual and you will *know* the essential things. Receive, believe, do—and you shall know; the spiritual things verify themselves to the spiritual man.

The greatest danger and abuse of such a principle, and consequent source of illusion and delusion, is to take or apply it individually, exclusively, or partially. Spirit is the most social, inclusive, and unifying—the most *semper, ubique, et ab omnibus*—thing in the world. In its most elemental principle or quality of Love, it is identical with unity, universality, and continuity. All confusion, disorder, error, lawlessness, evil, or sin in the universe come from breach of it. To think, feel, wish or will "in the spirit"—is to do so collectively or together. So the Church which is—"God, in Christ, by His Spirit, in the world," is primarily and essentially One and Catholic. Even its Holiness—or any other possible designation of it—is already implicitly included and expressed in its Unity: Holiness and Unity are identical, they are What God is.

I would define spiritual things then simply as Things of the Spiritual Man—the objects of his faith, his obedience, and his devotion. By the Spiritual Man I mean man in his unity with God, with himself, with all men and all things in the Church—the Body of Christ. The nearer we come to that unity of heart, mind, will, and act—the better judges are we in ourselves of the true things of the Spirit. There is still between us and the End—which is nothing less than God Himself—the atmosphere of earth, full of illusion and delusion, fallacies of sense, mind, and even spirit; but God has placed forever before our eyes, not the image but the Very Person of the Spiritual Man. We have not to ascend into heaven to bring Him down, nor to descend into the abyss to bring Him up; for He is with us, and near us, and in us. We have only to confess with our mouths that He is Lord, and believe in our hearts that God has raised Him from the dead—and raised us in Him—and we shall live.

Now all this was in my faith and in my life before ever I came face to face with the professed and the apparent contradictions of the new science and the new history and the new mind in general of the new time in which I was living. I believe I never was in doubt that God is as much in the world today as He was in the time of our Lord. And I believe He is as much in all the new learning and the new mind and the new truth as in the old facts and the old faiths of the world. I cannot think any real conflict between true religion, true history, true science or true anything else. And each of these has its truth—to which I want to stand in the right relation,—or, if not that, at least in the right attitude. This puts me necessarily in a position of uncertainty upon points or details about which I was certain before. My attitude is in many respects one of suspense. My subject as announced in the title is—My Faith in the Presence of Doubts; not Doubts that have Arisen in my Faith. So I shall not go into the matter or discussion of doubts, but simply refer to them in the discussion or statement of my faith.

There can be no question with any of us that—along with the new knowledge and the new mind of the present day has come a new attitude towards our faith. Miracles, from being the ground and support of our faith are becoming a stumbling-block and obstacle to the faith of many. I need not go into all the embarrassments of those who, true to the spiritual things which they have found so true to themselves, are nevertheless not satisfied to hold them in seeming—and much less in real—contradiction to truth everywhere or anywhere else in the one world of the One God.

I not only believe, but know, that all of God's truth is one, whether natural or spiritual—or what not. That which is true at bottom, or at the end, or in the whole, is true all through, and I should like at once to confess and pay homage to it. But we are creatures of a time and of a part, and can only worship the One and the All at a distance, and know by faith and not by sight that it is here as well as there.

I say then once for all that I know there is a truth of history, and a truth of science, a truth of philosophy and even metaphysics; I know also that there is a truth of God and of the spirit of man over and above all these; and I believe in no contradiction between or among them. Situated as we are at our one point in an eternal and universal process, we can only do our present part in each and have faith in the unity of all. Personally, while I feel my need on every side, I see no necessity nor any possibility of a whole-sale reconciliation.

A thousand times in the past half century I have gone through and over my Christian faith with the view of unify-ing and adjusting it to all the coordinate rest of truth. I go over it now, not in the order in which it formed itself in my life, because I cannot see that there was any order in that. I begin with a general survey and contemplation of the New Testament. Modern scholarship has made the most of its variety and diversity: How far even the Synoptics contrast and differ among themselves! How very diverse from the others is St. John! What a different atmosphere of thought and practice St. Paul brings us into! And then the Epistle to the Hebrews in contrast with the Apostle to the Gentiles!

I wonder at myself for wondering as I do, more and more, at the wonderful unity of the whole. From the beginning to the end of the New Testament I can see but one theme and one subject,—the Divine Human Personality in Whom heaven and earth, God and man, the natural and the spirit-ual, the actual and the ideal come together and are made One. Of course in all these effectuations of unity the focal point of interest and concern is in the attitude and issue of human freedom; the destiny of man is the matter in ques-tion. And in the very nature of finite spirit and the fact of its personal participation in the life and work of the world the quality and character and ultimate issue of things are of necessity conditional upon its free choice and action. God has given us to have life in ourselves, and as the means and to the end of that life He has made our world dependent upon our making it. But for the sake of our own making He will make it only what we do—that is, He will do all only in, with, through, and by us: All His will waits upon our willingness—"All things are ours,"—God Himself, and creation and nature are "ours"; the world is given us to do what we will with it, and in so doing to make what we will of ourselves. But we can make the "all things" ours only by making them, and our wills, God's. Our Lord in the first Beatitude declares the Kingdom of Heaven *ours;* but the condition of its possession is our poverty; that is, our possessing it only in, with, through, and by Him. He gives only through *us,* but we have only through *Him:* He and we must be *both* in it.

Now that is the theme of the New Testament; but the subject of it is Christ, by Whom and in Whom from beginning to end it is enacted and portrayed to us. God in His foreknowledge forepurposed our humanity to sonship to Himself (Rom. 8:29; Eph. 1:5). Christ in the process or evolution of this destiny is the Beginning and End, First and Last, Alpha and Omega, the predestination and the fulfilment in inheritance. But very much is He the very Process itself. Sonship, as I have often tried to say, is even more a personal than a natural relation; it is more in the act than in the fact; it only fully comes to itself in the realization and fulfilment. Even Christ (in the Epistle to the Hebrews) is described as having attained His sonship, begotten anew in it in His Resurrection from the dead—"a son perfected forever." To say that the sonship is in the act more than in the fact, in the perfection of the personal relation than in the prior and mere nature, is only to emphasize the steps between man and animal, and between spirit and flesh.

The Gospel of Christianity is not in its ethics,—it is in its personal relation to God as the essential source and condition of ethics: the Law is prior to the Gospel, but it is only the Gospel that makes the Law possible. "God with us, in us, through us, by us," is the whole truth taught by Christ, the whole work wrought by Christ,—negatively the whole meaning of His death and positively the completeness of His life in our humanity: "In that He died, He died to sin once; in that He liveth, He liveth unto God." It may be said that the first half of the New Testament is: Christ living the Gospel, manifesting God in our life, *being* our righteousness, accomplishing our sonship, effecting our redemption and resurrection from sin and death, entering upon our inheritance of eternal life. The second half of the New Testament is the promised ministry of the Holy Ghost—"taking of the things of Jesus and showing them" to His Church: the Word of God as the objective principle of God's personal revelation to us, the Spirit of God as the subjective principle of our personal appropriation of God. Once in possession of the whole Gospel, it seems to me that all the difficulties and so-called contradictions only enhance the truth along with the wonder of it.

But I undertook at the beginning to take some account of the difficulties and the doubts on the way to, if not in the way of, the Gospel. The question shall be as to the proper attitude towards these doubts. As to that I give no positive or general answer: I can only illustrate a single personal and tentative attitude. When, from time to time, I review my Christian faith, I rearrange it in some sort of order—as it has come to me on the whole and in the end: I go first through the personal life of Christ, and then through the Christian acceptance and interpretation of it in His Church. I will touch now only upon a few of the typical difficulties and doubts in it, and the attitude of my faith in regard to them.

I never begin the life of Christ without dwelling with a peculiar delight upon the double account which has been called The Gospel of the Infancy—or the Story of the Birth. In the first place there is such a divine charm in the story itself. But what strikes me even more is the background of spiritual—not only height and depth, but—inevitable truth in it. And yet I think I can partially understand the difficulty of the present day mind upon the subject of the miraculous element in the Birth record.

Meantime what of my Christian faith: what is honest

doubt doing with my Christian conviction as to the person of Christ? Everything depends upon how—with what eyes —we are looking upon the Virgin Birth. If we are doing so *only* with the eyes of sense or of science—i.e., of natural vision, if we are assuming that there is nothing of the supernatural in it at all, nothing of the spiritual or the divine,— then we are doing something more lowering to our nature and our intelligence, than any belittling of mere natural fact or historic truth that we can be guilty of. I beg not to sin against physical fact, but yet more earnestly I pray to be delivered from the more serious offense of spiritual blindness and denial.

The real miracle of the Gospel is the spiritual Jesus. That does not exclude—on the contrary it assumes—all the physical of our common humanity in Him. "He was made in all points like unto us—sin only excepted." And that exception was no mere fact of nature; it was an act in the nature (an act at once of faith, of obedience and of sacrifice) which accomplished and constituted its redemption and salvation. It was the human conquest of the spirit over the flesh. That was a human act, but it was none the less—on the contrary, it was all the more—a divine act. God and man are not mutually exclusive but mutually inclusive: they are most each and both when they are most one. The Church from the beginning refused to see in Christ only man. Moreover it insisted upon seeing in Him primarily and causally God in man, and only secondarily and by consequence man in God. The impression produced immediately by Jesus, and left permanently with His Church, is best and most fully, in its pure spirituality, portrayed in St. John, St. Paul, and the Epistle to the Hebrews. Not one of these refers to the physical features or incidents or explanations of His human genesis or generation. They describe Him as having been eternally God's foreknowledge or thought, fore-purpose or will of man; as having become in time God's not only revelation or manifestation but actual accomplishment and fulfilment of man's destiny through the sole process of self-realization in Him. We see ourselves now in the mind of God, in the act of God, and in the end or aim of God,—and by entering into and uniting ourselves with the divine process as seen in Christ, we attain our own and our only self-realization in eternal life.

The New Testament then, on the wholly spiritual side, sees all and more than all that the Story of the Birth undertakes to express in physical facts and terms. It sees that the True Jesus was born *into* but never *from* or *out of* humanity. Humanity could be His Mother but never His Father. The mother conceives, the father begets; the one receives, bears, produces, the other originates, engenders, quickens or creates. Life is from the father through the mother. But there is no life that does not come—immediately from, or mediately through *both*. There is no spiritual life that is not *both* from or of God, and through, with, and in man: there must be both, and it must be one.

Getting thus the spiritual truth or fact expressed in the story of the Birth, let us go on to note from the other side the spiritual exactness and felicity of both thought and language. The promise had been that "The Virgin (or maiden) shall conceive and bear a Son." Why "the Virgin"? Think now of the approaching birth of the Divine into the human —the soul of man so susceptible of the divine, so impotent and empty of it in or by itself,—what is virginity but an impotence and an emptiness! But lo! the Bridegroom comes: Hail thou favoured one, the Lord is with thee; and behold, thou shalt conceive and bear a Son, and shalt call His name Jesus. He shall be great and shall sit upon the throne of His Father and reign for ever. For it is He that shall save His people from their sins.—How shall this Almighty, Eternal, Divine Thing come to pass—does the poor, sorrowful, weak, and hungry human soul ask?—The Holy Ghost shall come upon thee, and power from on high shall overshadow thee. Wherefore the holy thing that is born of thee shall be called the Son of God. That which through the Love, the Grace, the Fellowship of God was to be born into every human soul, was born for all, and once for all, in the person of Jesus Christ, and is with Him in all the world in the Church which is His Body.

Where now are all the questionings and doubts of physical science and critical history as to this great miracle of the Gospel? They are here and they will remain here, just as the questionings and doubts as to free will and necessity are here and always will be. One side says: Why hesitate at God's transcendence of nature and law in the method and act of Incarnation, when finite freedom is a constant transcendence of it,—so much so that consistent science of the flesh or nature has no alternative but to deny *it* also? On the other side, both history and science say: We do not deny the possibility of anything; it is only the concrete actuality of the so-called miracles—the evidence or proofs of which we cannot allow as established. Is either issue of this controversy demonstrable? Can the question be for ever closed?

I think I can not only with sincerity but with honesty and fairness towards all the sorts of truth—spiritual and natural, as equally of God—say that none of these problems, difficulties and doubts, nor all of them together in the slightest degree diminish or interfere with my faith. On the contrary, as it is the highest as well as the hardest part of our probation to be thrown upon faith as against sight, and spirit as against letter, so, in general, problems, difficulties, and even doubts on the natural side may be the very occasions and stimuli that we need to drive us to evidences and proofs on the spiritual side. We say that Truth is mighty and will prevail: well, how will it prevail? Not by being attested by anything outside itself, but by self-verification within itself. There is a great deal more in being true than in being proved. We rest too much in the external for our faith, and it is for our good that the externals are allowed, if not made, more and more to fail us. "Man doth not live by bread alone"; even with our Lord the bread was withheld that the "Word" might suffice: and at the last, the flesh must die that the spirit may live.

Time was when I believed the New Testament upon the evidence of the miracles, and based the fact of the miracles upon the infallibility of the inspired record. Little by little I came to justify these exceptional miracles and inspiration upon the score of the One and Once for all Divine Act of Divine Incarnation and Human Fulfilment. At His Baptism was all that Jesus saw—and John: the heavens opened, the Spirit descending, the words spoken, "This is my beloved Son"—literally visible and audible?—Yet who of us now will surrender one trace of that vision or one breath of that utterance? In those forty days of Temptation in the wilderness, shall we take the encounter—the "grammatical vocables," the acts, movements, and questionings of the Devil, and our Lord's responses, as literally visible and audible? Yet we know that in that experience all the reason meaning and end of human temptation and probation is proposed—subsequently to be solved and expressed in human act and achievement—in the person of our Head and in the lives of all His members.

And coming at once to the crisis and the issue: The incidents, appearances, and records of the Resurrection stand and will stand, but how infinitely more we are to know of the eternal spiritual truth of the Resurrection! However inexplicable the physical Ascension, how luminous the spiritual! How impossible now would be the literal, physical, bodily presence of Jesus, in its ubiquity—how infinitely close and near to every one of us—nearer even than ourself, because Himself our closer and truer self—in the spiritual Body of our Risen Humanity.

The truest Glory of the Highest is not merely that He can humble Himself to behold the lowest, but that He can make Himself one with the vilest sinner in his return. That the humiliation of Jesus was His glorification, that His deepest passion was His highest action, His bitterest suffering His highest perfection, His death for the world the life of the world—in a word, that eternal life is through mortal death, who could have invented or discovered that depth or summit of human truth and destiny, but that God Himself had shown the way!

APPENDIX A

CHRISTIAN DEFENSE

Editor's Note: The following essay appeared in The Sunday School Teacher's Manual, *edited by W. M. Groton (Philadelphia: G. W. Jacobs, 1911). It reflects DuBose's thought in a period earlier than that in which he wrote* Unity in the Faith.

I propose only two things as possible within the scope of this essay. The first is to establish something of a general and tenable attitude toward all present-day criticism of Christianity. The second shall be to suggest an apologetic or answer which it will be in the power of us all to make our own and apply personally and actively in defence of our common Christianity.

I. THE PROBLEM

An indispensable preliminary. We need not undertake to answer questions about Christianity until we are in an attitude to understand them and in a temper to do them justice. To treat all questioning or criticism of Christianity as hostile attacks is an initial error fatal to any real answer to it. In order to place ourselves in a radical right relation to the whole business of modern criticism, we shall have to go so far back as to revise and revolutionize our entire popular conception of it. We shall have to learn to recognize under the forbidding guise of criticism and even of scepticism, the aspect of friends and not enemies to the truth we love. Let us remember how prone we are in the most every-day matters to reverse the truth as to good and evil; to rebel against that which is best for us and crave what is worst. It may seem a thing to be deplored that the one most intimate and sacred treasure of our religious faith may not be left in peace and security; that Christianity must expend so much of its thought and energy upon the vindication of its bare right to exist. But would that kind of rest or peace be desirable? What possession have we worth holding—especially what free, spiritual, personal possession: life, liberty, or happiness; mind, character, or standing—that we have not to preserve with all our diligence and defend with all our might? The trials, dangers, and pains to which our faith is unceasingly exposed, are themselves, so far from evils, the very conditions, occasions, and ministers of faith. A life or a faith that is independent of labour, danger, and pain; that is not the fruit of toil and strife and the need of victory, has nothing in common with that of Jesus Christ.

Modern scepticism and criticism. It cannot, of course, be denied that the rise of modern scepticism and criticism has given swift and wide occasion for their employment against Christianity by enemies and objectors of every sort. Possibly even a larger part of so-called scepticism and criticism may be only the expression of learned enmity or malicious ignorance. I admit the natural and deep provocation to look upon all doubt and questioning of Christianity as hostile attacks upon it. But

nothing absolves us from the high and difficult duty of recognizing the appearance and welcoming the application of a
true principle, and of a right and wise discrimination between its use and its abuse. And it is the use and not the
abuse of doubt and investigation with which we need to be
concerning ourselves. However painful and offensive to us
at the time, there is nothing in the end to be feared from any
form of ignorant and malicious, or of unfair and untrue, no
matter how subtle or able, scepticism and criticism. But the
only way in the world to escape the false applications of a
principle is to face and accept its true workings. There is no
escape from errors of any real movement but in honest alli-
ance with its truth. And there is a great truth in the things
which we just now ignorantly and cowardly most deprecate
and fear.

The origin and meaning of the two words. The origin and
meaning of the
two objectionable terms and things of which I have spoken
is this: *Skepsis,* our Greek Lexicon informs us, is examination, investigation, inquiry into, etc. *Scepticism* may be an
extreme or abuse of the spirit of inquiry and investigation;
but if so, it is the abuse of a good thing, and a thing which
in its use cannot possibly be carried too far. Let us accept
it not only as a fact but also as a right and a great fact, that
this age is an age of investigation and of verification. If
anything survives this age and comes out of it accepted, it
is going to be because it has a reason for survival and acceptance and because it is able and willing to prove its reason and establish its right. To complain or be afraid of
being put to the proof is weakness and faithlessness. *Krisis*
is the proper and only instrument of *skepsis.* There can be
no thorough investigation or verification, except through
separation, discrimination, analysis, testing, proving, trying,
deciding, judging. Let us not suppose that criticism, and
spiritual, religious criticism, has come into the world illegit-

imately, or that it has not the divinest of missions and tasks to perform in it. For criticism and separation and judgment, said our Lord, am I come into the world. He came with his winnowing fan in his hand, and is critical not only of the thoughts and intents of our hearts but of the deepest principles and foundations of our lives.

Christianity the great critic and final judge. Christianity is itself the great critic and final judge, and if it cannot endure criticism and judgment, it discredits itself in its own function and condemns itself at its own bar. No one will charge that the critical spirit, prior to its application to the sphere of religion, was in the world with evil intent, or that its initial and essential motive was other than the testing and proving and verification of truth and the exposure and correction of error. What has it accomplished, or what has it not accomplished, outside of its application to religion and Christianity? *Skepsis* and *krisis* were mighty implements and instruments applied by the modern spirit of truth to everything under the sun, and everywhere there followed a great severing and separation of true from false, of right from wrong, of good from bad. Now principles and processes which in everything and everywhere else wrought so much good could have had no essentially evil intention and could not have become altogether bad when they came to be applied to the highest truth and the best good. The first step in our right attitude is to know that scepticism and criticism were as necessary as they were inevitable when they came, and that they had a divine mission and task to perform as well in the realm of the spiritual as in that of natural truth and life. Our appeal in behalf of Christianity is from ignorant or inimical or wrong judgment; not to no criticism or judgment at all, but to fair and competent judgment. Let us believe that in itself judgment means justice, investigation means truth, verification means confirmation and establishment, not hostility and destruction.

What we have the right to demand. What we have the right to demand in all questions of Christianity is a judgment qualified and competent to deal with spiritual as well as natural evidence. Constituted and placed as we are, in a world which is like ourselves at once natural and spiritual, we cannot but be confronted with experiences of a mixed natural and spiritual character, and it requires faculties of both sorts to deal with them. There is no science or philosophy worthy the name that denies the possibility of there being, and being in actual correlation with what we call nature, a higher order of things that transcends nature. Natural knowledge can go no further than to question whether there is sufficient evidence or verification of such a superior system of things, or of its being in any actual vital relation with our natural experience. If at any point the higher spiritual order comes into such relation with the lower or natural, as to seem, upon evidence or testimony, otherwise sufficient, to supersede and replace the ordinary operation, as in the wholly exceptional case of the virgin birth or the bodily resurrection of our Lord, this would indeed be a miracle in the extreme sense of the term, if nature were all; but it would not be so upon the supposition involved,—namely, that it was the rational and significant entrance and evidence in nature of a higher operation. The question that then arose would not be one of purely natural probability. To make it such would be to assume the non-existence of the higher order and operation. The true question would be whether the spiritual probability is sufficient to outweigh the natural probablity. What we want, then, for a full and right judgment in the matter, is not only qualification and competence to weigh the natural improbabilities involved, but equal ability to appreciate and estimate the spiritual meanings and reasons and probabilities on the other side. Once admit even the possibility of a spiritual order both immanent in and transcending the natural order, and such a phenomenon as Christianity, and religion in general, is lifted above the issue of merely natural cause and effect. As against the improbability of such a dual order of experience in human life, we ought to remember that so far as we are concerned, the spiritual order would be impossible except in combination and correlation with such a natural order. A sphere of freedom and personality at all is possible only in connection with one of physical necessity and uniformity.

It comes then to this: the question of Christianity as a spiritual phenomenon, *the* spiritual phenomenon of the world; of Christianity as in its essence an incarnation, that is to say, the consummate presence and operation of the spiritual in the natural; above all, of Christianity as a spiritual operation of process at certain most significant and vital points of moments modifying or superseding the ordinary natural operations or processes;—this whole question of the supreme contact and correlation of the spiritual with the natural becomes more and more one of spiritual rather than merely natural probability or improbability. And the modern disposition to deal with it on purely or predominantly natural, historical, or scientific, grounds, is what we have not merely to object to or protest against, but to supplement and correct by a spiritual science competent to the task.

Let us illustrate, by example, the point of competence for the criticism of spiritual facts. Probably no English thinker was ever better qualified to weigh the natural improbability of a human resurrection from the dead than the philosopher Hume. So improbable was such an event that Hume assumed that no testimony or evidence on the other side could possibly outweigh it. Was Hume qualified or competent to weight the probabilities on the other side? With him it was only the question of the resurrection of a man. What conception had he in the argument of who the man was, or of what was the eternal significance of that resurrection. We hold that these were vital factors in the determination of the question of probability or improbability, and that no man is prepared to give the answer but one who speaks out of the fullest Christian knowledge of who Christ is, and out of the fullest Christian experience of what his resurrection means. For Christians to turn over the decision of these questions to the conclusions of physical or natural reasoning only, is to surrender the rightful claims of that side of our nature and life to which these facts of the spirit belong. On the contrary, let a man know the spiritual history of the race and the spiritual facts of his own nature; let him have grown to an adequate conception and experience of the truth embodied in the person and work of Jesus Christ and imparted to himself by personal relation and communion with him; let a man be so spiritually equipped, and although he be also at the same time the best endowed and qualified of natural sceptics and critics, yet in him the spiritual credibility of all the facts necessarily involved in the truth of our Lord's person and work will infinitely outweigh all their natural incredibility. Hume's once seemingly unanswerable arguments had and have meaning and pertinence only for those to whom the natural is all; they have none for those who are capable of weighing the meaning, the reason, the necessity of spiritual things. Scepticism does not go now the full length of Hume. No one holds that an incarnation or a resurrection is an inherently or essentially impossible or incredible thing. The question is one only of the sufficiency of the reason and the adequacy of the evidence. These we have to furnish from a better understanding and a deeper experience of the rightful claims and the evidential possibilities of the spirit.

The difficulty with apologetics in general. The difficulty with apologetics in general is that now again, as in the earlier ages when the faith of Christianity found catholic expression, critical thought has been carried to the point where it can be met only by an apologetic which is itself a science and an art. So subtle, searching, and thorough are not alone the hostile attacks but the honest tests and proofs to which Christianity is continuously subjected, that it is driven to justify, defend, or confirm its credibility and truth by a method and with a skill at least equal to that with which it is assailed. Nothing in the course of human thought has surpassed the delicacy, the dexterity, and exactness with which Christianity at the first defined and defended itself against every conceivable false conception and false expression. And the time has come when it shall have to recall and renew its ancient power of self-comprehension and its ancient skill of self-presentation, if it would hold its own in the arena of the present. It will not suffice it to have been once proved and approved; it must be capable of always anew proving and approving itself to the questionings of each new age. And it is no disadvantage to it to have always to answer for and give an account of itself.

It is of the very essence of an incarnation that it is an entrance of the supernatural or the divine into natural experience, into human history and human literature. It is impossible but that this should involve some modification or breach of the common in the course and in the records of human history. This brings Christianity legitimately under the scrutiny of scientific, historical, and literary criticism with regard to the facts involved. These must be subject to the necessity of verification, with only one distinct condition from the spiritual side: the possibility or probability of the supernatural or divine in the case must not be *ipso facto* excluded. On the other hand, the sufficiency of meaning, reason, or necessity on the spiritual side to establish a probability, the true *modus dignus deo,* is equally necessary to the furtherance of any such claim.

The general apologetics of the present, so far as it has

to meet the outward questionings of physical and meta-physical science, of literary and historical criticism, must largely remain in the hands of the experts, and consequently of the very few. I think we may safely leave it there, with the expectation that there will not be lacking the best expert attention to the high spiritual interests at issue. The zeal and devotion, the diligence and watchfulness, the learning, skill and genius of the defenders of Christianity are not going to lag behind those of its opponents. Truth will continue to be mighty and prevail; hatred or ignorance of it, falsehood or error, will not palm itself off permanently upon the acceptance and consent of humanity. The worst symptom of our Christianity is the faithless fear we show of everything which in succession questions or doubts or tries it. If we will but take care of our own faith, God will take care of his truth. Only let us be very sure that our faith is fixed upon his truth.

There is no greater injury to Christianity, no truer cause of its offence to much of the best thought and life of the world, than the weak and ignorant attitude that so many of us assume toward the legitimate function and benefaction of right criticism. The great multitude of us, not only holders but teachers of Christianity, are incapable—and should not be ashamed to confess ourselves incapable—of passing judgment or laying down conclusions upon many of the critical questions and controversies of the day. Of all the sciences that have tested the faculties of man, true criticism is the most difficult and delicate, the most de-pendent upon special gifts as well as upon consummate discipline and training. It seems to require almost the development of a new sense and the exercise of faculties not yet common to us all. Like other subtle and obscure sciences it doubtless furnishes a good field for imposture and charlatanry. Christianity cannot but be conscious of the manifest spiritual incompetence of very many who presume to pass judgment upon predominantly spiritual facts. But for all that, we had better possess our souls and hold our peace upon matters which we are as little competent, on the other side, to speak of. The truth will raise up for itself those who are competent on both sides, and at any rate prejudice and passion can never otherwise than injure or compromise its cause.

II. THE ANSWER

The supreme apologetic. Having divested ourselves, not of the duty of proper interest or intelligence in the matter, but of responsibility for, or (I think we shall show) dependence upon, the great mass of the more learned or expert controversy of the day, let us turn our mind to the apologetic which is infinitely the most important of all, a science which we may all acquire and apply, and upon which, after all, the present and the future of Christianity most depend. Christianity makes its real appeal to the common sense and the universal experience. At the first, not many of the wise or powerful or learned were called to it; but the weak and the foolish of this world who were its first representatives, were able to prove to the world of their day that it is the wisdom and the power of God. The ultimate burden of proof is upon us still, and although we may never solve all the difficulties that beset the correlation of the spiritual with the natural, yet we can take that first step from which in due time all the rest will come. We can find an evidence sufficient to convince ourselves of the reality, the power, the actual effects and results in us of our Christianity. When we have fully convinced ourselves, we shall have done that which will best and most certainly convince others.

Authority and human experience. The difficulty with Christianity in these days is less than ever from the direction of physical science. The philosophy of evolution is all on the side of the higher spiritual destiny of man along the lines of Christianity. From both sides, physical and spiritual, there is a drawing together toward a better interpretation and understanding of the so-called miraculous in religion. Between the natural and the supernatural, in the true sense of a lower and a higher or a further natural, it will eventually be seen that there is no real conflict. The battle rages now almost exclusively upon the field or ground of *authority* in religion. Has Christianity still and always to make good its claims at the bar of human experience and proof, or does it rest them properly only upon a divine authority, vested, say, in the Bible or the Church or both?

The above alternatives are not necessarily exclusive of each other. There may be a very real and high authority both of the Bible and of the Church, and yet these may not be independent of the added seal upon them of human experience. Of course such a thing is inconceivable as a divine authority for that which is not true; but on the other hand, is it not equally inconceivable that any authority whatever could permanently fix upon humanity as its true meaning and function and end that which is not so in reality? That then which has even so high authority as Christianity must be subject to the prior condition that it is true to the truest human experience.

Christianity has no ground for fear that there will be any reasonable demand upon it to surrender the principle of external authority, or to cease to reverence and respect the true bases of this to which it has been accustomed from the beginning. Authority may be better understood and more rationally and rightly exercised, but it will lose nothing from a freer and a higher reverence and obedience. Truly Christian students and scholars will always more and more know for themselves that there is a divine authority in the Scriptures for all the fullness of their faith in Jesus Christ. How the Scriptures are inspired may always be an open question; of the truth of their inspiration there will be no

question in the heart of Christian life or of Christian
scholarship. That there is a divine authority not only in the
Bible but in the Church need be as little as the other any
matter of doubt in the minds of Christians themselves. As a
matter of fact, the faith of Christendom is the faith of the
Church, and not that of individuals, even the most learned,
the most gifted, or the most spiritual. It is the resultant of
the organic life and thought of the body, the common sense
and consent of the whole, and not the mind or wisdom of
the members or the parts. There is a natural as well as a
divine ground for the authority of the Church, a natural as
well as a spiritual reason in the fact that our Lord's promises of truth and perpetuity were made to the Church and
not to individuals.

But however real or sufficient the principle of authority
may be for us who acknowledge it, it plays almost no part
in the mind or life of the world today. A positive and
absolute external authority was a fact and may have been
a necessity in the past; and the time is destined by truth
and propriety in the future, when a reasonable, real, historic
and corporate authority, an authority of organic consent
over the vagaries and diversities of pure individualism, a
principle of unity in infinite diversity, will reaffirm itself on
better foundations in our Christianity.

Authority in abeyance. Authority, as a working principle or
a practical means to anything like
actual universality or catholicity, is for the present at least
in temporary abeyance. If this be so, may there not be
divine as well as natural reasons why it should be so? There
are dangers, let us remember, in the undisputed control
over our minds and consciences of external authority, even
when it is the most reasonable and the most moderate.
Under its prevalence truth and right come to be with us mere
matters of external fact, quite independent of their reason
in themselves or of their essential and necessary relation

to ourselves. Is there not need from time to time that this blind or dead kind of acceptance or acquiescence should be broken up and a new and better kind of assent and valuation set up in us? What if God, in a time like this, should withdraw from his truth and his life in the world the outward prop and stay of preternatural attestation, and should leave them to stand alone upon their own inherent right and power to stand? Is not that faith a better faith which has not been allowed to rest upon the external fact that even God himself has pronounced its truth to be truth, but has been brought and has come to rest in it because it is the truth, and because itself has proved and found and knows it to be the truth? There is a wide and deep principle in this which needs such dwelling upon. If we recall the history and growth of human knowledge of all kinds in the world, we shall see that truth is ever transcending and surviving not only its changing forms but in temporary proofs and disproofs. Truth, in the long run, is not believed because it has been proved, but believed because it is true. The most important truth of all, that of human freedom and personality, can be neither scientifically proved nor disproved. It is theoretically much doubted, and practically not at all so. That truth and faith are practically independent of formal proofs is recognized by science in the importance it attaches to the principle of persistence. On that principle alone the most diverse forms of modern sceptical thought agree in not excluding religion as a permanent fact and a necessary factor in human life.

The needed form of Apologetic. Without then at all meaning to surrender what is true and right in external authority, let us for the present follow that form of apologetic which the times demand, and which therefore we believe God's providence prescribes. That apologetic must more than ever recognize and stand upon the principle that the truth which is going to be permanently accepted, which will persist, must be a truth which can make good its own claim upon human experience and life. We may not have been able of ourselves to attain to or discover that truth; we may have been indebted for it to external sources of authority, as the revelation of God in Christ, the Scriptures, and the Church. But once given us, it must be capable of self-verification. It must be true to us because it is true, and not because it has been given to us as true. We must be able to say of it that, independently of any ground of external authority for it, it is true in itself. God himself and the Scriptures have laid down that principle of final and complete verification: If a man will do the truth, he shall know that it is the truth;—that is said only of what is so true in itself as to be able to be its own proof.

There is a second principle involved in that first one. Every being is made for its truth, as its truth exists for it; and each is a criterion or test or measure of the other. If, for example, it is true, as St. Augustine says, that we are made for God and God therefore is that for which we are made, there is no final and complete verification of that fact except in the actual experience of it; except, that is, in the realization and experience of the relationship in which God is actually ours and we his. Suppose it be true in itself that it is in Christ that the truth is realized that we are made for God, that He is ours and we are his, He in us and we in him,—no external authority for it, nothing but the actual being in Christ and the experience of all that means, can be the final or complete verification of the fact of the truth. Now God himself would not have us stop short of that final and only real proof. He himself will withdraw from us all other assurances and dependences and throw us only upon that. He will say to us: Do the truth, live the truth, and you shall know it. You will see that this is primarily a proof to ourselves alone. But a very fruitful consequence follows from it: it is only those who know themselves who can make others know; the apologetic which will first convince ourselves will be the best with which to convince others. Let us make Christianity a presence and power in the world in ourselves, and we make it so far beyond ourselves.

Man is made for his own truth, and his truth exists for him; how shall we bring these two together that they may mutually interpret and establish each other? Can we so present Christianity to the open mind of men as that it shall be its own sufficient proof to them? Can we make them see as we see, that it is God's own eternal meaning and truth and purpose of themselves, and that they can find and realize themselves only in it? To the mind that is not open and receptive, of course no proof will be sufficient. Even our Lord could not ensure that all minds should be open to himself; but He did assure them that, if any were so, the truth was sufficient in itself to satisfy and convince them. He assumed that that would be the real test and evidence of truth. He claimed the right to be believed and accepted for himself, for what their own minds and hearts, if they were open, could and would see and hear and know him to be. Only secondarily did He ever appeal to any external attestation to him even from God himself. He would have men find themselves in him simply because He was to them the way, the truth, and the life of themselves. We must endeavour to reveal him as He would reveal himself, and give him the higher opportunity to be his own sufficient proof rather than adduce for him only the inferior proofs.

The definition of religion. Given the fact of religion, and a fair chance to know it for what it is, I believe no open human mind will resist or reject the claim of Jesus Christ to be its adequate or complete expression. To measure the truth of this statement, it is necessary first to define for ourselves the meaning of religion, to determine clearly what must of necessity be the aim and end of religion. The function of religion is to solve, not only theoretically but practically or actually, the problem or mystery of man's nature, life, destiny. Religion will have accomplished its task when man shall have attained his end. Human completion or perfection, nothing less, is the meaning and truth of the thing, must be its eternal goal. Now it is just this which, first of all, Christianity sees in Jesus Christ—humanity perfected and completed, after its kind, along the true line of its higher nature. It is the nature of man to be more than nature, to have had a higher origin and to have a higher destiny than belong to his only natural life, because the purpose of God, therefore also the nature of man, predestines him from the beginning to the final full realization of a divine sonship which we see first humanly attained and revealed in the person of Jesus Christ as the head of humanity. Sonship, in its highest and proper meaning, is not a mere fact of nature; it is an act of personality. It is not enough that it be physically generated; it has to be personally apprehended and freely exercised and realised. We do not simply be sons; we have got to become or, make ourselves such. Sonship like every other properly human relation is such, or becomes such, only as it is *self*-realized and *self*-exercised. It is the free, personal self-activity of sonship, and not the mere natural basis of it or constitution for it, that is the essence and the real meaning of it. Thus nature constitutes us to become, in a sense even more real than any earthly relation, sons of God. There is of course a natural basis for this relationship, for otherwise it could not arise. There must be a true sense in which we are already by nature sons of God. "Finite spirits are not products of nature but children of God." I cannot find, however, that this natural sonship, as a mere fact of nature, is anything more than a mere capacity or potentiality of becoming, in the actual and true sense, sons of God. St. Paul says that we are predestined unto sonship through Jesus Christ; that is, that Jesus Christ is not only the actualization and manifestation to us of the divine destiny potential in our higher God-related nature, but is the medium of imparting to us that higher destiny through our union with him in faith. What God predestinated us to become, what our nature constitutes or capacitates us to become, that Jesus Christ enables us to become, and it is just our eternal spiritual task in life, in union and communion with him, to become.

It is now apparent that our answer for Christianity is not to be a refutation of arguments against it, nor yet a production of arguments for it. It is not to deal with proofs or disproofs, but only so let it appear itself that it may be able to prove itself its own best proof. Spiritual things for the spiritual man, and the spiritual man for spiritual things. Each is the best test of the other, and each will best prove itself to the other. I said that Jesus Christ is first human completion or perfection. And He is so first in himself, and then, secondly, in us through the grace and power that comes to us by our union with him. Christ is our High Priest, who mediates between God and us to the end of effecting our union with God. He stands for men in things pertaining to God, in that He has fully realized in himself the whole truth of us and perfectly represented and presented it to God. He is the beginning of the consummation in the end of the divine sonship to which God and our nature predestinated us in the beginning. Having been himself humanly perfected in the way in which we need to be perfected, He becomes not merely the outward revelation and revealer, but the inward power and author of the self-same perfection and eternal salvation in us. *The New Testament is all the story of how our Lord before us, the author, leader, captain, forerunner, of our salvation, was himself first perfected by the things He suffered, was himself glorified by his victory over all the conditions and experiences of human life, himself accomplished the perfect human sonship to God through a life and death of entire love, service and sacrifice;—and then, this accomplished for us, He proceeds to accomplish it all in us; how, through the quickening, transforming and new-creating power of His Spirit acting through our faith, He works in us all that He wrought, and becomes in us all that He was and is in himself.* Already, as St. Paul says, we see ourselves by faith completed in him who is our head. To know ourselves so now in faith, will be to know ourselves so in the end in fact. For the faith of Jesus Christ has the power not only to realize future fruition in present hope but to fulfil present hope in future fruition.

Religion completed in Christ. A larger and longer vision has enabled Christianity to see in Jesus Christ not only the end and completion of humanity, but the end and completion of all creation, so far as creation comes within our knowledge and experience. It is a scientific fact that man is the end or head of natural creation, or of what we now call evolution. It is no mere stretch of scientific imagination to claim that evolution, having already passed from the mere physical stage to the psychical, is destined to pass, and is passing, from the mere psychical to the spiritual. The further evolution of nature is the evolution of man, and the further evolution of man is to be along the line of his spiritual faculties and powers. To know nature through the senses is not the final act or attainment of man; it is to know God through the spirit—the spirit of man which relates him to God as his senses relate him to nature. Adam is the expression to us of our psychical or natural manhood; Jesus Christ is the truth to us of our spiritual, God-related, divine manhood, our predestined sonship to God. As humanity psychically or naturally culminated in Adam, or man as he is in himself or in nature, so humanity will spiritually culminate in Christ, or man as he will be in God. Jesus Christ, as He is the immediate end or goal of man, is more remotely the end or goal, and so the completion or fulfilment, of the whole creation which naturally terminates and comes to its natural end in man.

So Jesus Christ becomes to us the naturally as well as the supernaturally predestinated and constituted end and meaning of the whole creation. As nature ends in man, so man ends in Christ, and through Christ in God. But it will be no blasphemy to go yet further and say that, in a very real though limited and relative sense, not only the creation, natural and spiritual, but God himself, finds his end and fulfilment in Jesus Christ. What we mean is this: that if it is God's purpose to fulfill himself in creation, then it is in Jesus Christ, and him alone, that He finds or accomplishes that self-fulfilment. For the Christ of Christianity is nothing to us if He is not God revealed to us as fulfilled in humanity and so in the creation which comes to its end and meaning in humanity. God is indeed all that He is in himself, eternally and absolutely. But without himself, as self-fulfilled in his creatures, He is all himself, all Father, all love, all God, only in Jesus Christ. How otherwise can we define religion than as that in which God, nature, and man are finally at one, each perfect in all and all in each. And where else or how else can this be found than in Jesus Christ?

So soon as we have conceived Christianity as completion, and more particularly as human completion, of necessity there arises another conception beside it and inseparable from it. Perfection for man, or completion, is not a simple straight unfolding from less to more, from beginning to end. From the very first it needs to be not only a growth in good but a cure from ill. Human life is always as much a preservation from evil as a conservation in good. We need not waste words about the existence and prevalence of evil, in every sphere and at every point of our earthly life. Even as only an idea or an illusion, yet as such or whatever it be, it is always with us and always evil, and therefore always something from which to be saved. Deliverance, redemption, salvation, word and thing, are inseparable from human experience, and therefore inseparable from the function of human religion.

Christ the power of God unto salvation. Now Jesus Christ, and He alone, reveals to us the true meaning, the true way, and, in himself, the true accomplishment or attainment of redemption or salvation. To begin with, there is no possible salvation from evil except through personal conquest of it. It is here to be met and overcome, and the meeting and overcoming it is not only the condition of our redemption but no less the instrument and means of our completion or perfection. For there is no other way for us to grow in good than through meeting and overcoming and surviving evil. Jesus Christ is human good or goodness, human holiness, righteousness, life —only because He was the human conqueror and conquest of sin. There is no other wise in which He could have become so. He wrought for us human redemption in the only possible way in which it could be wrought. He did it by being human himself, and in his humanity overcoming, destroying and abolishing sin in the only way in which sin can be abolished—by a faith, a hope, a love, a holiness, a righteousness, a life, superior to and victorious over sin. Jesus Christ came not to save us from the necessity of ourselves overcoming and abolishing sin; He came to save us by revealing and imparting to us the grace and the power of ourselves overcoming and abolishing sin. He showed us how to do it himself; He enables us to do it ourselves. We see in him the power of God unto salvation, that is, unto holiness, righteousness, life. That power in him is God's power in us, made ours by God's grace and our faith, which means by God's gift and our acceptance. If we believe that; that is to say, if we believe God, then—everything to the contrary notwithstanding—we already see and know ourselves in Christ saved and free from sin. The hope anticipates the reality; the reality will justify and realize the hope. For God so surely makes things what they are by his word, that his word already calls things that are not yet as though they already were.

The Cross of Christ a thing inseparable from human redemption. It means that by which we die to sin and live to God; and it is only by our own dying to sin and living to God that we can be redeemed or saved. Good or evil is all within ourselves. There is no real or essential good or evil but the good or evil will, the good or evil person. There is no good or evil *thing;* to the good will or person all things will be good. Make man good, and the earth will cease to be evil; abolish sin, which is personal, and all so-called natural evil will be converted into pure good. Therefore the only real redemption or salvation for us is to be changed, transformed, new-created ourselves. And only ourselves, our own will and personal action, can change ourselves. We cannot change ourselves, it is true, without union and co-operation with God; but neither can God change us except through our own will and act in changing ourselves. You cannot sever or distinguish *us* from our own will or action. What we see in Jesus Christ is humanity redeemed, saved, made holy, living the life of God. All this is of course the will and action of God in it. Yes, but it is the will and action of God *become,* and now inseparable and indistinguishable from, its own will and action. The Cross of Christ is not a thing only; it is a will and an act. In the first instance, that is, in our Lord himself, it was the will and act which was in itself human salvation, the will and the act in which humanity *at-one'd* itself with God, *redeemed* itself from sin, *raised* itself from death. The Cross of Christ is man's perfect attitude toward sin and holiness, acted out to its perfect end or limit; the resistance unto blood, the obedience unto death, the love that lays down its life. The Cross was not for our Lord alone. It was for him only because it is the only thing for us. We are already saved, in faith or in hope; for we see our salvation accomplished and provided in Christ. But salvation in faith is only the provision and the condition of our salvation in fact. And we shall be saved in fact only as we drink his cup and are baptized with his baptism; only in the fellowship and power of his Cross; only when we have repented unto the death of sin and have believed unto the life in God and the life of God. As there is no religion for us without redemption, so there is no redemption for us but by the Cross of Christ. It alone is the attitude toward sin which saves from it; it alone is the attitude toward holiness which attains it; it alone is the attitude toward God which brings us to him. Put to death in the flesh and quickened, made alive, in the spirit, is the only formula of human salvation.

The Atonement. There is another word and thing, equally inseparable from any possible concept of religion. It is the word and the thing Atonement. The word originally is and means at-one-ment, reconciliation. The thing itself can never get above or beyond that meaning. Who can go beyond at-one-ment with God? What short of that will express or fulfil the meaning or end of religion? There has never been a fundamental ethics, much less religion, which did not begin with the necessity of at-one-ment—with ourselves, with things, with our neighbour, with God, or with all. The end of the Greek ethic was to be at one with ourselves. Unity, harmony, proportion, symmetry, of body, mind, character, life—that is for us truth, beauty, goodness, happiness. We are not at one, at peace, at harmony, with ourselves; our fundamental need is at-one-ment. The end of Hebrew moral and religious thought and life was at-one-ment with the Law, which is God's, which is God,—the law of righteousness. Oneness with that is our only truth, good or goodness, life, blessedness. We are not at one with that eternal and universal law of God; and at-one-ment with it is our infinite necessity. The end of Christ and of Christianity is oneness not with ourselves only, though that also; not yet with human or divine law only, yet that too of necessity in the end. It is oneness with God himself;—nothing less than that is truth or beauty or goodness or life or blessedness for man. We are not at one with God; oneness with God is our one completion or perfection; at-one-ment with God is our one necessity. We can make ourselves at one with God only as God first makes himself at one with us. For himself He has done this in Christ. His part is consummated and complete. For our part, He can make himself at one with us even in Christ, only through our own will and act making ourselves one with him in Christ. As with Christ as one of us, so with us as one with Christ, the only will and act of at-one-ment with God is that of the Cross, the death to sin and new life to God.

The Incarnation. The above conceptions involve and cannot stop short of another, which includes them all, and is no less than they inseparable from the completed notion or fact of religion. It is, word and thing, what we call the Incarnation. Christianity is everything to us Christians, or else it is nothing; it is the whole truth of God in the world and in ourselves. It is unique enough, and universal enough, and great enough incident or event in the eternal history or evolution of the universe to have been introduced or consummated in the world by any mystery or natural impossibility of virgin birth and of bodily resurrection that our Scriptures record. When the naive and natural response of the maiden faith to which it was first addressed could do no more than, How can these things be?—the answer from above was, With God no word shall be impossible. Without attempt to explain the possibility or the mode of the facts which we call virgin birth and resurrection, we simply know these two things: the life which was Christ and is Christianity was born *of* God and *in,* not *of,* humanity or

man. It was begotten of God, its Father; and only conceived and born in humanity, its mother. All spiritual or
divine life is *of* God *in* us: that is the meaning of regeneration, and Christianity is a regeneration, a birth from without
ourselves, from above, a birth of God in man, and so of a
new life of man in God. That is the first great thing in
Christianity that we know; and the second is this: that the
mystery or natural impossibility which we express in the
term resurrection is not too much or too great to be pre-
dicated of humanity as the result of the birth and life of God
in it.

The highest proof. Let us try in a word to sum up the whole
                         matter. True religion is God's truth of
us; consequently we are the best test and proof of it, as it
is of us. We may never have discovered it, but we are the
best and only final judges of it when it has been discovered
to us. Its proof consists in its perfect correspondence with
ourselves, as our judgment will turn, and our truth to ourselves be measured, by our correspondence with it. The
function of religion is not merely a right theory but an
actual fulfilment of the meaning and end of human life. We
are distinctly forewarned at the beginning that nothing will
verify the truth of religion but actual experiment or experience of it. We must live it in order to know it. So long
as we are not applying this only direct and real test, no
amount of learning or skill expended in the study of external
evidences will satisfy or settle our minds. How shall we
apply the one only test or proof as a general apologetic?
We cannot, as has been said, ensure minds open to the truth,
even of themselves; but we shall go a great way if we bend
all our efforts to so presenting and commending the truth
to the mind as it may best reveal itself and be its own proof.
Let men see and know what religion is, and how truly and
exactly our Christianity is it,—and Christianity will better

prove and commend itself, than it will by all other methods combined.

This is of course a practical rather than a theoretic or scientific apologetic; but it may be the latter also in the very best sense. There is the highest science as well as art in bringing before men the spiritual truth of themselves, in making them feel and know their deepest need of self-realization or completion, of redemption, of oneness with God, of the Cross of Christ, of eternal life. There is the truest science in bringing men to know both theoretically and practically that in the selfless love, service, and sacrifice for others we most truly find and fulfill ourselves. It is the last reach of spiritual science to learn how all these and all other truths meet and unite and come to their fulfillment only in the truth of truths, the end of ends, the fact of the Incarnation, the self-realization of God in his creation, of the whole creation in God.

APPENDIX B

BIBLIOGRAPHY

The books of the Reverend Dr. William Porcher DuBose appeared as follows:

The Soteriology of the New Testament.
    New York: The Macmillan Company, 1892
The Ecumenical Councils.
    New York: The Christian Literature Company, 1896
The Gospel in the Gospels.
    New York: Longmans Green, 1906
The Gospel According to St. Paul.
    New York: Longmans Green, 1907
High Priesthood and Sacrifice.
    (Paddock Lectures in the General Theological Seminary)
    New York: Longmans Green, 1908
The Reason of Life.
    New York: Longmans Green, 1909
Turning Points in My Life.
    New York: Longmans Green, 1911
"Christian Defense" in *The Sunday School Teacher's Manual*.
    Philadelphia: G. W. Jacobs Company, 1911
Articles in *The Constructive Quarterly,* here republished.

247-457-C-3.5